The Philosophical Challenge of September 11

☝METAPHILOSOPHY

METAPHILOSOPHY SERIES IN PHILOSOPHY

Series Editors Armen T. Marsoobian and Brian J. Huschle

The Philosophical Challenge of September 11

Edited by

Tom Rockmore
Joseph Margolis
and
Armen T. Marsoobian

Blackwell
Publishing

First published in *Metaphilosophy* 35, no. 3 (April 2004), except for "Terror and the Attack
on Civil Liberties", "Civilizational Imprisonments" and "Afterword".

350 Main Street, Malden, MA 02148-5018, USA
108 Cowley Road, Oxford OX4 IJF, UK
550 Swanston Street, Carlton, Victoria 3053, Australia

First published 2005 by Blackwell Publishing Ltd

Library of Congress Cataloging-in-Publication Data has been applied for

ISBN 1-4051-0893-2

A catalogue record for this title is available from the British Library.

For further information on
Blackwell Publishing, visit our Web site:
http://www.blackwellpublishing.com

CONTENTS

Notes on Contributors

Davis B. Bobrow is professor of public and international affairs and political science at the University of Pittsburgh. He is a past president of the International Studies Association, a former member of the Defense Science Board, and a recipient of the Secretary of State's Open Forum Distinguished Public Service Award. Among the books he has written, edited, or co-written are *Prospects for International Relations* (1999), *Policy Analysis by Design* (1987), *Understanding Foreign Policy Decisions* (1979), *International Relations: New Approaches* (1972), *Weapons System Decisions* (1969), *Computers and the Policy-Making Community* (1968), and *Components of Defense Policy* (1965).

Drucilla Cornell is professor of political science, women's studies, and comparative literature at Rutgers University. She is the author of numerous works of political philosophy and feminist theory, including *Beyond Accommodation, The Imaginary Domain, At the Heart of Freedom*, and most recently *Between Women and Generations: Legacies of Dignity*. She is currently working on two book projects—one about the future of critical theory, the other about the future of ideals in political theory and left-wing activism.

Ronald Dworkin is Frank Henry Sommer Professor of Law and Philosophy at New York University and Quain Professor of Jurisprudence at University College, London. His books include *Taking Rights Seriously, Law's Empire, Life's Dominion,* and *Sovereign Virtue.*

George Leaman is director of the Philosophy Documentation Center in Charlottesville, Virginia. His main research interest is in German philosophy and National Socialism, and he is the author of *Heidegger im Kontext: Gesamtüberblick zum NS-Engagement der Universitätsphilosophen, The Holdings of the Berlin Document Center: A Guide to the Collections*, and numerous articles.

Domenico Losurdo is professor of history of philosophy at the University of Urbino, director of the Philosophical and Pedagogical Sciences Institute, and coordinator of the doctoral-degree courses in philosophy for the university. He is president of the Internationale Gesellschaft Hegel-Marx fuer Dialektisches Denken, codirector of *Topos* (Cologne), and a member of the scientific committee of *Dialektik* (Hamburg), of *Archives de Philosophie* (Paris), and of *Nord-Sud XXI, Droits de l'homme, Liberté* (Geneva). He is the codirector of the "Socrates" series edited by Guerini (Milan). He has given seminars and lectures in several European and Latin American universities and has been a member of examining committees for the selection of university teachers in France (the Sorbonne) and in Finland (Oulu University). He has also supervised CNR projects and 40 percent research projects.

Joseph Margolis is currently Laura H. Carnell Professor of Philosophy at Temple University. The most recent of his many books are *The Unraveling of Scientism: American Philosophy at the End of the Twentieth Century* (2003) and *The Advantages of a Second-Best Morality: Moral Philosophy after 9/11* (forthcoming).

Armen T. Marsoobian is professor of philosophy at Southern Connecticut State University. His primary areas of research are American philosophy, aesthetics, Peircean semiotics, and metaphysics. His articles on Dewey, Peirce, Buchler, Emerson, and aesthetics have appeared in a variety of journals and anthologies. He has co-edited two books in systematic metaphysics, Justus Buchler's *Metaphysics of Natural Complexes* and *Nature's Perspectives: Prospects for Ordinal Metaphysics*. Most recently he co-edited *The Blackwell Guide to American Philosophy*. He is editor in chief of *Metaphilosophy*. Currently he is working on a manuscript on aesthetic meaning and opera.

Andrew Norris is assistant professor of political science at the University of Pennsylvania. His essays have appeared in *Constellations, Diacritics, Political Theory, Polity, Radical Philosophy, Telos,* and *Theory and Event*. His article "Beyond the Fury of Destruction: Hegel on Freedom" is forthcoming in *Political Theory*, and his edited collection *Politics, Metaphysics, and Death: Essays on Giorgio Agamben's Homo Sacer* is forthcoming from Duke University Press. He is currently writing a book on the concept of the political.

Angelica Nuzzo is associate professor of philosophy at Brooklyn College, City University of New York, and in 2000 and 2001 was a fellow at the Radcliffe Institute for Advanced Studies at Harvard. She is the author of two books on Hegel *(Rappresentazione e concetto nella logica della Filosofia del diritto* and *Logica e sistema)*, the monograph *System*, the forthcoming *Kant and the Unity of Reason*, and numerous essays on German Idealism, modern philosophy, and political philosophy.

Tom Rockmore is professor of philosophy at Duquesne University. The most recent of his many books is *Marx after Marxism* (Blackwell). His *Hegel, Analytic Philosophy, and Idealism* is forthcoming from Yale University Press.

Joseph M. Schwartz is associate professor and chair of political science at Temple University. He writes in the areas of democratic theory and

American politics and is the author of *The Permanence of the Political: A Democratic Critique of the Radical Impulse to Transcend Politics* (Princeton, 1995) and *The Future of Democratic Equality: Reconstructing a Politics of Social Solidarity in the United States* (Routledge, forthcoming).

Amartya Sen is Lamont University Professor at Harvard University and was until recently Master of Trinity College, Cambridge. Winner of the Nobel Prize in Economics, he has served as president of the Econometric Society, the Indian Economic Association, the American Economic Association, and the International Economic Association. He formerly served as honorary president of OXFAM and is now its honorary adviser. He was Drummond Professor of Political Economy at the University of Oxford, a Fellow of All Souls College, and professor of economics at Delhi University and the London School of Economics. Among his many books are *Collective Choice and Social Welfare* (1970), *On Economic Inequality* (1973, 1997), *Poverty and Famines* (1981), *Choice, Welfare and Measurement* (1982), *Resources, Values and Development* (1984), *On Ethics and Economics* (1987), *The Standard of Living* (1987), *Inequality Reexamined* (1992), and *Development as Freedom* (1999). His most recent book, *Rationality and Freedom,* will be followed by a companion volume, *Freedom and Justice.* He has received honorary doctorates from major universities in America, Europe, Asia, and Africa, as well as numerous awards, including the Bharat Ratna (the highest honor bestowed by the president of India), the Eisenhower Medal, the Honorary Companion of Honour (U.K.), and the Nobel Prize. He is a Fellow of the British Academy and a foreign honorary member of the American Academy of Arts and Sciences.

Shibley Telhami is Anwar Sadat Professor for Peace and Development at the University of Maryland, College Park, and nonresident senior fellow at the Saban Center at the Brookings Institution. He served as an adviser to the U.S. Mission to the United Nations and as a member of the U.S. delegation to the Trilateral U.S.-Israeli-Palestinian Anti-Incitement Committee. He was a member of the U.S. Advisory Group on Public Diplomacy for the Arab and Muslim World, which was appointed by the Department of State at the request of Congress, and codrafted the report of its findings, "Changing Minds, Winning Peace." He also codrafted several Council on Foreign Relations reports on U.S. public diplomacy, on the Arab-Israeli peace process, and on Persian Gulf security. He is a member of the Council on Foreign Relations and serves on the boards of Human Rights Watch, Seeds of Peace, the Education for Employment Foundation, and Neve Shalom/Wahat al-Salam; he also served on the board of the U.S. Institute of Peace. He is author of the best-selling book *The Stakes: America and the Middle East* (Westview Press, 2003; updated edition, 2004).

1

INTRODUCTION

TOM ROCKMORE and JOSEPH MARGOLIS

Most people are aware—and agree—that September 11, 2001, collects a terribly important series of events. But at this early date, opinions about their meaning diverge sharply, conflict, perseverate, admit confusion and uncertainty. Ever since Socrates, who claimed to know that he did not know, lacked knowledge, intellectuals have been less careful, less willing to take the measure of their ignorance, too quick to settle for appearances. In addressing 9/11, we are literally forced to acknowledge our ignorance of the right way to come to grips with the powerful new questions that confront us—questions unlike anything in recent memory, perhaps uniquely so, at any rate outside the pale of standard questions and conceptual resources.

For many, 9/11 is simply more of the familiar world, a variation on a well-known theme, something already encountered and digested by past experience. For others, it represents a break with the past, a leap into the unknown, a radically new situation, something never quite encountered before. Though there have been other catastrophic events, 9/11 now looms as distinctly sui generis—fundamentally so. In the United States, perhaps the most recent comparable event was the assassination of President John F. Kennedy in 1963. There is no doubt that it was a shock, an instance of national tragedy. Yet there was an orderly, planned transition that followed it. In comparison, 9/11 looms larger, and its effects, which are still largely unknown, may well affect for many years to come, and in ways that cannot yet be fathomed, not just the United States but the entire world. It is too soon to know with certainty about it, too soon for any agreement about its main features, their causes, significance, future significance, relation to particular themes, political repercussions, justification, and the like.

It is not very hard to identify whole regions of ignorance about 9/11. One difficulty concerns how to establish exactly what occurred, that is, the facts—and how to approach them. The supposed facts that we have, which have been collected mainly by governments, or governmental agencies eager to establish one or another thesis, are hardly unbiased. There is very little known about the events leading up to the attacks on American targets that could sustain a close historical analysis or an analysis in a court of law. We do not even possess the facts reliably. The U.S. media were distinctly biased in their reporting. The media responded spontaneously to pressures to be patriotic in their accounts and agreed in the most natural way with the analysis that issued from government sources. There was pressure as well to toe the line on pain of possible difficulties in renewing broadcast licenses.

What was the cause of 9/11? The answers are murky. The U.S. governement's view that 9/11 was not wholly unanticipated yet lacked any "real" cause—that is, that it was a bolt from the blue, an event that did not answer to any prior event—seems self-serving at best. To treat 9/11 as if it were an event without rhyme or reason renders it quite meaningless. The idea that it was a reaction of the jealous poor among Arab peoples cannot possibly be the whole story. A causative factor may be abstracted from long-term economic trends—for instance, the failure of liberal economics to narrow the gap between rich and poor, North and South. Another may relate to the so-called clash of civilizations suggested by Samuel Huntington, whose religious corollary suggests that Islam is an outmoded religion when compared to Christianity.

Additional difficulties arise about the future significance of 9/11, both for the United States and for the world at large. For we obviously do not know how the interpretation will go. If we distinguish between the actual events of that September day and what followed shortly thereafter, we see how problematic the causal connection is. Up to the end of 2003, the two main events that followed in the wake of 9/11 were the war in Afghanistan and the second war in Iraq, unleashed in March 2003. The first, which is close to 9/11 in time, is clearly related to it in causal terms. It is harder to analyze the second war against Iraq in comparable terms. It is true that it follows on and is presumably related to the first war against Iraq. But it answers to more general American interests in Israel and the Middle East. (One must not ignore the matter of access to Iraqi oil.) There is also a rather vaguely formed punitive question. There is also the question of the neoconservative agenda set out in position papers well before the Bush government came to power—which includes what is now euphemistically called regime change. There are likely to be further lines of speculation that have not yet shown themselves: 9/11 is simply too recent, too inexplicit to be fully fathomed.

This bears, of course, on the justification of U.S. and other responses to 9/11. The verdicts are mounting, but their final validity is surely uncertain. The indefinite detention of foreign and U.S. nationals without trial or explicit charge appears to go contrary to U.S. law and long-term U.S. policy. The narrowing of civil liberties under cover of defending them is troubling. The American military response to Iraq is especially problematic. Can the invasion of a soverign state be justified on the bare charge of clear and present danger or where the supporting evidence is affirmed but not actually shared or publicly examined? Must the deciding evidence be appraised by an independent tribunal? Can one justify a preemptive military strike where the supporting argument is seriously disputed?

One wonders whether we are prepared to address 9/11 in accord with the familiar terms and categories of our tradition, or whether they are even adequate to the task. We are no longer certain about our analytic instruments. In the West, modern political philosophy begins with Hobbes's theory of the state as the source of public power mediating between the destructive tendencies of individuals pitted mercilessly against one another. The continuing tradition is remarkably homogeneous: for example, virtually every political philosopher from Locke to Rawls fastens on the problem of property. Rawls is generally acknowledged to be one of the most important Anglo-American political philosophers of the past century; and yet the new events that command our political reflection seem pointedly unrelated to anything in Rawls's writings. Political philosophy as we have known it now seems outdated, seems unable to help us in our hour of need.

One suspects that the impasse extends to other domains. All of our ready conceptual assurances are confounded by 9/11. The assumption that we have captured the world in our theories has been stalemated by the world itself. The world has changed in ways no one could have foreseen. We cannot diagnose the events of 9/11 by any simple application of the usual tools. They defy our sense of legible order, and we cannot say when our categories will adjust again.

The essays that follow, which in the main were commissioned for this collection, do not reflect any single analysis, or assured set of inferences, or correct conclusion. Each records a considered reflection on the still-inchoate import of a nest of puzzles that political reality has thrust upon us in the wake of 9/11. This is a time not for settled answers but for a search among new options, a time not for indifference but for a review of fundamental convictions and alternative visions. We are searching for a sense of a better order that we cannot possibly claim to know—or know how to find. In the final analysis, the engagements with 9/11 simply confront us in an unavoidable way; that is, in a new way, with unforeseen and unforeseeable implications. We are, in fact, at the very point of initiating a responsible philosophical reflection about an uncharted world. That is the single most important feature of the effort we make here.

2

IRAQ, AMERICAN EMPIRE, AND THE WAR ON TERRORISM

GEORGE LEAMAN

It is abundantly clear that the administration of George W. Bush, supported by its ally in London, misrepresented its case for war with Iraq in an effort to win support from the American public, the U.S. Congress, and the U.N. Security Council. Iraq did not present a grave military threat to the United States or Britain; it was not connected with the 9/11 atrocities; and it did not have a massive stockpile of biological or chemical weapons.[1] Yet planning for the removal of Saddam Hussein and the occupation of Iraq began immediately after Bush's inauguration,[2] and several Bush administration officials had been advocating this course for years.[3] Why? What does the invasion of Iraq have to do with the war on

---

[1] Misleading and apparently false statements about the Iraqi threat to the United States were made by George W. Bush on the following occasions: "Address to the Nation," Mar. 17, 2003; "State of the Union Address," Jan. 28, 2003; "President Bush Outlines Iraqi Threat," Remarks by the President on Iraq at the Cincinnati Museum Center, Oct. 7, 2002; "Iraqi Regime Danger to America is 'Grave and Growing,'" Radio Address by the President to the Nation, Oct. 5, 2002; United Nations Address, Sept.12, 2002. The failure to find weapons of mass destruction in Iraq raises the possibility that President Bush lied to Congress and the public about the reasons for going to war with Iraq. If so, he may be legally vulnerable to a federal charge of conspiracy under Title 18, Section 371, of the United States Code. See John W. Dean, "Missing Weapons Of Mass Destruction: Is Lying About The Reason For War An Impeachable Offense?" *FindLaw's Writ: Legal Commentary*, June 6, 2003, at www.findlaw.com.

[2] According to former U.S. Treasury Secretary Paul O'Neill, Iraq was discussed at the first National Security Council meeting after Bush's inauguration. See Suskind 2004, 85–86. The Bush administration also discussed plans for war with Iraq and the distribution of its oil resources as early as February 2001. See p. 96: "Documents were being prepared by the Defense Intelligence Agency . . . mapping Iraq's oil fields and exploration areas and listing companies that might be interested in leveraging the precious asset. One document . . . lists companies from thirty countries . . . their specialities, bidding histories, and in some cases their particular areas of interest. An attached document maps Iraq with markings for 'supergiant oilfield,' 'other oilfield,' and 'earmarked for production sharing,' while demarking the largely undeveloped southwest of the country into nine 'blocks' to designate areas for future exploration. The desire to 'dissuade' countries from engaging in 'asymmetrical challenges' to the United States—as Rumsfeld said in his January articulation of the demonstration value of a preemptive attack—matched with plans for how the world's second largest oil reserves might be divided among the world's contractors made for an irresistible combination, O'Neill later said."

[3] For example, on Jan. 26, 1998, a group of neoconservatives wrote on open letter to President Clinton arguing that the United States should adopt a strategy for removing Saddam Hussein from power in Iraq. Signatories to this letter include several prominent

terrorism announced after 9/11? In this essay I argue that both the invasion of Iraq and the war on terrorism are part of an effort to secure continuing American military and economic supremacy on a global scale over the long term. I also argue that this imperial project is an extension of established policies, and that there are significant continuities between the actions of the Bush administration and those of its predecessors. I conclude by examining some of the things that need to be done to change this situation, which threatens the continuing viability of democratic government in the United States.

With the end of the cold war and the collapse of the Soviet Union, the United States assumed a position of military dominance unparalleled in world history. It possessed the most powerful air, land, and sea forces ever assembled, and its overwhelming military advantages were extended by a combination of major reductions in Russian military spending and continuing U.S. spending on a massive scale. While Soviet (and Russian) military spending declined by approximately 90 percent from 1987 to 1997,[4] U.S. military spending remained at cold-war levels.[5] The United States spent more than $2 trillion on its military from 1992 to 2000, and by the late 1990s U.S. military spending was absorbing more than half of all discretionary spending in the federal budget. These huge expenditures

people now serving in the Bush administration, including Elliott Abrams, Richard Armitage, John Bolton, Paula Dobriansky, Zalmay Khalilzad, Richard Perle, Peter Rodman, Donald Rumsfeld, William Schneider Jr., and Paul Wolfowitz. The text of this letter is available at the Web site of "The Project for a New American Century," at www.newamer icancentury.org/iraqclintonletter.htm. In June 1996 Richard Perle and two others now serving in the Bush administration (Donald Feith and David Wurmser) argued for the removal of Saddam Hussein in a study prepared for a Jerusalem-based think tank after the election of Benyamin Netanyahu as prime minister of Israel. See "A Clean Break: A New Strategy for Securing the Realm" from the Institute for Advanced Strategic and Political Studies at www.israeleconomy.org/strat1.htm. See also Kathleen and Bill Christison, "The Bush Administration's Dual Loyalties," in *The Politics of Anti-Semitism* (Oakland, Calif.: AK Press, 2003), pp. 127–43.

[4] According to the Stockholm International Peace Research Institute, Soviet and Russian military expenditure fell "from an estimated $257 billion in the USSR in 1987 to $24.1 billion in Russia in 1997, and as a proportion of GNP from 16.6% in 1987 to 3.8% in 1997." See *SIPRI Yearbook 1998: Armaments, Disarmament and International Security* (Oxford: Oxford University Press, 1998), appendix 6D.

[5] According to the Center for Defense Information, average annual U.S. military spending for the years 1945 to 1996 was $298.5 billion (in 1996 dollars). See Center for Defense Information, "U.S. Military Spending, 1945–1996," July 9, 1996, at www.cdi.org/ issues/milspend.html. In 1997, U.S. military spending was approximately $260 billion, more than half of all discretionary spending by the federal government that fiscal year. See Center for Defense Information, "Discretionary Spending, Fiscal Year 1997," Sept. 10, 1996, at www.cdi.org/issues/discret.html. This number does not include other military-related spending, such as foreign military aid, international peace keeping, additional retirement pay, veterans' benefits, the military portion of the space program, and the military share of interest on the national debt. In FY 1997 these costs were estimated to be an *additional* $231 billion. See Center for Defense Information, "Military Costs: The Real Total," Aug. 8, 1996, at www.cdi.org/issues/realtota.html.

continued in the absence of a plausible military threat from any other country and without any meaningful political discussion of their continuing necessity.[6]

This situation illustrates two things about U.S. military spending and security planning. First, U.S. military spending has a political life of its own separate from the arguments used to justify it. Over many decades massive cold-war military spending has created vested interests throughout the U.S. government and economy that want to see it continue, for whatever reason. This is simply due to the vast amounts of money involved, and hundreds of U.S. corporations and their shareholders, as well as the military bureaucracies, depend on military spending as a primary source of revenue. U.S. spending on what Eisenhower called the military-industrial complex is widely distributed throughout the country, in all fifty states and virtually all Congressional districts, thus ensuring some measure of political support from elected politicians at the federal, state, and local levels. This huge spending has created expectations of its own necessity on the part of those who benefit from it, and in practice it may be very difficult to stop.[7] Still, the level of U.S. military spending remains so high that it demands some continuing political justification, and since the disappearance of the Soviet threat a compelling rationale for this spending has been lacking. From the perspective described above, the best possible rationale is one that allows the gravy train to continue indefinitely without question or challenge. I shall return to this point in a moment.

Second, U.S. security planning has long been based in part on criteria that have nothing to do with the Soviet Union or actual military threats to U.S. territory from other countries. Over many years the U.S. built a system of alliances, military deployments, and capabilities that allow it to influence political events all over the world, to foster global "stability" in a manner consistent with a particular understanding of the U.S. national interest. A principal objective of these arrangements was explained years ago in a State Department planning document:

We have about 50% of the world's wealth but only 6.3% of its population. This disparity is particularly great as between ourselves and the peoples of Asia. In this situation, we cannot fail to be the object of envy and resentment.

---

[6] Both the first Bush administration and the Clinton administration "avoided any public discussion of what role the United States should play in the world. . . . As a result, today, over a decade after the end of the Cold War, there is still no common understanding about the fundamental purposes of the American military establishment or the principles by which the United States will decide whether to use military power in pursuit of the national interest." Richard H. Kohn, "The Erosion of Civilian Control of the Military in the United States Today," *Naval War College Review* 55, no. 3 (summer 2002): 13.

[7] Ibid., pp. 15–16: "If one measures civilian control. . . by the relative influence of the uniformed military and civilian policy makers in the two great areas of concern in military affairs—national security policy and the use of force to protect the country and project power abroad—then civilian control has deteriorated significantly in the last generation."

Our real task in the coming period is to devise a pattern of relationships which will permit us to maintain this position of disparity without positive detriment to our national security. To do so, we will have to dispense with all sentimentality and day-dreaming; and our attention will have to be concentrated everywhere on our immediate national objectives. We need not deceive ourselves that we can afford today the luxury of altruism and world-benefaction.[8]

This was written in 1948 and remains a remarkably honest assessment of a continuing U.S. security challenge—how to increase U.S. access to world markets and resources under highly favorable terms despite massive disparities in the global distribution of wealth.[9] U.S. foreign policy and security planning sanction "stability" and "responsible" or "moderate" behavior on the part of foreign governments, in pursuit of highly favorable environments for U.S. investment, production, and trade.[10] The concept of the national interest at the center of this thinking is thus closely identified with the interests of the American business community, which generally regards the external world in terms of opportunities for, or threats to, open-ended profit maximization.[11] The cold war obscured this U.S. interest in its "sphere of influence," which is comparable to the past British interest in overseas colonies or the Roman interest in outlying provinces. With the end of its rivalry with the Soviet Union the U.S. has been able to extend its sphere of influence, and it is free to act unilaterally in support of efforts to force global economic integration on its terms.[12]

The new Bush administration came into office with priorities similar to those of the Reagan administration in the 1980s: the transfer of resources from the poor to the rich; large increases in the military spending that subsidizes many U.S. industries; and open rejection of any international constraints on U.S. action.[13] However, it must be remembered that the

[8] George Kennan, U.S. State Department Policy Planning Staff Document PPS 23, Feb. 24, 1948. This document was published in *Foreign Relations of the United States, 1948*, vol. 1, pp. 509–29, and the full text is available online at www.geocities.com/rwvong/future/kennan/pps23.html.

[9] By 1993, the richest 10 percent of the people in the United States had an income equal to that of the poorest 43 percent of the people in the entire world. Put another way, the income of the richest 25 million Americans was equal to that of almost 2 billion people. In 2000, the United States had approximately 4.7 percent of the world's population. See United Nations Development Programme, *Human Development Report 2002* (Oxford: Oxford University Press, 2002), pp. 19, 162–65.

[10] See Richard Du Boff, "Business Ideology and Foreign Policy: The National Security Council and Vietnam," in *The Pentagon Papers, Volume V: Critical Essays* (Boston: Beacon Press, 1972), p. 17.

[11] Ibid.

[12] Chalmers Johnson, *Blowback: The Costs and Consequences of American Empire* (New York: Henry Holt, 2000), p. 7.

[13] See Chomsky 2002, xi. The following is from the introduction to the 1986 edition of this work, and it is a fair summary of the policies of the Bush administration: "The [Reagan] Administration was committed to three related policies, all achieved with considerable

policies of the Bush administration, while extreme, are not entirely different from those of previous administrations. The Clinton administration arguably violated Constitutional and legal limits on the president's authority;[14] used military force outside the confines of international law;[15] made the removal of Saddam Hussein a national priority as a matter of law;[16] and supported U.S. military planning for "full-spectrum dominance" of every military situation anywhere in the world.[17] Like the Bush administration, Clinton sought major reductions in social spending, the extension of international free-trade agreements, changes in environmental regulations desired by the business community, and the deregulation of financial markets. While Bush has continually advocated policies that benefit the rich, it is also true that the distribution of wealth in the U.S. became more skewed during the Clinton years than at any time in the previous forty years.[18] It is not the priorities of the Bush administration that make it stand out relative to its predecessors but rather the fact that it seized on 9/11 as an opportunity to take radical action in an effort to expand U.S. power.

success: 1) transfer of resources from the poor to the rich; 2) a large-scale increase in the state sector of the economy in the traditional way, through the Pentagon system . . . ; and 3) a substantial increase in U.S. intervention, subversion, and international terrorism (in the literal sense). Such policies cannot be presented to the public in terms in which they are intended. They can be implemented only if the general population is properly frightened by monsters against whom we must defend ourselves."

[14] Clinton was sued in 1999 by seventeen Congressional representatives, Democrats and Republicans, who charged that he had committed U.S. forces in Serbia without a declaration of war and that he had violated the terms of the War Powers Act. See *Tom Campbell et al. v. William Jefferson Clinton*, United States District Court for the District of Columbia.

[15] The United States, "the only country in the world with the power to do so, has shifted decision-making on international interventions out of the hands of the UN, in favour of illegal reliance on NATO as an authorising power, and ultimately on unilateral US action." See Phyllis Bennis, "Law of Empire: The US Undermines International Law," in *Le monde diplomatique*, December 1999, at http://mondediplo.com/1999/12/02bennis.

[16] In October 1998 Clinton signed the Iraq Liberation Act, which declared that the U.S. objective in Iraq was to "remove from power the regime led by Saddam Hussein and to promote the emergence of a democratic government."

[17] "The ultimate goal of our military force is to accomplish the objectives directed by the National Command Authorities. For the joint force of the future, this goal will be achieved through full spectrum dominance—the ability of U.S. forces . . . to defeat any adversary and control any situation across the full range of military operations. . . . The label full spectrum dominance implies that U.S. forces are able to conduct prompt, sustained, and synchronized operations with combinations of forces tailored to specific situations and with access to and freedom to operate in all domains—space, sea, land, air, and information. Additionally, given the global nature of our interests and obligations, the United States must maintain its overseas presence forces and the ability to rapidly project power worldwide in order to achieve full spectrum dominance." See Joint Chiefs of Staff, Director for Strategic Plans and Policy, *Joint Vision 2020* (Washington, D.C.: U.S. Government Printing Office, June 2000), p. 6.

[18] Robert Pollin, *Contours of Descent: U.S. Economic Fractures and the Landscape of Global Austerity* (London: Verso, 2003), pp. 6–7.

The United States faced a genuine threat from the perpetrators of the attacks on September 11, who managed to kill thousands of people and cause billions of dollars of damage in less than five hours. The visually shocking impact of the attacks caused an outpouring of national solidarity, as people all over the United States donated blood for the injured, supplies and equipment for the rescue workers, and money for the families of the victims. Millions of Americans asked thoughtful questions about these carefully coordinated attacks, wanting to know how they had been possible, who was behind them, and why. There was also widespread rage against the perpetrators, fear, and an understandable public demand for effective government action in response. What this response should be was a matter of considerable public discussion. In its initial response, the Bush administration identified Al Qaeda as the organization behind the attacks and announced a war to destroy it as well as "every terrorist group of global reach."[19] Questions about the history, motivation, and objectives of the attackers were dismissively addressed in terms of a general hatred of political freedom, hostility to Israel, and a desire to overthrow existing governments in the Middle East. The Bush administration did not define terrorism or say exactly who terrorists were, but it promised a decisive fight against all terrorists who plot or commit "evil" around the world. This was the beginning of the Bush administration's war on terrorism, and from then on public fear and rage were focused on those identified by the government as terrorists or their supporters. At the same time, public attention was directed to future U.S. action in Afghanistan and elsewhere, and further questions about the background and motivation of the attacks were avoided or suppressed. Despite the lack of clarity, this initial administration response was generally well received by the American public, which rallied to the support of U.S. political institutions after the attacks.[20]

September 11 thus created a political situation that gave the Bush administration wide latitude to use violence as an instrument of foreign policy, as well as a new political justification for massive increases in U.S. military spending. Administration officials, who as early as January 2001 had discussed the preemptive use of military force to "dissuade" other countries from challenging U.S. interests, now viewed military action in Afghanistan "as a 'demonstration model' of what other countries that

[19] George W. Bush, Address to a Joint Session of Congress and the American People, Sept. 20, 2001. Regarding the assumed responsibility of Al Qaeda for the attacks, it should be remembered that there has been "a prima facie case from the outset, though little credible evidence has been produced despite what must be the most intensive investigations ever by the coordinated intelligence services of the major powers." See Chomsky 2002, 145.

[20] Bush's public approval ratings soared in the weeks after 9/11, dispelling the lingering cloud of the 2000 election fiasco. See James Zogby, "The Ups and Downs of George W. Bush," Apr. 22, 2003, at Media Monitors Network, www.mediamonitors.net/zogby84.html.

were considered hostile to the United States might face."[21] This was complemented by approval of a broad plan for covert activity in Afghanistan and "around the globe, including plots and assassinations— a plan to neutralize people disposed against the U.S. government by any means necessary."[22] The success of the military campaign in Afghanistan quickly led to a widening U.S. focus on uncontrollable third-world countries believed to be *potential* threats to U.S. interests, including Iraq, Iran, and North Korea, who in January 2002 were identified as an "axis of evil" that threatened world peace.[23] Making Iraq the rhetorical center of the so-called axis of evil had nothing to do with 9/11. It was instead a continuation of the internal administration discussions of January and February 2001 that matched a desire to "dissuade" countries from engaging in "asymmetrical challenges" to the United States with plans for the division of the world's second-largest oil reserves among the world's contractors.[24] The effort to destroy "every terrorist group of global reach" quickly became a much larger effort to leverage U.S. military power to long-term economic and political advantage, something that had been advocated by many neoconservatives even before Bush was elected.[25] This larger effort has nothing to do with preventing further terrorist attacks, and it was quickly pursued because administration officials were encouraged by the military success in Afghanistan to expand the scope of U.S. military action.[26]

The war on terrorism has offered a political opening for further large increases in U.S. military spending, which even before 9/11 was higher than the combined spending of the next fifteen military powers.[27] Like the

---

[21] Suskind 2004, 81–82, 187.

[22] Ibid., 190.

[23] George W. Bush, The State of the Union Address, Jan. 29, 2002.

[24] Suskind 2004, 96.

[25] See, for example, *Rebuilding America's Defenses*, Project for a New American Century, September 2000, p. iv. Signed by several people now serving in the Bush administration, including Stephen Cambone, I. Lewis Libby, Paul Wolfowitz, and Dov Zakeim, this report argued for increased military spending precisely because the United States was the world's dominant power and faced no serious military challenge. "This report proceeds from the belief that America should seek to preserve and extend its position of global leadership by maintaining the preeminence of U.S. military forces. Today, the United States has an unprecedented strategic opportunity. It faces no immediate great-power challenge; it is blessed with wealthy, powerful and democratic allies in every part of the world; it is in the midst of the longest economic expansion in its history; and its political and economic principles are almost universally embraced. At no time in history has the international security order been as conducive to American interests and ideals. The challenge for the coming century is to preserve and enhance this 'American peace.' Yet unless the United States maintains sufficient military strength, this opportunity will be lost."

[26] According to Paul O'Neill, Donald Rumsfeld and Paul Wolfowitz pointed to "the ease with which the Taliban had fallen as evidence of how doable Iraq would be." Suskind 2004, 204.

[27] See Center for Defense Information, *Defense Monitor* 30, no. 7 (August 2002), p. 4. See also Chomsky 2002, 157.

war on terrorism, these huge increases are open ended and are justified with general appeals to the incalculable value of freedom and domestic security. In January 2002, President Bush told Congress that his budget for the war on terrorism "includes the largest increases in defense spending in two decades—because while the price of freedom and security is high, it is never too high. Whatever it costs to defend our country we will pay."[28] Military planning expanded with the budgets after 9/11, reflecting the preparation for global military commitments over the long term.[29] By fiscal year 2004 annual U.S. military spending had reached $400 billion, not including an additional $87 billion appropriation for U.S. operations in Iraq, Afghanistan, and elsewhere. Over the next five years the Bush administration plans to spend $2.3 trillion on the U.S. military, with annual budgets to exceed $500 billion, not including related military spending, such as foreign military aid, veterans benefits, the military portion of the space program, or the military portion of the national debt. The mobilization of public opinion against the countries of the axis of evil serves the same rhetorical and political purpose as the "evil empire" in the 1980s—scaring the public into lavishing public funds on military contractors, who now include virtually all of the large industrial and hi-tech firms in the country. From the perspective of those who benefit from this spending the war on terrorism is a great gift, an open-ended commitment to massive public subsidies on terms defined largely by the military and the intelligence agencies. It's not hard to see that any attempt to decrease this spending will be resisted by those feeding at this trough. There are powerful vested interests in the perpetuation of a terrorist threat from which we need to be protected, and in the control of political activity that might alter or challenge this situation.[30]

This situation is dangerous, and as citizens we need to think carefully about it. We can start by recognizing that the Bush administration decided to invade Iraq for reasons that have nothing to do with 9/11, and that greed and a desire to extend American power are motives in U.S.

[28] George W. Bush, The State of the Union Address, Jan. 29, 2002.

[29] "In the fifty-six years since the first Unified Command Plan, our combatant command structure has been expanded geographically and empowered legally. The 1986 Goldwater-Nichols Defense Reorganization Act strengthened the role of our combatant commands, and with UCP' 02, the last remaining unassigned regions of the world—Russia, the Caspian Sea, Antarctica, and the countries of North America—were finally placed within our combatant commanders' areas of responsibility (AORs). Now the entire globe is encompassed within the AORs of our five regional commands." See Richard Myers, "Shift to a Global Perspective," Naval War College Review 56, no. 4 (autumn 2003): 12.

[30] In this context it is useful to remember the anthrax attacks after 9/11, which had a tremendous public impact and may have facilitated passage of the U.S. Patriot Act. While those responsible for the attacks and their motives remain unknown, it is possible that someone targeted two political opponents of the Bush administration, Senate Majority Leader Tom Daschle and Senate Judiciary Committee Chairman Patrick Leahy, for assassination.

planning. We can also acknowledge that the Bush administration and its allies are trying to silence criticism of the war on terrorism,[31] which is being used for maximum political advantage, and demand answers to reasonable questions that remain unaddressed. U.S. citizens do indeed face a danger from the plans of highly motivated and intelligent groups that want to attack the country, and there is a legitimate public desire for safety and security. But it is simply a matter of civic prudence to recognize that the desire for safety can be exploited by those in power for their own ends, and that some people have an interest in the perpetuation of a threat from which we need to be protected at great cost.[32] At Nuremberg Hermann Goering famously observed that it was an easy matter to use external threats to bring people to do the bidding of their political leaders. "All you have to do is tell them they are being attacked and denounce the pacifists for lack of patriotism and exposing the country to danger. It works the same in any country."[33] This is essentially what the Bush administration has done to mobilize U.S. public opinion for the invasion of Iraq (and perhaps the other countries of the axis of evil) as part of its war on terrorism. It is a cynical betrayal of the public trust and the good-faith willingness of most Americans to make sacrifices for the common good in the aftermath of 9/11. In Iraq thousands of people have been killed or wounded in demonstration of U.S. power and in pursuit of U.S.

---

[31] For example, in testimony before the Senate Judiciary Committee in December 2001 Attorney General John Ashcroft accused critics of new antiterror measures of "aiding terrorists" and "eroding national unity." Other administration officials have continued to resist questions or criticism with similar statements. See, for example, "Rumsfeld: Criticism at Home, Abroad Harms War on Terrorism," *Washington Post*, Sept. 8, 2003. In early 2002, Republican leaders in Congress responded to mild questions from Democratic Senator Tom Daschle about the direction of the war on terrorism with particular hysteria. Senate Minority Leader Trent Lott said, "How dare Senator Daschle criticize President Bush while we are fighting our war on terrorism, especially when we have troops in the field?" Representative Thomas Davis III, chairman of the House Republican Campaign Committee, said Daschle's "comments have the effect of giving aid and comfort to our enemies." House Majority Whip Tom DeLay called Daschle's remarks "disgusting." See "Lott Calls Daschle Divisive," *Washington Post*, Mar. 1, 2002. There are many other examples, and these tactics will certainly continue, because they are effective.

[32] While this matter is being discussed here in the context of the war on terrorism, it should also be recognized that the United States faced the same situation for much of the cold war. The Soviet threat was often manipulated for political purposes in the United States and other Western countries. As a starting point in the literature on this matter see Andrew Cockburn, *The Threat: Inside the Soviet Military Machine* (1983), and Alan Wolfe, *The Rise and Fall of the Soviet Threat* (1984). There are numerous other well-documented examples of the exaggeration and manipulation of alleged foreign threats in U.S. political history, including the cases of Nicaragua, El Salvador, Vietnam, Cuba, Angola, Chile, Grenada, the Dominican Republic, and many others.

[33] G. M. Gilbert, *Nuremberg Diary* (Cambridge, Mass.: Da Capo Press, 1995), pp. 278–79. We should be aware that these same words might be applied to elected members of Congress and other politicians, who could be brought to do the bidding of the military and the intelligence agencies in the same manner.

control of oil, and the destruction of lives continues with no end in sight. We need to acknowledge this and deal with the consequences. We also need to look much more closely at the objectives and consequences of the campaign in Afghanistan.

As a next step we can demand answers to the many reasonable questions about the attacks of September 11 that remain unaddressed; we obviously need to understand their true origins in order to prevent future attacks. This will be difficult, as both of the major U.S. political parties and many current and former government officials have an interest in obscuring the details of past U.S. support for Islamic fundamentalism.[34] According to former National Security Advisor Zbigniew Brzezinski, the U.S. effort to recruit, train, arm, and supply volunteers from several Muslim countries to fight the Soviet Union and its allies in Afghanistan began in July 1979.[35] Following the logic that the enemy of my enemy is my friend, the United States supported militant Islamic organizations fighting in Afghanistan in an effort to harm the Soviet Union, in cooperation with the governments of Saudi Arabia, Pakistan, Egypt, and China. A thorough investigation into the causes of the attacks of 9/11 should include an examination of this history, as well as assessment of the long-term costs and benefits of this thinking, which was eagerly supported by both Democrats and Republicans over the course of several U.S. administrations.

We can also demand a public discussion of the objectives of the U.S. war on terrorism, which was actually declared twenty years ago "by the Reagan-Bush Administration, with similar rhetoric and much the same personnel in the leading positions."[36] It is clear that the current Bush administration has had several objectives in its response to 9/11, and that some of these have nothing to do with Al Qaeda or the attacks in New York or Washington. The Bush administration has seized on the attacks as an opportunity to use violence in pursuit of long-established foreign-policy objectives, and as political cover for huge increases in military spending that subsidize much U.S. industry. Military action is the Bush administration's desired instrument in this situation not merely because

---

[34] The difficulty of examining this history has also been increased by new restrictions on public access to the records of past U.S. administrations. See, for example, Executive Order 13233—Further Implementation of the Presidential Records Act, Nov. 5, 2001.

[35] Interview with Zbigniew Brzezinski, "How Jimmy Carter and I Started the Mujahedeen," translation of interview with *Le nouvel observateur* (France), Jan. 15–21, 1998, p. 76. Reproduced at www.counterpunch.org/brzezinski.html. In this interview Brzezinski is quoted as saying the following: "According to the official version of history, CIA aid to the Mujahedeen began during 1980, that is to say, after the Soviet army invaded Afghanistan, 24 Dec. 1979. But . . . it was July 3, 1979 that President Carter signed the first directive for secret aid to the opponents of the pro-Soviet regime in Kabul. And that very day, I wrote a note to the president in which I explained to him that in my opinion this aid was going to induce a Soviet military intervention."

[36] Chomsky 2002, 2.

the means are at hand in the form of huge U.S. military advantages. "The central tragic fact is simple: coercion works; those who apply substantial force to their fellows get compliance, and from compliance draw the multiple advantages of money, goods, deference, access to pleasures denied to less powerful people."[37] This is learned behavior, and we should not be surprised that the leaders of powerful countries resort to violence, since they have the superior means to do so at their disposal. Such people seem unprepared for situations in which the use of force does not result in the desired outcome, as was the case with the Soviet Union in Afghanistan and the United States in Vietnam.[38] In such situations they learn their lessons at the expense of their own troops and the populations they are trying to control, who all suffer as a consequence of imperial ambition. The U.S. occupation of Iraq may prove to be another such situation, something the Bush administration (like any powerful government) will not easily admit as it continues to try to impose a political solution that will allow it to dominate the region and control Iraq's oil over the long term.

To change this situation fundamentally, we must insist that the United States abide by its professed commitments to justice and the rule of law, and that it accept the same standard of behavior that it demands of other countries. That standard should be based on a simple principle, that other people should be treated in the same manner we wish to be treated—this is the basis of justice between people and between nations. In the war on terrorism this means that the U.S. must be willing to consider the interests of others and forego actions that it condemns in others. At the moment this is not the case, and the U.S. government explicitly reserves the right to use force in any manner and for any purpose it sees fit. It identifies "terrorism" not by a particular set of actions or practices but by the perpetrators of such actions, and sanctions *the lawful use* or threatened use of violence by itself regardless of means.[39] The United States has a

---

[37] Charles Tilly, *Coercion, Capital, and European States* (Oxford: Blackwell, 1990), as quoted in Chomsky 2002, 144.

[38] "No one at high levels seemed to question the assumption that U.S. political objectives in South Vietnam could be attained through military victory." See "U.S. Ground Strategy and Force Deployments, 1965–1968," in *The Pentagon Papers,* vol. 4 (Boston: Beacon Press, 1971), p. 604.

[39] There is no official U.S. definition of terrorism, and different government agencies operate with different definitions. The Department of Defense defines terrorism as the "the *unlawful* [emphasis added] use of—or threatened use of—force or violence against individuals or property to coerce or intimidate governments or societies, often to achieve political, religious, or ideological objectives." See U.S. Army Field Manual FM 100-20, *Military Operations in Low-Intensity Conflict,* Dec. 5, 1990, chap. 3 ("Combating Terrorism"), as well as the DOD *Dictionary of Military and Associated Terms* (JCS Pub. 1-02). The FBI also uses this definition. However, the Department of State has for many years been using a definition contained in Title 22 of the United States Code, Section 2656f(d): "The term "terrorism" means premeditated, politically motivated violence perpetrated against noncombatant targets *by subnational or clandestine agents* [emphasis added], usually

right to defend itself, as any country does, and this is not in dispute. But we should insist that if necessary it do so openly, without concealed motives, without greed and a desire for imperial expansion, and with an explicit commitment to live by the ideals we profess. The commitment to treat others the way we wish to be treated sometimes requires from the powerful a willingness to do what is right instead of what is possible. The many neoconservatives in the Bush administration have nothing but contempt for such thinking, which they regard as a form of weakness. They view the exercise of power as its own justification, following the old logic that "large countries do what they wish, while small nations accept what they must."[40] This is the logic of empire, and there are no moral barriers to the use of force in such thinking, just the practical limits of available forces and resources. If the United States is successfully able to impose its will on Iraq, we should be prepared for further U.S. military action in other countries as part of a continuing effort to extend American power. This is morally unacceptable.

Finally, we can work to change U.S. energy policy and the long-term dependence on imported oil, which has led to continual U.S. support of the largest oil-rich dictatorships in the Middle East, including Iran, Iraq, and Saudi Arabia. The political life of each of these countries has been a matter of intense interest to the United States for decades, and the continuing U.S. efforts to control the region have had far-reaching consequences. Massive U.S. support for the shah of Iran ultimately resulted in the Islamic revolution, which legitimated an authoritarian theocracy and energized hostility to the United States throughout the region. Past U.S. support for Saddam Hussein during the worst periods of domestic oppression in his country, motivated by a desire to limit the spread of the Iranian revolution, makes a mockery of present U.S.

---

intended to influence an audience." See, for example, the annual "Patterns of Global Terrorism" reports of the State Department Office of the Coordinator for Counterterrorism. The White House has used different definitions at different times. In 1986 it defined terrorism as "the unlawful use or threat of violence against persons or property to further political or social objectives." See *Public Report of the Vice President's Task Force on Combating Terrorism*, February 1986, p. 1. In September 2002 it defined terrorism as "premeditated, politically motivated violence against innocents." See *The National Security Strategy of the United States of America*, September 2002, p. 5. This general definition, which did not exclude U.S. actions, was apparently a mistake, as it was qualified several months later. "The enemy is terrorism—premeditated, politically motivated violence perpetrated against non-combatant targets by subnational groups or clandestine agents." See *National Strategy for Combating Terrorism*, February 2003, p. 1. The two consistent themes through these documents are the equation of terrorism with the *unlawful* use or threatened use of violence, and the identification of terrorists as *subnational or clandestine agents*. In either case *the lawful use* or threatened use of violence by governments is sanctioned, for whatever purpose and regardless of means. This demands public discussion.

[40] Thucydides, as quoted in Chomsky 2002, 147.

expressions of humanitarian concern for the well-being of the Iraqi people. After helping to build Saddam Hussein's government into a regional power as a bulwark against Iran, the United States had to fight its creation after it became uncontrollable and invaded oil-rich Kuwait. U.S. desire for Saudi oil has created close relationships of mutual dependency between U.S. government and industry and the Saudi royal family. Despite the fact that fifteen of the nineteen hijackers of September 11 were Saudi nationals, and that Saudi support for Islamic radicalism in the Middle East and Central Asia helped fuel the creation of Al Qaeda, the Taliban, and other groups, toppling the government of Saudi Arabia is not on the U.S. agenda. The United States already has what it wants from that country, and it seems that Al Qaeda is much more interested than the U.S. in fundamental change in Saudi Arabia. Access to Middle East oil on favorable terms remains a national-security priority for the U.S. government, and Saudi Arabia will be a U.S. ally so long as the Saudi government cooperates with U.S. efforts to maintain a steady flow of reasonably priced oil.[41]

A war on "every terrorist organization of global reach" will not change any of this. To address this situation we need to reduce energy consumption, something not favored by either the oil-producing countries, U.S. energy companies, or a host of others who benefit from the present arrangements and above all else want to maintain the existing revenue streams and the power that goes with them. Environmentally sustainable energy consumption should be a national objective, but it will be resisted precisely because it challenges entrenched economic and political power.

All of this should be kept in mind as we listen to the statements of our government officials, many of whom have established records of manipulative lying to facilitate the use of force to extend American power for private benefit. It also should be kept in mind the next time there is an attack in the United States, something that is highly likely given both the existence of groups like Al Qaeda and the huge interest some have in the perpetuation of threats from which we need to be protected at great cost. The United States is the most powerful state in world history, and its present leaders are using the attacks of September 11 as political cover for an effort to expand this power. This is about greed and empire, and

---

[41] Alan P. Larson, "Economic Priorities of the National Security Strategy," *U.S. Foreign Policy Agenda* (Electronic Journal of the Department of State) 7, no. 4 (December 2002), at http://usinfo.state.gov/journals/itps/1202/ijpe/pj7-4larson.htm: "We need to secure reliable supplies of energy at reasonable prices in order to foster economic growth and prosperity, and to ensure that oil cannot be used as a weapon. We must deal with some hard facts about the international oil markets. Two-thirds of proven world oil reserves are in the Middle East. Europe and Japan, like the United States, rely on imports to meet a growing portion of oil needs. Aftershocks from global oil supply disruptions will ripple through the global economy. Finally, problem states control significant amounts of oil."

democratic government is threatened by the lying, fraud, and violence necessary to sustain this project.[42]

References

Chomsky, Noam. 2002. *Pirates and Emperors: Old and New*. Cambridge, Mass.: South End Press.

Suskind, Ron. 2004. *The Price of Loyalty*. New York: Simon and Schuster.

---

[42] President Bush brought the contempt with which government officials treat the American public to new heights in an interview on the ABC News program *prime time* with Diane Sawyer, December 16, 2003, available at http://abcnews.go.com/sections/primetime/US/bush_sawyer_excerpts_2_031216.html. The excerpt is from a discussion of U.S. intelligence and weapons of mass destruction in Iraq:

> DIANE SAWYER: But let me try to ask—this could be a long question. . . . When you take a look back, Vice President Cheney said there is no doubt, Saddam Hussein has weapons of mass destruction, not programs, not intent. There is no doubt he has weapons of mass destruction. Secretary Powell said 100 to 500 tons of chemical weapons and now the inspectors say that there's no evidence of these weapons existing right now. The yellow cake in Niger, in Niger. George Tenet has said that shouldn't have been in your speech. Secretary Powell talked about mobile labs. Again, the intelligence—the inspectors have said they can't confirm this, they can't corroborate.

> PRESIDENT BUSH: Yet.

> DIANE SAWYER: —an active—

> PRESIDENT BUSH: Yet.

> DIANE SAWYER: Is it yet?

> PRESIDENT BUSH: But what David Kay did discover was they had a weapons program, and had that, that—let me finish for a second. Now it's more extensive than, than missiles. Had that knowledge been examined by the United Nations or had David Kay's report been placed in front of the United Nations, he, he, Saddam Hussein, would have been in material breach of 1441, which meant it was a *causus belli*. And look, there is no doubt that Saddam Hussein was a dangerous person, and there's no doubt we had a body of evidence proving that, and there is no doubt that the president must act, after 9/11, to make America a more secure country.

> DIANE SAWYER: Again, I'm just trying to ask, these are supporters, people who believed in the war who have asked the question.

> PRESIDENT BUSH: Well, you can keep asking the question and my answer's gonna be the same. Saddam was a danger and the world is better off cause we got rid of him.

> DIANE SAWYER: But stated as a hard fact, that there were weapons of mass destruction as opposed to the possibility that he could move to acquire those weapons still—

> PRESIDENT BUSH: So what's the difference?

> DIANE SAWYER: Well—

PRESIDENT BUSH: The possibility that he could acquire weapons. If he were to acquire weapons, he would be the danger. That's, that's what I'm trying to explain to you. A gathering threat, after 9/11, is a threat that needed to be de—dealt with, and it was done after 12 long years of the world saying the man's a danger. And so we got rid of him and there's no doubt the world is a safer, freer place as a result of Saddam being gone.

DIANE SAWYER: But, but, again, some, some of the critics have said this combined with the failure to establish proof of, of elaborate terrorism contacts, has indicated that there's just not precision, at best, and misleading, at worst.

PRESIDENT BUSH: Yeah. Look—what—what we based our evidence on was a very sound National Intelligence Estimate. . . .

DIANE SAWYER: Nothing should have been more precise?

PRESIDENT BUSH: What—I, I—I made my decision based upon enough intelligence to tell me that this country was threatened with Saddam Hussein in power.

DIANE SAWYER: What would it take to convince you he didn't have weapons of mass destruction?

PRESIDENT BUSH: Saddam Hussein was a threat and the fact that he is gone means America is a safer country.

This entire conversation is bogus, as we now know from Paul O'Neill. See note 2 above.

3

"US" AND "THEM":
THE POLITICS OF AMERICAN
SELF-ASSERTION AFTER 9/11

ANDREW NORRIS

The war is then considered to constitute the absolute last stand of humanity. Such a war is necessarily unusually intense and inhuman because, by transcending the limits of the political framework, it simultaneously degrades the enemy into moral and other categories and is forced to make of him a monster that must not only be repulsed but also utterly destroyed. In other words, he is no longer an enemy who must only be compelled to retreat into his borders.

—Carl Schmitt

Either you are with us, or you are with the terrorists.

—George W. Bush

What is the meaning of 9/11? To ask that question in the United States today is immediately to call forth images of the destruction wrought by the terrorist attacks of 2001, first of the collapse of the World Trade Center and then perhaps of the simultaneous attack upon the Pentagon, or even of the plane commandeered by terrorists that crashed that day in a field in western Pennsylvania. But there is no question in anyone's mind *which* September 11 is being referred to. Almost no one will even momentarily recall that September 11 is the anniversary of the 1973 U.S.-supported military coup in Chile, in which the democratically elected government of Salvador Allende was overthrown by General Augusto Pinochet, whose fifteen-year military dictatorship became notorious for its extraordinary human-rights abuses.[1] Though hardly surprising, on reflection this fact is perhaps even more striking than the idea that what is widely seen as an assault upon the United States is more closely associated with the destruction of a symbol of international capitalism than it is with an attack upon the actual center of operations for the American military; for it illustrates how profoundly disconnected the American people are from the history of what has been done with

---

[1] As late as June 1976 Henry Kissinger was assuring Pinochet, "In the United States, as you know, we are sympathetic with what you are trying to do here" (Kornbluh 1999). About as many will remember this sordid history as will recollect that the 11th is Theodor Adorno's birthday. Perhaps they will even be the same people.

their money and in their name. It is not that "our" trauma has blotted out the memory of "theirs," along with our complicity in it, but that there was little there to blot out to begin with. It is in part this disconnect that makes possible the deep sense of victimization that has gripped the United States in the wake of the attacks of September 11, 2001. Far too few asked—or ask—*why* these attacks took place, what *reasons* could be given for them. Instead of an attempt to understand what had happened and how it might be averted in the future, there was a rush to demonize the attackers and those who either supported or condoned them.

This was, no doubt, easy enough: the people who committed these terrible deeds had demonstrated an utter disregard for human life and for many of the values that make life worth living. But, precisely because these were political acts rather than isolated criminal deeds, no understanding of the private personal motivations and character of the terrorists in the planes and the people who gave them material aid could fully account for these deeds. Not every murder is a political assassination, least of all a terrorist deed that, as one is told again and again, forever changed the world. For it to be a political assassination, the act must resonate with many people other than the perpetrators, it must find at least tacit support elsewhere, and it must spring from conditions other than those of personal pathology. (If, for instance, Jackie Kennedy had killed JFK in a fit of jealous rage, it would not have been a political assassination, or even a political act, but a private, criminal act with enormous political repercussions.) That one of the conditions that made possible the attacks of September 11, 2001—one of the reasons for this attack—might be a widespread resentment of the United States' subversion of democracy abroad and its casual disregard of the standards to which it holds other nations accountable, as in the example of Chile, is a possibility that has not been widely enough considered in the United States.[2]

This is particularly true of the second Bush administration, which has responded to the attacks in a moralistic and deeply unhelpful manner, calling for a "war" to "rid the world of evil."[3] It is not difficult to see how this approach undermines any attempt to respond with anything other than violence. Indeed, Elaine Tyler May has argued convincingly that the

[2] David Campbell argues that "the idea that US foreign policy alone offers an explanation for the event is questionable. With no clear statement of grievances or claim of responsibility from anyone on behalf of those who undertook the suicide highjackings, Christopher Hitchens rightly observes that acting as a 'self-appointed interpreter for the killers' is rather rash" (Campbell 2002, 4). But one need hardly claim to be a privileged "interpreter" for the dead highjackers to ask what might motivate such people or lead their acts to be anything but universally condemned, any more than claiming that U.S. foreign policy is an important part of what produces the conditions for such actions and such support (however qualified) amounts to claiming that U.S. foreign policy "alone offers an explanation for the event." To suggest otherwise is to attack straw men.
[3] I quote here Bush's address at the National Cathedral on September 14, 2003, but this has been a recurrent theme of his and his cabinet's.

Bush administration's rhetoric of war succeeded in cutting off whatever self-reflection had been provoked by the attacks. And it did so with the aid of hysterical media that reported as facts mere speculations about what "we" felt (righteous anger) and what we needed (revenge, blood) in the wake of the attacks, which only helped to make them so (May 2003, 36–37 and 45). It is only in retrospect that this process could appear to be an instantaneous one, as in George Weigel's hyperbolic and somewhat silly claim that, "in less than two hours, between the first attack on the World Trade Center and the crash of the fourth highjacked airliner in rural Pennsylvania, Americans discovered, or rediscovered, moral absolutes. . . . There was good, and there was evil. We could tell the difference again, and we could use those words again" (Weigel 2002, 14). Americans have always used those words, though not perhaps so easily and so often as they do now, or as their leaders and spokesmen in the government and the press do. Even this is not, however, so positive a development as Weigel suggests in his defense of the relevance of the Catholic tradition of the just war. War calls for combat, not self-scrutiny; and one does not reason with evil or seek to compromise with it—one does not, as Noam Chomsky has put it, "consider realistically the background concerns and grievances, and . . . try to remedy them, while at the same time following the rule of law to punish criminals" (Chomsky 2002, 62–63; compare 123). Evil is not a crime but a sin; its origin is a mystery of theology, not poverty or political oppression, and one *fights* it; if one is lucky, one destroys it.

This makes the use of the rhetoric of evil extremely problematic for those who would otherwise resist the Bush administration's Manichean impulses, as is evident in William Schulz's generally fine book, *Tainted Legacy: 9/11 and the Ruin of Human Rights*. Schulz, the executive director of Amnesty International U.S.A., begins his first chapter by agreeing with Bush that the terrorists who acted on 9/11 were "evil." But since he wants to argue that their acts must be "punished" (Schulz 2003, 15–16), as if evil were a violation of positive law, rather than stamped out as instances of the demonic, Schulz is driven to splitting hairs among forms of evil, as when he asks rhetorically, "If something is considered *overwhelmingly, irredeemably, incomprehensibly* evil, the very embodiment of the Satanic, then may we not be justified in using virtually any means to eradicate it?" (21, emphasis added). Presumably we shall not be justified if we can see the terrorists as *less than overwhelmingly, redeemably,* and *comprehensibly* evil—an evil, in short, with which we could live. The retreat from the agreement with Bush on the simple evil of the terrorists is completed when Schulz admits that "we do not punish them for *being* evil; we punish them for committing specific, identifiable crimes" (22), which more or less puts "evil" into a black box of irrelevance. This allows Schulz to say that it is wrong—which it surely is—to suggest that "those whose humanity we can question—those who are part of the 'world of evil' in the president's words, or, more graphically, 'barbarians,' in the vice president's—have forfeited their rights by forfeiting their humanity" (121). "In order to inflict torture, you must on some emotional level understand your victim to be subhuman and therefore not eligible to claim human rights. 'Barbarians,' Vice President Cheney's word, does nicely" (121). Given Schulz's rejection of this, and given the fact that he ultimately agrees with many of the criticisms of Bush I shall advance here, his initial agreement may have as much to do with his attempt to draw in as wide an ideological array of readers as possible as it does with any substantive commitments on his part. However, the difficulties this involves Schulz in point to the dangers of a moralistic, comic-book account of a battle of "good guys" against evil. Especially given the nature of the "good guys" in question, it is surely more helpful to begin by setting aside such simplistic terms and oppositions.

This point does not apply just to moral or theological language but to any that might do the same work. Consider in this regard Schulz's definition of "terrorism" as "non-state actors . . . committing acts of violence against 'non-combatant targets,' involving violations of those targets' human rights, for some larger political or religious purpose" (Schulz 2003, 178). Why, one wonders, should it be possible only for "non-state actors" to commit acts of terrorism? Sharon's Israel and Bush's America are surely guilty of "committing acts of violence against 'non-combatant targets,' involving violations of those targets' human rights, for some larger political or religious purpose." Schulz's response to this is to describe it as an attempt at "sidetracking" the real issue and to claim, with no argumentative support whatsoever, that "if we are to keep the use of the word 'terrorism' within manageable boundaries, it makes sense to limit its application to groups separate from the state (except of course where a state is so closely identified with terrorists or acquiescent in terrorism, as Libya was in the Lockerbie bombing, that it is impossible to tell the state and the terrorists apart, in which case we can properly speak of 'state-sponsored terrorism')" (82). But this is only more "manageable" if we find it difficult or inconvenient to see our government as engaging in the sort of "evil" conduct it attacks. In this context it is helpful to recall the U.S. cold-war policy of Mutually Assured Destruction, or MAD, which required threatening the populations of the Soviet Union, and indeed the world at large, with the most terrifying destruction so as to ward off any nuclear attack upon the United States or its client states. As Michael Walzer puts it, "It is immoral to make threats of this kind. . . . [It is] an immorality we can never hope to square with our understanding of justice in war. Nuclear weapons explode the theory of just war" (Walzer 1977, 278 and 282).[4] Likewise, the Allied "terror bombing" of German cities during World War II and, more to the point, Clinton's bombing of the El Shifa pharmaceutical plant in Sudan are

---

[4] That Walzer immediately adds "we move uneasily beyond the limits of justice for the sake of justice" does nothing to deny that this use of terrifying threats is unjust or immoral.

accurately described as acts of terror that slaughtered, maimed, or indirectly killed thousands (Walzer 1977, 255–63 and 323; Shaw 1988, 78–79; Mahajan 2003, 35ff.). To acknowledge the United States' own use of terror in such cases would automatically make it impossible to rally the nation to fight "evil" in the name of "the war on terror." The point being not to play tit for tat but to resist moralistic oversimplifications of complex political phenomena.[5]

It is not easy to do this in a society in which the main forum for public debate is televised programs. As the sociologist Zygmunt Bauman observes, the mass media, particularly television, the dominant medium in our time, are naturally drawn to the presentation of *narratives* of *individual actors*, as these adapt themselves easily to visual presentation: a battle between individuals can be shown on television as a careful analysis of differences; complex policies cannot. Bauman cites Martin Esslin's pithy summation, "Drama is always action; its action is that of human beings. In drama we experience the world through personality" (Esslin 1973, 20). The consequences of this structural feature of the medium help to determine a large part of what will be said about politics in the forum that dominates political discussion in our time: "Among things left outside ["the media world," the world as presented by the mass media] is a large part of politics: . . . all the more abstract, principal matters of policy choices or historical trends which pertain to the systematic rather than the personal dimension of human life, and for this reason do let themselves be easily translated into images, passion dramas, personal interest stories" (Bauman 1988, 80).[6] This structural drive toward the celebration of personalities, characters, and plotted narratives that move either backward or forward, toward victory or defeat, favors the politician who demonizes his opponents and presents his struggle against them ready packaged for the medium, with an easily understood and clearly delineated plot and a stark, dramatic choice. It thus encourages a moralistic politics, if not a moral politics, a simplistic politics of good versus evil in which shades of gray are washed away, either in the course of the "show" or, for those with weaker skills or interests, before the

[5] One is reminded of George Orwell's comment, "Political language has to consist largely of euphemism, question-begging and sheer cloudy vagueness. Defenseless villages are bombarded from the air, the inhabitants driven out into the countryside, the cattle machine-gunned, the huts set on fire with incendiary bullets: this is called *pacification*" (Orwell 1962, 153). Or *Operation Iraqi Freedom*, conducted by a military which keeps no count of the number of Iraqis it kills and for which Iraqi lives, in this setting at least, literally don't count.

[6] For an excellent complementary account of the way the structural conditions of the private, corporate ownership of the mass media produce both a formal and a substantive subsumption of culture, political deliberation, and the general "marketplace of ideas" under the capitalist mode of production and hence corporate interests, see Jhally 1989. It is precisely this sort of structural account as opposed to individually motivated action that Bauman and Esslin argue television silently discourages.

program has even begun.[7] As Bush put it soon after the attacks, "You are either with us or against us."[8]

No doubt this is only a tendency. That other modes of evaluation and responses are possible even in our televised world, and even in the face of horrible acts of terror, is made plain by the U.S. response to the destruction of the Oklahoma City Federal Building. While the initial assumption that this was the work of Middle Eastern terrorists led to widespread calls for a violent response, when it was proven to be the work of domestic rightwing zealots this reaction quickly died down and "there was no call to obliterate Montana and Idaho" (Chomsky 2003, 24; and see May 2003, 37–38). Instead, it became a criminal matter and was dealt with by the courts. One reason for this quite different outcome has to do with the difference in status accorded to what have been widely described as varieties of fundamentalism, the "foreign" Islamic variety and the domestic Christian one. The difference in status is in part a matter of the dominance of conservative ideology in the United States, where a terrorist who threatens international capitalism will always be more terrifying than one who does not. But part of the difference is a more fundamental matter of maintaining a common identity. To treat abortion-clinic bombers as soldiers fighting in a war, as Bush almost does members of Al Qaeda, would be tantamount to fighting a civil war.[9] The Bush administration seeks to take the country in precisely the opposite direction, making use of 9/11 to forge a new unity, as if the only alternative to civil war were submersion in a common identity. (That this is a matter of this particular administration's overall strategy explains why the earlier attack on the Twin Towers in 1993 did not generate a similar mobilization of the nation.) As Attorney General John Ashcroft has put it, any criticism of the administration's decisions or its handling of "the war on terror" only serves to "aid terrorists [and] erode our national unity and diminish our resolve" (cited in May 2003, 49). Such a stark and on the face of it utterly unreasonable attempt to defend a democratic nation by squashing public debate about its government and policies will hardly be adequately

---

[7] For a good account, by a journalist, of the ways journalism serves the state by dividing the world between "the forces of light and the forces of darkness," an attack upon authentic moral consciousness that amounts to "the destruction of culture," see Hedges 2003, 62ff. and 144.

[8] As Richard Falk notes, "The president's good-versus-evil rhetoric also denies shades of gray," and "implies too much clarity in a world that's much messier than that." "It shows a lack of respect for the sovereignty of other countries and may place them between contradictory pressures." Cited in Jordan 2001. Jordan quotes a South American diplomat as saying, "If you ask whether we condemn the Sept. 11 attack, we're with you. But is more violence the best answer? The Americans don't leave room for alternative opinions. When will countries speak out: after 1,000, 100,000, or 1 million more are killed?"

[9] I say "almost" because, as I shall discuss further below, Bush won't grant prisoners in Guantánamo and other such holding facilities accused of being "enemy combatants" the rights due soldiers under international law.

challenged by a citizenry sporting "United We Stand" bumper stickers in the windows of their SUVs.

Both the leaders and the led seem to be adopting a Hobbesian logic that poses the sacrifice of plurality and argumentative deliberation as the cost of heading off perpetual civil war and dispersed impotence in the face of threats from abroad.

> The only way to erect such a Common Power, as may be able to defend them from the invasion of Forraigners, and the injuries of one another . . . is, to conferre all their power and strength upon one Man, or one Assembly of men, that may reduce all their Wills, . . . unto one Will: which is as much to say, to appoint one man, or Assembly of men, to beare their Person; and every one to . . . submit their Wills, every one to his Will, and their Judgements, to his Judgement. This is more than Consent, or Concord; it is a real Unitie of them all, in one and the same Person. [Hobbes 1968, 227]

So much for the Aristotelian idea that human beings are political animals because they can and must speak with one another about questions of justice and injustice (Aristotle 1978, 10–11)! For Ashcroft as for Hobbes, the teaching of such doctrines as Aristotle's only produces "a habit (under a false shew of Liberty), of favouring tumults, and of licentious controlling of the actions of their Soveraigns" (Hobbes 1968, 267). In the United States today the need to avoid anything that hints at civil war or fundamental disagreements about what our common identity might be (Christian? pro-"life"? pro-"choice"?) dovetails with the creation of a personality that might star in a narrative drama. This fits well with Hobbes's account of sovereignty, in which the sovereign "personates" the community, and where "person" plays upon its theatrical roots as the mask that identifies a play's character: "A multitude of men, are made *One* Person, when they are by one man, or one Person, represented. . . . For it is the *Unity* of the Representer, not the *Unity* of the Represented, that make the Person *One*" (Hobbes 1968, 220; see 228). "We" see ourselves in the person who represents us. In America, only the president represents all Americans. Thus far the separation of powers has meant that the executive is not the sovereign, but that may be changing, as the assertion of the person who "we" are unfolds in the drama that is its struggle against evil. As Bush has put it too, "Either you are with us, or you are with the terrorists."[10]

The expert in Islamic law Khaled Abou El Fadl has noted the irony that this reactive posture is also typical of a large current of the contemporary Islamic world. A "siege mentality" has set in, whereby many Muslims in the postcolonial world accept the binary oppositions which defined that world, the West versus its "Other," the orientalist's East. On Abou El Fadl's account, the results have been remarkably

---

[10] http://www.suntimes.com/terror/stories/cst-nws-main21.html.

similar to those we see in America under Bush: questions of power have usurped questions of principle, whose "universalism" is too often cast as a "Western" colonial imposition.

> Therefore, instead of Islam being a moral vision given to humanity, it becomes constructed into the antithesis of the West. In the world constructed by these groups, there is no Islam: there is effectively only opposition to the West. This type of Islam that the radicalized groups offer is akin to a perpetual state of emergency where expediency trumps principle and illegitimate means are constantly justified by invoking higher ends.

He goes on to note that even in this state of mutual siege one can hardly speak of a clash of civilizations à la Samuel Huntington: "Considering the numerous cultural interactions and cross-intellectual transmissions between the Muslim World and Europe, it is highly likely that every significant Western value has a measure of Muslim blood in it" (Abou El Fadl 2003, 79, 80, 81).[11] Given the role that Islam, and Baghdad in particular, played in the recovery and preservation of the Greek philosophical heritage, this is hardly an exaggeration.

Moreover, as Abou El Fadl notes, both of these "worlds" are quite diverse. Jews and Christians do not agree about everything, the recently developed notion of the Judeo-Christian heritage notwithstanding; even in the extraordinarily religious and largely Christian United States there are millions of atheists, not to mention Buddhists, Hindus, and so on. And the Islamic world—part of which lives in New York, and Philadelphia, and London—is also extremely diverse. Abou El Fadl does an excellent job of laying this out, as well as drawing attention to the way that the legacy of postcolonialism has encouraged an exaggerated role for the unitary state or nation that is foreign to Islam. Not coincidentally, reactionary developments in Islam, such as Wahhabism, have been profoundly influenced by such themes.[12] It is little wonder that some

---

[11] From a somewhat different angle, Noam Chomsky also points out that speaking of a clash between Islam and the West "makes little sense" in this context: "The most populous Islamic state is Indonesia, a favorite of the United States ever since Suharto took power in 1965, as army-led massacres slaughtered hundreds of thousands of people, mostly landless peasants, with the assistance of the U.S."; "the most extreme Islamic fundamentalist state, apart from the Taliban, is Saudi Arabia, a U.S. client state since its founding"; and, most pertinently perhaps, "in the 1980s the U.S. and the U.K. gave strong support to their friend and ally Saddam Hussein—more secular, to be sure, but on the Islamic side of the 'clash'—right through the period of his worst atrocities, including the gassing of the Kurds" (2002, 78–79).

[12] As the Saudi example makes plain, even the most reactionary "Islamic" regimes will not simply mirror the United States, if only because they have to appease reactionary and potentially subversive forces in their own population that respond—quite understandably—with rage to the combination of impotence in domestic politics, where democratic institutions are weak and compromised, and humiliation abroad, where the United States flaunts its power and its indifference to the effects it might have on others. Even the Indonesian government now has second thoughts about the Bush response to 9/11. In a

have concluded that that what 9/11 has been used to bring about—what it now means for those living in a world structured by responses to it—is a battle between forces that deeply resemble one another, even a two-sided fundamentalist Jihad (e.g., Hedges 2003, 4).

The moralistic oversimplifications central to each "side" are all the more to be resisted given the fact that the rhetoric of a war against evil does not just condemn one's enemy to the status of the inhuman but, as many have pointed out, also presents the enemy of evil—Bush, Ashcroft, "us"—as necessarily "good," an insinuation that has not helped Americans think clearly about the Patriot Act, the war in Iraq, or the use of torture in offshore holding facilities like Guantánamo Bay (which the U.S. government either engages in or gets done by its proxies, such as Egypt, and which according to some polls 45 percent of the population now supports, given the proper conditions).[13] "The enemy of my enemy is my friend" is a dangerous adage, and it is both a paradox and an inevitability that, in a struggle to rid the world of evil, one will end up with friends and clients like Pinochet, as the Bush administration's alliance in its "war on terrorism" with antidemocratic forces throughout the world reminds us. It is not an inevitability that the same government would, in the service of this struggle, publicly embrace political assassination in the absence of any trial (so-called "extra-judicial executions"), but this is not particularly surprising.[14] Indeed, the announcement of this

December 8, 2003, speech, Indonesian Foreign Minister Hassan Wirajuda acknowledged, "The situation in Iraq today shows that smart bombs and air cover cannot turn the tide against terrorism. Terrorists have no fixed addresses that can be obliterated once and for all with surgical strikes." "An arbitrary pre-emptive war has been waged against a sovereign state—arbitrary because it is without sufficient justification in international law. Does that mean that any state may now individually and arbitrarily decide to use force pre-emptively against any other state perceived as a threat?" (*New York Times*, December 8, 2003).

[13] Schulz 2003, 154–70, provides an excellent and thoughtful discussion of the moral and pragmatic issues surrounding the renewed debate on torture (see also Zizek 2002, 102–4). But Schulz also, as above, provides a good model of someone who does not adequately criticize the broader context of such debates. I noted above his compromising use of the rhetoric of evil. This is matched by his suggestion that "the World Trade Center victims . . . were good people. . . . Theirs was an honorable legacy" (Schulz 2003, 17–18). With all due respect for the dead, what might possibly justify such a sweeping claim? Are all innocent victims for that reason good or honorable people? Schulz does not even try to answer this, announcing instead that "when those 3,000 [*sic*] people died on September 11, 2001, the meaning of their individual lives was immediately transposed in the minds of hundreds of millions of people around the world into something larger, a symbol of the best of the American tradition, a proud legacy of liberty, generosity, freedom, and respect for human rights" (Schulz 2003, 197–98). This is simply the flip side of the demonization not just of the terrorists but of all who fail to understand their deed as anything but an attack on this "proud" and "honorable" legacy—and understand it instead as, say, a case of political actors engaged in a struggle with an empire.

[14] "CIA Told to Do 'Whatever Necessary' to Kill Bin Laden; Agency and Military Collaborating at 'Unprecedented' Level; Cheney Says War Against Terror 'May Never

policy has not led to any widespread expression of outrage or shame in the United States. Moralistic rhetoric and immoral deeds seem here to call each other forth, and, for all of the evident fundamentalist religiosity of leading members of the Bush administration, the meanings of the political terms in play—*terrorist, freedom fighter, liberation, prevention,* even *war*—seem to be determined less by objective or even simply enduring criteria than by the exigencies of a conflict between "us" and "them."[15] Our acts are reactions, and as such they are determined by what they oppose. In ordinary circumstances, no doubt, constitutional prohibitions against torture, wars of aggression, and violations of privacy and so on apply. But in the extraordinary circumstances of the war on terror—a war that Cheney for one has suggested may never end—these prohibitions must be relaxed. In this perhaps permanent state of emergency, more Machiavellian principles apply, and the defense of legality and morality will require extralegal if not immoral acts. The responsibility for this is that of the original actor, who has forced this devil's choice upon us.[16] This takes popular form in the widespread notion that terrorists attack the United States because they envy us. Here, as in our blissful ignorance of our own history, we are passive: we are simply enjoying our economy and our freedom; it is the others who observe us with envy and then act to tear us down.

Bush is on record as claiming that Jesus Christ is his favorite political philosopher. Given the Machiavellian nature of the compromises he insists upon, there is reason to doubt whether he has read his favorite philosopher's words as carefully as one might hope. But one might well

End,"' Bob Woodward, *Washington Post*, October 21, 2001. Cited in Mahajan 2003, 197. As Kennedy's well-known plans to assassinate Castro testify, U.S.-sponsored assassination is not a new idea, but it has not been so openly proclaimed in the past. As with the "war on terror," which every repressive regime in the world now uses as a cover for its violence, U.S. public acceptance of the idea of political assassination will only encourage this practice by others. Israel, for instance, has long practiced assassination of suspected terrorists, with U.S.-provided gunships; but it has only recently publicly floated the idea of assassinating Arafat himself.

[15] For a deeply religious man, Bush was profoundly unconcerned by the resistance of so many church leaders to his planned war on Iraq.

[16] In his Web-site "testimony" of his faith (www.pray4bush.com), Bush declares: "My faith frees me. Frees me to put the problem of the moment in proper perspective. Frees me to make decisions that others might not like. Frees me to try to do the right thing, even though it may not poll well. . . . The death penalty is a difficult issue for supporters as well as its opponents. I have a reverence for life; my faith teaches that life is a gift from our Creator. In a perfect world, life is given by God and only taken by God. I hope someday our society will respect life, the full spectrum of life, from the unborn to the elderly. I hope someday unborn children will be protected by law and welcomed in life. I support the death penalty because I believe, if administered swiftly and justly, capital punishment is a deterrent against future violence and will save other innocent lives." Here, as in the war, it is not Bush himself who fails to respect life when he takes it, or orders it taken, but those whom he condemns to death. It is because they, and perhaps "our society" at large, do not respect life that he must take it.

argue that even a careful reading of the Gospels that focused on Christ as a teacher of either good deeds or love would not be the most helpful place to look for a political as opposed to a moral lesson. Indeed, the distinctively moral lesson to be learned here is one that would still encourage precisely Bush's drive toward an American community of unity and common identity. As Hannah Arendt argues in *The Human Condition*,

> The one activity taught by Jesus in word and deed is the activity of goodness, and goodness obviously harbors a tendency to hide from being seen or heard. Christian hostility toward the public realm, the tendency of at least early Christians to lead a life as far removed from the public realm as possible, can also be understood as a self-evident consequence of devotion to good works, independent of all beliefs and expectations. For it is manifest that the moment a good work becomes known and public, it loses its specific character of goodness, of being done for nothing but goodness' sake. [1958, 74]

This not only encourages a turning away from the public realm, which is the site of public deliberation not just in Arendt but in the Aristotelian tradition as a whole; it also leads to an excessive emphasis upon actors' *intentions*. Consider in this regard the contrast mentioned in my opening paragraphs above, between the personal motives of the terrorists and the underlying causes of terrorism, such as domestic political oppression in countries like Saudia Arabia that are supported by the United States (Schulz 2003, 26–27); if terrorism is seen as entirely a moral matter, the latter will readily appear as little more than a distraction from questions concerning the goodness of one's will and the categorical nature of moral imperatives.[17] (The language here is of course Kantian, but the Christian roots of this mode of moral thought should be equally obvious.)

Love is similarly at odds with an appreciation for the nature of distinctively political action: "Love, by virtue of its passion, destroys the in-between which relates us to and separates us from others. . . . Love, by its very nature, is unworldly, . . . not only apolitical but antipolitical" (Arendt 1958, 242). A community of good Christians who love one another is one opposed in principle to a public realm that celebrates

---

[17] Arendt's own alternative to such moral evaluation of the individual will is her account of political space as an arena in which principles and public persons reveal themselves in an audience's judgments. According to Arendt, principles are distinct from motives just as private selves are distinct from public persons: "Action, to be free, must be free from motive on the one side, from its intended goal as a predictable effect on the other. . . . Action insofar as it is free is neither under the guidance of the intellect nor under the dictate of the will—although it needs both for the execution of any particular goal. . . . Unlike the judgment of the intellect which precedes action, and unlike the command of the will which initiates it, the inspiring principle becomes fully manifest only in the performing deed itself." This principle is what the audience responds to, and it is only in the judgments of the audience that the political act is completed and the principle revealed and understood. Failing to evoke their judgment, the behavior of private individuals never rises to the level of the act of a public person (1968, 151–52).

plurality and diversity of perspectives. "The unpolitical, non-public character of the Christian community was early defined in the demand that it should form a *corpus*, a 'body,' whose members were to be related to each other like brothers of the same family" (53). Unity here, as in Hobbes and as in Ashcroft's vision of a united front against terror, is achieved at the cost of the diversity that makes public deliberation possible and worthwhile. On the one hand we have the body of Christ that is the church, and on the other we have the body politic (Norris 2000a). Where all are the same, and none occupies a different perspective, there is no need for discussion. "Being seen and being heard by others derive their significance from the fact that everybody sees and hears from a different perspective. This is the meaning of public life" (Arendt 1958, 57). "United we stand" is the slogan for a group that *asserts it*self, rather than a group of people who ask what *they* want and who *they* are—where they are characterized by internal differences as well as commonalities.[18] And in the absence of public discussion and public deliberation such self-assertion can be directed only in a hierarchical, authoritative mode that allows for the achievement of a single voice that might speak for the political unit, where the rest "submit their Wills, every one to his Will, and their Judgements, to his Judgement." Little wonder that 9/11 has produced a resurgence of the executive branch's power in America (Arato 2002) and the public's willingness to trust it (May 2003, 40).

So even on a sympathetic interpretation Bush's stated commitments in political philosophy are of a piece with the disastrous push for unity and submission being carried forward by his administration. But given how little Bush, Ashcroft, and Wolfowitz have concerned themselves with either love or good deeds, it seems unlikely that a sympathetic interpretation will best bring out the real picture of this administration's attempts to translate 9/11 into a political form. Indeed, the political philosopher most readily brought to mind by the Bush administration's language of reactive decisions taken in exceptional circumstances and in the context of a larger struggle between friends and enemies is not Jesus Christ but rather the lapsed Catholic and erstwhile Nazi Carl Schmitt. It will repay our time to consider this comparison in some detail.

Schmitt's most famous book, his 1927 *Concept of the Political*, argues that the political is distinguished from other spheres of human activity by virtue of its guiding concept. Where the economic is a matter or profit and loss, the moral a matter of good and evil (*Böse*), and the aesthetic a matter of beautiful and ugly, "the specific political distinction to which political actions and motives can be reduced is that between friend and enemy. This provides a definition in the sense of a criterion, and not as an exhaustive definition, or one indicative of substantial content" (Schmitt

---

[18] I sketch one way of understanding this model of a reflective community in Norris 2002.

1996a, 26).[19] The "friend" in question is neither the sentimental companion of modern life nor the Aristotelian *philos* but one with whom one
shares membership in a hierarchical mode of association in which the
voice of the unified political entity (*Einheit*) alone possesses "the *jus belli*,
i.e., the real possibility of deciding in a concrete situation upon the
enemy," as well as "the right to demand from its own members
the readiness to die and to kill enemies" (45 and 46). Conversely, the
"enemy," as Schmitt repeatedly emphasizes, but as too many of his
readers have failed to note, "is not merely any competitor or just any
partner of a conflict in general. He is also not the private adversary whom
one hates. An enemy exists only when, at least potentially, one fighting
collectivity of people confronts a similar collectivity. The enemy is solely
the public enemy" (28). Individual citizens have neither the authority nor
the responsibility to declare war against the public enemy, the declaration
of which is a sovereign decision.

Schmitt does not concern himself in *The Concept of the Political* with
the criteria of the legitimacy of the sovereign. But he does make clear, if
only indirectly, that sovereignty is a necessary condition of the political as
he understands it. In the absence of a sovereign voice that might declare
war and command the citizenry to fight, the unified political entity would
be unable to defend itself. The political mode of association is distinguished from other modes of association by virtue of that central concern
with the *survival* not of the individual, whose life may sacrificed in war,
but of the way of life of the collectivity (Norris 1998). Such questions
cannot be answered, according to Schmitt, by appeal to either impartial
judges or abstract norms, such as international law: "Only the actual
participants can correctly recognize, understand, and judge the concrete
situation and settle the extreme case of conflict. Each participant is in a
position to judge whether the adversary intends to negate his opponent's
way of life and therefore must be repulsed or fought in order to preserve
one's own form of existence [*die eigene seinsmäßige Art von Leben*]"
(Schmitt 1996a, 27; 1932, 15). The political way of life is *seinsmäßig*,
measured by the standard of its own being, and not any standard it might
share with a political enemy that by definition "is, in a specially intense
way, existentially something different and alien" (1996a, 27).

The decision the sovereign makes in naming the threat and the enemy
is one that declares a state of emergency. As Schmitt puts it in his earlier
Political Theology, "The Sovereign is he who decides on the (state of)
exception [*Ausnahmezustand*]," and

the exception appears in its absolute form when a situation in which legal
prescriptions can be valid must first be brought about. Every general norm
demands a normal [*normale*] everyday frame of life to which it can be factually

---

[19] I modify the translation of Schmitt's texts throughout when accuracy demands.

> applied and which is subjected to its regulations. The norm requires a
> homogenous medium. . . . For a legal order to make sense, a normal situation
> must exist, and he is sovereign who decides whether this normal situation
> actually exists. [1985, 5; 1996b, 13]

In the latter volume, this claim is repeated, in essentially the same
language, in the context of a discussion of "the decision emanating
from the political entity" to fight for its existence, independence, and
freedom:

> The endeavor of a normal state consists above all in assuring total peace within
> the state and its territory. To create "tranquility, security, and order" and
> thereby establish the normal [normalen] situation is the prerequisite for legal
> norms to be valid. Every norm presupposes a normal situation, and no norm
> can be valid in an entirely abnormal situation. [1996a, 46]

If the sovereign takes the view that the normal situation does not obtain,
then he must impose order in an extralegal fashion: "The decision frees
itself from all normative ties and becomes in the true sense absolute. The
state suspends the law in the exception [Ausnahmefall] on the basis of the
right of self-preservation [Selbsterhaltungsrechtes]" (1985, 12; 1996b, 18).
The sovereign decision determines whether what counts as a normal
situation for a given unified political entity obtains; or, conversely,
whether there is a state of exception or emergency. The question of the
norm and that of the exception are in truth one question, with two sides.
This is the reasoning that underlies Schmitt's dismissal of international
law. On his account, international law would have to be founded in the
constituting power of a sovereign decision. But the existence of a plurality
of nation-states belies the existence of any such sovereign. "A world state
which embraces the entire globe and all of humanity cannot exist" (1996a,
53). This means that international relations are more or less in a constant
state of crisis, in which only one side of the two-sided coin of law or
exception is revealed. As Locke, Hobbes, Hegel, and many others agreed,
international affairs remain in a state of nature.

What is particularly striking in the present context is the way Schmitt
emphasizes this and relates it to domestic politics. It is in its ability to
maintain order and to protect the polity from external and internal
threats that the sovereign fulfills its existential function. "The *protego ergo
sum* is the *cogito ergo sum* of the state" (Schmitt 1996a, 52). This
effectively identifies the domestic enemy (46) and the external political
enemy: "For to the enemy concept [zum Begriff des Feindes] belongs the
ever present possibility of combat" (1996a, 32; 1932, 20). It is in part for
this reason that Schmitt describes sovereignty as "a borderline concept
[Grenzbegriff]" (1985, 5; 1996b, 13). The sovereign decision on the state of
exception determines what will count as normal for the polity, and this
will determine the identity of the group: what it will mean here to be
political friends, and hence who is a friend and who is either a domestic or

an external political enemy. The decision, the *Entscheidung,* separates (*scheiden*) who belongs from who does not: it establishes the border, the *Grenze.* In doing so, and in determining the condition for law as such, the sovereign's decision "must necessarily be unlimited [*unbegrenzte*]" (1985, 5; 1996b, 13; cf. Norris 2000b). Straddling the limits of law and community identity, "the sovereign . . . stands outside the normally valid legal system, [but] nevertheless belongs to it, for it is he who must decide whether the constitution needs to be suspended in its entirety" (Schmitt 1985, 7).

The sovereign thus functions as a potential or actual sovereign dictator. By virtue of his union of the law (as constituted power) and the sovereign decision (on the state of exception as constituting power), Schmitt effectively undermines the authority of the law: being an effect or expression of the sovereign decision, the law is by its nature subservient to it. As many have noted, this violates Schmitt's own insistence in his book on dictatorship (written only a year before *Political Theology*) on the importance of distinguishing between sovereign dictatorship and the Roman model of commissarial dictatorship (McCormick 1997, 121ff.) In stark contrast to the sovereign dictator, the Roman commissarial dictator was appointed by a body other than himself for a limited amount of time to address a specific crisis (such as a plague, invasion, or rebellion) identified by the appointing body, not by the dictator's own sovereign decision. Norm governs exception, rather than vice versa.[20]

We are less concerned here with Schmitt's own reasons for violating his strictures on the necessity of not conflating these types of dictatorship than we are with how his position in *Political Theology* and *The Concept of the Political* might compare with the Bush administration's posture since 9/11. The resemblances are many, and striking: the emphasis upon the necessity of exceptional measures in reaction to a perceived threat to the very existence of the political way of life;[21] the demand that these measures require a mode of authority that precludes the active participation and explicit prior consent of the governed; the denial that the

[20] In characteristically counterintuitive fashion, Zizek argues that it is precisely the commissarial form of dictatorship or emergency powers that is to be condemned: "There is one feature common to all reactionary proclamations of a 'state of emergency': they have all been directed against popular unrest ('confusion') and presented as a decision to restore normality. In Argentina, in Brazil, in Greece, in Chile . . . " (Zizek 2002, 108). Following Walter Benjamin's distinction in the eighth of his "Theses on the Philosophy of History" between the "real" and the unreal state of emergency, Zizek proposes "a radical political Act" that will break us out of our current "deadlock" rather than restoring us to the grip of global capital (2002, 152). Interesting as this is, Zizek's enthusiasm for Lenin is in this regard troubling, to say the least.

[21] In ways this central rallying cry is the most open to criticism. It is patently obvious that, terrible as attacks such as those of 9/11 may be, they will threaten the *way of life* of the American people only in their indirect effects on the way the American people, their government, or their press behave.

governed can in principle identify the normal situation or a threat to it, and hence judge and regulate the executive or sovereign; the suggestion that the state of emergency is permanent, if only latently so; the rejection of international law (manifest in the Bush case both in its denial that the prisoners in holding facilities, such as those at Guantánamo Bay, are protected by the Geneva Conventions and in its rejection of the International Criminal Court, or ICC); the emphasis upon the unity of the community, in America the "homeland" since September 11, 2001;[22] and the bellicose, militaristic nature of that posited community.[23]

Even more ominous than all of this is the way the Bush administration echoes Schmitt's "borderline concept" of sovereignty. To some extent this is a matter of the administration's taking advantage of weaknesses and lapses in the U.S. Constitution, which does not establish a well worked out institutional framework for identifying and addressing states of emergency and constituting a commissarial as opposed to sovereign dictator to meet it. Andrew Arato rightly argues this would require that the dictator, for lack of a better word,

> not be self-appointed, and that emergencies be declared and ended by a body he does not control. . . . [A]ll such devices are merely technical and procedural, and . . . behind them "must stand an alert people, a real constituent power." But it is also true that well-designed rules would provide road signs for coming dangers for an alert citizenry and its organizations. . . . In the United States today, however, none of these principles are satisfied. The rules for emergency powers are extraordinarily flexible; they are determined without consultation, and are subject only to judicial scrutiny that usually comes too late. The president declares the emergency in which he alone exercises its powers. While Congress could end emergencies without fear of veto, and there are no statutory time limits, these provisions are mostly a dead letter. There are thus no legal signposts for public scrutiny of emergencies, and opposition is

[22] For a brilliant discussion of the nuances of the rhetoric of "the homeland," see Kaplan 2003.

[23] In a thoughtful consideration of the rise of rule by presidential fiat, Rudi Teitel also draws our attention to the Schmittian premises of these developments (2003, 204). Teitel also argues, however, that the state of exception in which the administration pictures itself acting is an international as opposed to national one: "The current administration's paradigm regarding law is really a form of 'law of the exception' and that . . . is associated with the regime's conception of the itself as the 'sovereign police.' It sees the role of the United States in the world as that of the one and only 'superpower.' In this world vision, the United States has sovereign power over the 'law of the exception'" (2003, 198). This would mark a break with Schmitt in ways that Teitel does not note; as I argue above, Schmitt can dismiss international law because law for him is coextensive with sovereignty, and there is no world sovereign. In a similar way, the current administration establishes a state of exception for aliens and, ultimately, citizens that it exposes to executive fiat; but it does not propose itself to be the world state or the world sovereign. This is not to say that the United States does not try to act in the name of humanity and in ways that undermine the sovereignty of other states, only that it does not by so doing establish itself as a police force that as such enforces law or anything like it. It does not intervene everywhere, only where its interests are at stake.

mostly driven into the inevitably mistaken, fruitless, and unpopular track of condemning all restrictions on civil liberties even in genuine emergencies. [2002, 471][24]

The president can thus with seeming legitimacy present himself as acting lawfully, or at least not in violation of explicit Constitutional provisions, when he claims extraordinarily sweeping emergency powers for himself. (Though this is of course hotly contested.) The Schmittian nature of this comes out even more clearly when one considers "unlawful combatants," the most striking objects of Bush's emergency measures after 9/11. Prisoners have been held incommunicado, without being formally charged, without access to counsel, and without any judicial review, potentially subject to courts established at the command of the president in which the executive branch claims the right to play judge, jury, and executioner. As David Cole rightly notes, "If another country were to lock up and try hundreds of people in secret, we would not hesitate to call the detainees 'disappeared'" (Cole 2002–2003). It is hardly a coincidence that Guantánamo Bay is itself a case of what Amy Kaplan describes as "legal limbo,"

> a geographical area in which both national and international laws are suspended, leaving it hovering in a realm that is neither domestic nor foreign. The United States has total jurisdiction over this space that the [federal appeals court that denied a writ of habeas corpus on behalf of a prisoner in March 2003] considers extraterritorial; Cuba has nominal sovereignty but no jurisdiction over the same territory it has leased in perpetuity to a foreign power with which it has no diplomatic relations. [2003, 65–66]

Although the administration has made token amendments to its sweeping claims to executive discretion in order to mollify the public, it is in principle committed to an extreme version of what seems to amount to a permanent state of exception in which U.S. citizens as well as aliens are subject, among other things, to indefinite detention at the command of the president without the right to consult a lawyer (Teitel 2003, 203).[25] I say "permanent" here because the administration has openly suggested that this war against evil and terror—which, like all wars fought by the United States since 1945, is one that the U.S. Congress did not even declare—may never end.

This declared state of exception mirrors the ambiguous nature of Schmitt's, where the sovereign and his actions define a border that is neither within nor without the constitutional order. While, as I have argued above, we are better off viewing the terrorist attacks as violations

---

[24] Arato is quoting Carl Friedrich's *Constitutional Government and Democracy*. For a thoughtful account of the general guidelines that would allow for a constitutional state of emergency that escapes the dangers of Schmitt's state of exception, see Schulz 2003, 183ff.

[25] As I write this early in 2004, there are promising signs from federal appeals courts in Manhattan and California that the judiciary will not allow this to go unchallenged.

of national and international law than as acts of war committed by nonstate actors, this is not to say that the matter is completely unambiguous. And this ambiguity opens itself up to the sort of arguments we have seen Schmitt making about the state's responsibility to establish a state of exception so as to develop the "homogenous medium" that makes possible the application of norms (Schmitt 1985, 13). As law professors Christopher Eisgruber and Lawrence Sager observe in a thoughtful piece on "the blurred boundary between domestic law and foreign affairs after 9/11," the attacks of 9/11 were in one sense a domestic criminal matter and in another a matter of foreign affairs. This is difficult terrain for U.S. law, as "judges have traditionally granted Congress and the presidency almost complete discretion over questions about immigration, the military, espionage, and many other aspects of foreign affairs" (Eisgruber and Sager 2003, 163). As I have emphasized, the Bush administration has made heavy and effective use of the language of war in this regard; but its practice has been considerably less straightforward, and it has not consistently treated these attacks and the defense against future such attacks as a matter of foreign affairs rather than domestic law. Instead, "the Bush administration has created a third track for detention of suspected terrorists and enemy agents, one that features neither the protections of the ordinary criminal process nor the protections of ordinary prisoner-of-war status" (172).

Eisgruber and Sager suggest that the courts should not in response to this abandon their responsibilities, and that they cannot give the executive branch as much leeway here as they have allowed in the past in matters unambiguously concerned with foreign policy.

> Courts might . . . not only play a gatekeeping function with regard to prisoner-of-war status, but also insist that the government choose between the criminal law track and the prisoner-of-war track. Such a doctrine would demand that in order for the government to hold people as prisoners of war, it must specify conditions that, if satisfied, would constitute an end to the "war" and hence entitle the prisoners to release. If the government were unwilling to do that, and wanted the power to incarcerate people indefinitely on the basis of the dangerous plots in which they had been engaged, then it would have to try them for crimes. [2003, 172]

In its open resistance to such judicial oversight, the Bush administration comes dangerously close to establishing itself as a Schmittian creature of the border, one that is neither within nor without the constitutional order, and that places "enemy combatants" and others in a permanent state of exception in which they are subject neither to domestic legal norms nor to the rules of international law but only to its sovereign decision.[26]

---

[26] For an interesting if somewhat excessive account of accused enemy combatants as the objects of a sovereign decision, see Giorgio Agamben's forthcoming *State of Exception*. I

If the comparison to Schmitt is helpful because of the starkness and clarity with which he expresses positions he shares with Bush and Ashcroft, it is also helpful for the limits he proposes to these dangerous views. The administration has made it plain that wars such as that being fought in Iraq are in large part at least a matter of spoils to be won and shared by the victors. Wolfowitz's memo appealing to national security as the grounds on which those nations, such as France, Germany, and Russia, who did not support the United States' preemptive war in Iraq will be barred from bidding for reconstruction contracts is only the most shameless expression of this. The more general problem concerns the privatization of the war business in America. As Chalmers Johnson makes painfully clear, the outsourcing of "every conceivable kind of service except firing a rifle or dropping a bomb" has produced a situation in which "the potential for private profit in U.S. warmaking has become . . . almost impossible to exaggerate. The war [in Iraq] has been a bonanza, for instance, for both Halliburton, the energy holding company, and for Bechtel, the number-one construction contractor in the United States. Dick Cheney was CEO of Halliburton from 1995 to 2000. George Shultz was Bechtel's president for eight years before becoming Ronald Reagan's secretary of state." With such a revolving door between companies that profit from war and the occupation of defeated lands and the government, particularly the executive branch, it is not to be expected that wars will cease any time soon. As Johnson puts it, "When war becomes the most profitable course of action, we can certainly expect more of it" (2003, 57, 54, and 58). Schmitt's probable response to this is indicated by his bitter comment in *The Concept of the Political* that "to demand seriously of human beings that they kill others and be prepared to die themselves so that trade and industry may flourish for the survivors or that the purchasing power of the grandchildren may grow is sinister and crazy" (1996a, 48). Schmitt himself may not give us much help in resisting this or any other encroachment of the market upon political matters (Marcuse 1968), but he at least reminds us of the impropriety of what is fast becoming business as usual.

But, of course, the demand to kill and die is never put in these harsh terms to the largely underprivileged men and women serving in the U.S. military. In a remarkably prescient moment in *The Concept of the Political*, Schmitt observes how the sinister lunacy of slaughter and military sacrifice for financial gain leads inexorably to its opposite extreme, that of a war fought in the name of humanity. "A war waged to protect or expand economic power must, with the aid of propaganda, turn into a crusade and into the last war of humanity" (1996a, 79). To fight in the name of humanity does not eliminate enmity, it only makes

discuss Agamben's use of Schmitt in my 2003. A more measured if equally disturbing account of the treatment of "unlawful combatants" can be found in Schulz 2003, 93ff.

one's enemy the representative or embodiment of the inhuman. "Evil,"
"barbarian," "inhuman": such an opponent is worthy of no respect, and
can justly be tortured or even exterminated.[27]

For all of the danger of many of his doctrines, even Schmitt recognizes
that

> humanity as such cannot wage war because it has no enemy, at least on this
> planet. The concept of humanity excludes the concept of the enemy, because
> the enemy does not cease to be a human being. . . . To confiscate the word
> humanity, to invoke and monopolize such a term probably has certain
> incalculable effects, such as denying the enemy the quality of being human
> and declaring him to be an outlaw of humanity; and a war can thereby be
> driven to the most extreme inhumanity. [1996a, 54]

Schmitt mentions in this regard the extermination (*ausrotten*) of the indigenous North Americans, and he speculates that, "as civilization pro-
gresses and morality rises, even less harmless things than devouring
human flesh could perhaps qualify as deserving to be outlawed in such
a manner. Maybe one day it will be enough if a people were unable to pay
its debts" (1996a, 54). The irony is heavy here, in the reference to a moral
progress that demands outlawing a people and their way of life "in such a
manner," that is, by extermination. Gopal Balakrishnan puts the matter
well when he says that Schmitt's response to this is to propose for
politics "a minimal ethic: not love your neighbor, but respect your
enemy" (2000, 108).

No doubt it will be hard indeed to respect anyone who does not join us
in wholeheartedly condemning the attacks of September 11, 2001. And
the fact that this is a struggle against terrorists will make it impossible to
end the "war" by compelling the enemy "to retreat into his borders," as
the epigraph from Schmitt to this essay puts it (1996a, 36). The terrorists
have no state of their own—indeed, as John Gray has argued, "unconventional warfare of the kind practiced by Al Qaeda has its breeding
grounds in the zones of anarchy that flow from failed states," such as are
found in "much of Africa, parts of post-communist Russia, in Afghanistan and Pakistan, in Latin American countries such as Columbia and
Haiti and in regions of Europe such as Bosnia and Kosovo, Chechnya
and Albania" (2003, 73–74). This argues against conceiving of the
struggle against terror as a war. It should also remind us that we shall
have to help the people in these sites of chaos give themselves borders and
states if we want them to feel anything but victimized and righteously
angry—if, in other words, we want them to have political alternatives to
terrorism, alternatives that will allow them the autonomy and security

---

[27] Schmitt does maintain in *The Concept of the Political* that "all genuine political theories
presuppose man to be evil ['*böse*']" (1996a, 61; 1932, 49). But Schmitt, in contrast to Bush, is
talking about *all* human beings, not just those in the enemy camp. And immediately he goes on
to specify, "i.e., by no means an unproblematic but a dangerous and dynamic being."

enjoyed by those of us who, by an odd coincidence, do not feel driven to self-destructive acts of terror, those of us who are not yet "evil" (Schulz 2003, 26–27). This will require the nation building (or, better, state building) that Bush initially condemned and now practices in a unilateral and opportunistic fashion. And that will in turn require international cooperation and perhaps even some compromises in the United States' own sovereignty. But sovereignty is not necessarily safety, nor is it justice. And it is a fool's gamble to seek safety in injustice—just as it is a fool's gamble to assume that one's enemy is wholly irrational, and not motivated by an anger and frustration that one might share, and that one might help alleviate. This will no doubt be difficult. But it is not as hopeless a task as ridding the world of evil, nor is it as likely to undermine our own legal and moral order.

References

Abou El Fadl, Khaled. 2003. "9/11 and the Muslim Transformation." In *September 11 in History: A Watershed Moment?* edited by Mary Dudziak. London: Duke University Press.

Arato, Andrew. 2002. "The Bush Tribunals and the Specter of Dictatorship." *Constellations* 9, no. 4 (December): 47–471.

Arendt, Hannah. 1958. *The Human Condition*. Chicago: University of Chicago Press.

———. 1968. "What is Freedom?" In *Between Past and Future: Eight Exercises in Political Thought*, enlarged edition. New York: Penguin.

Aristotle. 1978. *Politics*. Translated by Ernest Barker. Oxford: Oxford University Press.

Balakrishnan, Gopal. 2000. *The Enemy: An Intellectual Portrait of Carl Schmitt*. London: Verso.

Bauman, Zygmunt. 1988. *Freedom*. Minneapolis: University of Minnesota Press.

Campbell, David. 2002. "Time is Broken: The Return of the Past in the Response to September 11." *Theory and Event* 5, no. 4, http://muse.jhu.edu/journals/theory_and_event/v005/5.4campbell.html.

Chomsky, Noam. 2002. *9–11*. New York: Seven Stories Press.

Cole, David. 2002–2003. "Their Liberties, Our Security." *Boston Review* 27, no. 6 (December/January), http://www.bostonreview.net/BR27.6/cole.html.

Eisgruber, Christopher, and Lawrence Sager. 2003. "Civil Liberties in the Dragon's Domain: Negotiating the Blurred Boundary between Domestic Law and Foreign Affairs after 9/11." In *September 11 in History: A Watershed Moment?* edited by Mary Dudziak. London: Duke University Press.

Esslin, Martin. 1973. *The Age of Television*. San Francisco: W. H. Freeman.

Gray, John. 2003. *Al Qaeda and What It Means to Be Modern*. New York: New Press.

Hedges, Chris. 2003. *War Is a Force That Gives Us Meaning*. New York: Anchor.

Hobbes, Thomas. 1968. *Leviathan*. Edited by C. B. Macpherson. New York: Penguin.

Jhally, Sut. 1989. "The Political Economy of Culture." In *Cultural Politics in Contemporary America*, edited by I. Angus and S. Jhally. New York: Routledge.

Johnson, Chalmers. 2003. "The War Business: Squeezing a Profit from the Wreckage in Iraq." *Harpers* 307, no. 1842 (November): 53–58.

Jordan, Michael J. 2001. " 'With or against us' war irks many UN nations: Bush's intention to broaden the war beyond Afghanistan fails to galvanize UN." *Christian Science Monitor*, November 14, http://www.csmonitor.com/2001/1114/p7s1-wogi.html.

Kaplan, Amy. 2003. "Homeland Insecurities: Transformations of Language and Space." In *September 11 in History: A Watershed Moment?* edited by Mary Dudziak. London: Duke University Press.

Kornbluh, Peter. 1999. "Kissinger and Pinochet." *The Nation* (March 29), http://www.thirdworldtraveler.com/Kissinger/KissingerPinochet_Nation.html.

McCormick, John P. 1997. *Carl Schmitt's Critique of Liberalism: Against Politics as Technology*. Cambridge: Cambridge University Press.

Mahajan, Rahul. 2003. *Full Spectrum Dominance: U.S. Power in Iraq and Beyond*. New York: Seven Stories Press.

Marcuse, Herbert. 1968. "The Struggle against Liberalism in the Totalitarian View of the State." *Negations: Essays in Critical Theory*. Boston: Beacon Press.

May, Elaine Tyler. 2003. "Echoes of the Cold War: The Aftermath of September 11 at Home." In *September 11 in History: A Watershed Moment?* edited by Mary Dudziak. London: Duke University Press.

Norris, Andrew. 1998. "Carl Schmitt on Friends, Enemies, and the Political." *Telos* 112 (summer): 68–88.

———. 2000a. "Jean-Luc Nancy and the Myth of the Common." *Constellations* 7, no. 2 (June): 272–95.

———. 2000b. "Carl Schmitt's Political Metaphysics: On the Secularization of the Outermost Sphere." *Theory and Event* 4, no.1 (summer), http://muse.jhu.edu/journals/theory_and_event/voo4/4.1norris.html.

———. 2002. "Political Revisions: Stanley Cavell and Political Philosophy." *Political Theory* 30, no. 6 (December): 828–51.

———. 2003. "The Exemplary Exception: Philosophical and Political Decisions in Giorgio Agamben's *Homo Sacer*." *Radical Philosophy* 119 (May/June): 6–16.

Orwell, George. 1962. "Politics and the English Language." *Inside the Whale and Other Essays*. New York: Penguin.

Sager, Lawrence, and Christopher Eisgruber. 2003. "Civil Liberties in the Dragon's Domain: Negotiating the Blurred Boundary between Domestic Law and Foreign Affairs after 9/11." In *September 11 in History: A Watershed Moment?* edited by Mary Dudziak. London: Duke University Press.

Schmitt, Carl. 1932. *Der Begriff des Politischen*. Munich: Duncker und Humblot.

———. 1985. *Political Theology*. Translated by George Schwab. Cambridge, Mass.: MIT Press.

———. 1996a. *The Concept of the Political*. Translated by George Schwab. Chicago: University of Chicago Press.

———. 1996b. *Politische Theologie*. Seventh edition. Berlin: Duncker und Humblot.

Schulz, William. 2003. *Tainted Legacy: 9/11 and the Ruin of Human Rights*. New York: Nation Books.

Shaw, Martin. 1988. *Dialectics of War: An Essay in the Social Theory of Total War and Peace*. London: Pluto Press.

Teitel, Rudi. 2003. "Empire's Law: Foreign Relations by Presidential Fiat." In *September 11 in History: A Watershed Moment?* edited by Mary Dudziak. London: Duke University Press.

Walzer, Michael. 1977. *Just and Unjust Wars*. New York: Basic Books.

Weigel, George. 2002. "The Just War Tradition and the World After September 11." *Logos: A Journal of Catholic Thought and Culture* 5, no. 3:13–44.

Young, Marilyn. 2003. "Ground Zero: Enduring War." In *September 11 in History: A Watershed Moment?* edited by Mary Dudziak. London: Duke University Press.

Zizek, Slavoj. 2002. *Welcome to the Desert of the Real: Five Essays on September 11 and Related Dates*. New York: Verso.

4

MISREADING ISLAMIST TERRORISM:
THE "WAR AGAINST TERRORISM" AND JUST-WAR THEORY

JOSEPH M. SCHWARTZ

We live in an age of imperial war, in which the lone global superpower endeavors to impose upon the world "free market" liberalism as the only tolerated path to "freedom." A likely outcome of this Sisyphean effort by the United States to transform the world in its own image could well be the very anti-Western Islamic rebellion against "liberty and democracy" that American policymakers erroneously claim is already in full swing. "American," rather than "Western," values now constitute the litany of imperial virtues. Much of Western Europe holds to a more nuanced conception of the democratic state's responsibility to regulate transnational capital. Thus, the United States government is so isolated in its imperial arrogance that its only reliable allies are its junior partner in the Anglo-American alliance and a "new Europe" of states that formerly lived under the hegemony of the deceased alternative empire (the USSR). These regimes, often governed today by a kleptocratic nationalist (former Communist) apparat, have yet to establish democratic traditions comparable to those of the Western European nations that express severe doubts about the new American *imperium*.

While some terrorist movements pose a security threat to innocent civilians across the globe, the imperial overreach of the neoconservative cabal within the Bush administration promises to exacerbate that threat (Atlas 2003; Lind 2003). An adequate response to the neoconservative claim that there exists a massive Islamist (that is, fundamentalist Islamic) threat to American freedoms necessitates a rational critique of both the neoconservative misreading of the origins of anti-Western Islamist terror (until recently Islamist terror has almost exclusively been visited upon other Muslims) and the neoconservative doctrine of "just" preemptive wars (National Security Council 2002). According to the neoconservatives, there exists an imminent, massive threat to the American way of life from cooperation between "terrorist states" and stateless terrorists. Such a threat can only be deterred by a unilateral U.S. global war against both enemies. Such a literal war of massive military force—not simply a metaphorical war of intelligence and espionage—can be justly waged, according to the new National Security Doctrine, against any sovereign state that fails to conform to the foreign-policy prescriptions—or moral values—of the United States (National Security Council 2002).

1. The End-of-the-Cold-War Origins of Global Islamist Politics

The U.S. global-war strategy—begun in Afghanistan, accelerated in Iraq—has transpired despite the reality that terrorist organizations are extremely decentralized; their strength is hard to estimate; and they operate frequently in weak states that can neither police terrorist organizations nor significantly aid them. The origins of the Al Qaeda terrorist network can be rationally discerned, even if we may not find particularly coherent or achievable its rhetorical goals of defeating the infidel West. Mideast experts, including the Middle East historian Bernard Lewis, the bête noire of many on the left, admit that the immediate demands of Al Qaeda, enunciated in its "Declaration of the World Islamic Front for Jihad Against the Jews and the Crusaders" issued on Febraury 23, 1998, are less "irrational" than their maximalist rhetoric promoting the conversion—or extermination—of all infidel Christians and Jews. The three demands of the global declaration are feasible (and two of them are about to be achieved!): the withdrawal of U.S. troops from Saudi Arabia; an end to sanctions against Iraq; and Islamic control over Muslim holy sites in Jerusalem (Lewis 1998). The extent to which Al Qaeda could recruit significant numbers of cadres if all three demands were satisfied is an intriguing question, even if the totalistic ideology of Al Qaeda envisions an endless war against infidels within the Muslim world and around the globe (Berman 2003a, 2003b).[1] Just as fears of "Islamic terror" misread the particular origins of Islamist politics, so does the doctrine of "just war" against terrorism threaten the excessive use of state military force instead of an efficacious, nuanced police response to a decentralized terrorist network. In order to comprehend how a small, defeated wing of Arab Islamist politics transformed itself into a global terrorist network, the analyst must deploy forms of historical and ethical analysis more particular and less global than the rhetoric of "the war against terror."

The seeds of Al Qaeda and an Islamist politics with global—rather than purely national—ambitions arose from the denouement of the Soviet empire and the cold war. The events analyzed below exported Islamist politics beyond the borders of the Arab world. In 1979 and 1980, the Shi'ite Iranian revolutionary overthrow of the shah's oppressive,

---

[1] Paul Berman locates the main intellectual inspiration for Al Qaeda in the writings of the Islamist intellectual Sayyid Qutb, who was put to death by Nasser's Egypt in 1966 (Berman 2003a and 2003b). Berman admits—but then goes on to ignore—that Qutb focused almost all of his ire on "infidel" traitors among the leadership of Arab regimes. Also, while Islamism may well be as totalistic an ideology as Berman claims—and a modernist one that draws on vanguardist and nationalist elements of both Bolshevism and fascism—the absence of its holding national state power in regimes as powerful as Nazi Germany and the Soviet Union severely limits its power and reach. Terrorism is a weapon of the dispossessed and weak, not of strong states.

modernizing, pro-Western regime brought the first Islamist state to power. That historic event, combined with the week-long Islamist takeover of Mecca in the fall of 1979, provoked a brutal response against Islamist politics among the authoritarian (often pro-American) regimes of the Middle East. The Saudi government brutally put down the Islamist revolt in Mecca by killing more than one thousand religious rebels. Following the Islamist threat to the Saudi regime, Syria, Algeria, and Egypt cracked down on their Islamist oppositions, with Syria's President Hafaz al-Assad murdering twenty thousand people in the opposition stronghold of Hama. This repression led to the involuntary exiling of many Arab Islamist militants, who found a useful outlet for their repressed energies as mujahedin in the holy war against the Soviet invasion of Afghanistan. Saudi Arabia, along with the United States, heavily financed the mujahedin, as part of a long-term Saudi effort to export its fundamentalist Islamist Wahhabite ideology. To this day, the corrupt, Westernized Saudi elite—which blatantly violates the very Wahhabite puritanical practices it preaches in its government-controlled schools and mosques—gains cover for its domestic depredations by financing Islamic virtue abroad and exporting its disillusioned youthful idealists to foreign battlefields.

The other main sponsors of this *jihad* against the infidel Soviets were, of course, the U.S. Central Intelligence Agency (CIA) and the Pakistani secret service. The mujahedin were considered pro-Western according to the inane cold-war logic that "the enemy of my enemy is my friend." The mujahedin might have continued to accept U.S. largesse absent the collapse of the Soviet Union and its withdrawal from Afghanistan in 1991.

The collapse of the Soviet empire from 1989 to 1991 represents the second crucial historic origin of a global Islamist terrorist network. This collapse enabled the triumph of Islamist mujahedin in Afghanistan (only the second success of Islamist politics—and its first armed triumph). Most Western observers fail to note that the mujahedin in Afghanistan were disproportionately Sunni Muslim and that Iran backed the Shi'ite-dominated Northern Alliance, not the majority Pushtan insurgents supported by Pakistan (with its large Pushtan ethnic group) and the CIA. The ensuing warlord and tribal conflict in Afghanistan ended in the 1996 conquest of Afghanistan by the Taliban. The Taliban's own inability to govern Afghanistan securely provided the third cornerstone for the emergence of Al Qaeda. The Taliban was more a fundamentalist religious movement than a fully governing party. Much of its military muscle came through a tactical alliance with the remaining foreign mujahedin, most of them loyal to Al Qaeda. Meanwhile, the post-Soviet-era repression by authoritarian governments that succeeded the fall of Communism gave rise to Islamist tendencies within broader nationalist movements opposed to post-Communist authoritarian regimes in Bosnia, Kosovo, Georgia, Chechnya, Dagistan, and the former Soviet Central Asian republics (Kepel 2002; Roy 1995).

Prior to 1991, the Soviet Union's support of anti-American, nationalist Arab authoritarian regimes (most notably Algeria, the Baathist regimes of Syria and Iraq, and Nasser's Egypt) frequently led the United States to back Islamist oppositions as anti-Soviet surrogates. The United States preferred the politics of the Muslim Brotherhood (and the Wahhabite Saudi aristocracy) to the Arab nationalism of Nasser. The Americans initially supported the Baathists (and Saddam) as an alternative to the powerful Iraqi Communist Party, the main opposition to the post–World War II Hashemite monarch of Iraq (Telhami 2002). Perhaps the most notable, but underrecognized, collusion of the United States with Islamist forces came via the CIA's sponsorship of anti-Chinese Indonesian Islamists in the anti-Sukarno Indonesian uprising of 1965. In the eyes of the U.S. foreign-policy establishment, the major sin of the semi-authoritarian, populist regime of Sukarno had been its tactical alliance with the (predominantly ethnic-Chinese) Indonesian Communist Party. In the week-long military and mob uprising against Sukarno, Islamist Indonesian mobs, spurred on by their mullahs and CIA "handlers," slaughtered five hundred thousand ethnic Chinese. Most of the slaughtered were merchants and their families rather than members of the Indonesian Communist Party (Mortimer 1974).

The third watershed mark in the reversal of traditional U.S. support for antisecular Islamist politics came with the 1991 Gulf War. The disintegration of the Soviet Union negated the presence of a competing superpower, one often (opportunistically) allied with third-world nationalist regimes. This absence enabled the United States to create a broad global coalition against Iraq's violation of Kuwaiti sovereignty. Fearing its own Islamist opposition and the radicalization of underemployed college-educated youth, the Saudi government agreed, for the first time, to host American air bases and forward-positioned ground troops and supplies. In addition, the 1992 Algerian military overturning of the democratic election victory of the Islamic Salvation Front (a diverse Islamist party ranging from moderate and pragmatic elements to extreme Islamists) gave rise to the armed opposition of the Islamic Armed Group (Ghadbian 2000). In the next decade, more than twenty thousand Algerians—mostly civilians—would perish in this civil war. Despite this oppression, a moderate Islamist party, the Movement of Peace, currently cooperates with the secular coalition government in Algeria.

This hosting of infidel American troops within the Hijaz (the area of Saudi Arabia proximate to the holy cities of Mecca and Medina), combined with Muslim anger at the disastrous public-health consequences of the unduly tight economic sanctions against Iraq, radically increased anti-American sentiment within the Islamic world. (The banning of the importation of water-treatment-plant replacement parts, due to their alleged potential military applications, contributed to the death of tens of thousands of Iraqi children.) Even if Saddam's Baathist clique monopolized much of the oil-for-food revenues, the increased mortality rate caused by the broad sanctions even led Secretary of State Colin Powell, upon taking office in winter 2001, to call for "smarter sanctions" that would limit the damage to the civilian population.

The United States further incurred the ire of the Islamic world by its refusal to use its economic and military-aid leverage to pressure the Israelis to fulfill the 1993 Oslo accords by withdrawing most settlements from the West Bank and Gaza Strip. Thus, by 1995, in the eyes of even moderate Muslims, the Hijaz had been occupied by infidel troops; the possibility of regaining control over the Holy Rock in Jerusalem had faded from view; and a predominantly Islamic country suffered not only from the rule of a Baathist authoritarian nationalist regime but also from U.S.-inspired U.N. economic sanctions. By the time of Al Qaeda's 1998 "Declaration of the World Islamic Front for Jihad against the Jews and Christians," anti-American sentiment in the Islamic world was at an all-time high. While the number of individuals willing to act on Al Qaeda's call may be relatively small (two thousand to three thousand individuals by many guesstimates), their actions reflect a much broader base for an Islamist politics that no longer predominantly involved domestic opposition to corrupt Arab regimes. The realignment of global politics after the collapse of the Soviet Union and a U.S. foreign policy insensitive to Islamic sensibilities engendered a new form of global Islamism.

2. The Western Ideological Misreading of the Islamist Threat

The Islamist ideology of purity, sobriety, and patriarchy has clear affinities with the antimodernist reactionary politics of Western fascism and far-right Christian fundamentalism. The restrictive regulation of female sexuality is a common theme among moral-reform movements reacting to the social dislocation of modernization, urbanization, and mass education. Islamist politics, as with European fascism, is both a reaction against modernity and a product thereof. Absent modern means of communication, mass literacy, and postcolonial nationalism, there would be no global Islamism. For anti-Westernism depends upon an encounter with the West. But within the Arab world the reaction to modernity and the uprooting of rural traditionalist societies has varied, as has its tell-tale indicator—the status of women. The Baathist regimes of Syria and Iraq provided university education and professional opportunities for women; even Khomeini's Iran did not completely outlaw professional women (though it restricted them to serving only women).

The diversity within the Muslim world should come as no surprise to those who know the basic history of Islam. Much of Islamic history occurred under the Ottoman Empire and its *millet* system, which granted considerable cultural autonomy to regions. Islam is a decentralized religion; while there is no coherent doctrine of separation of church and state within

Islam, there is also no central religious hierarchy. While the caliphates of the Ottoman Empire claimed to unite religion with state authority, ever since Islam's founding in the seventh century there have been numerous rebellions against central authority conducted in the name of Islam. These antistate rebellions usually reflected regional desires for political autonomy. On the other hand, it would be naïve to deny the element of "combat fundamentalism" present within Islam. Islam expanded globally across the centuries, mostly through conversion along trading routes but also through military conquest. But this armed conquest was mostly limited to preexisting tribal and kinship conflicts within the Arabian Peninsula. The Ottoman Empire's expansion had an economic and political dynamic similar to other empires, *interesting* and it did not force upon its subjects a uniform or particularly fundamentalist form of Islam. But periodically competing caliphs used the ideology of Islamic "combat fundamentalism" to justify their expansionist aims (Mann 2001; Euben 2002). *mixed ... some used islam to expand, some were economic/normal, u/ islam unsec*

The decentralized nature of the Islamic clergy and the divisions between Shi'ite and Sunni and between orthodox and moderate Islamic tendencies demand that any analysis of Islam and politics focus on the particular and the local (Geertz 2003a; 2003b). Western social scientists in the 1950s and 1960s often noted the relatively passive, apolitical nature of the Islamic clergy (particularly in rural areas, prior to mass literacy) (Telhami 2002). The fundamentalist emphasis on personal purity often takes an individual rather than a collective and political expression. If fundamentalism inherently possessed an overt political message, the corrupt Saudi regime would not be willing to spread Wahhabite orthodoxy to leading Sunni mosques and university centers across the Middle East, including the Al Azhar mosque in Cairo, the theological center of Sunni Islam (Foer 2002).[2]

The very concept of jihad has been contested throughout the history of Islam. The dominant tendency has been to interpret "the greater" jihad as a personal quest for religious rectitude (jihad's most literal translation is "struggle") (Euben 2003, 6–7). The predominant reaction to Western colonization of the Islamic world—from the religious schools, or *madrasas*, of South Asia to the Wahhabist traditionalist reaction to colonization in the Arabian Peninsula—has been a retreat into private moral rectitude. While traditional Islam does not doctrinally separate the political from the religious, there is also a long tradition of Islamic revivalist withdrawal from politics, as well as opportunist Islamist political accommodation with dominant, nonfundamentalist political

[2] For an analysis of the Saudi funding of the "ahl-ah-hadith" (puritanical literalist) tendency in Islamic theological circles and this tendency's control of the Al Azhar mosque, see Foer 2002. Foer's article provides a good introduction to contemporary Islamic theological conflicts among rationalists (*mu-tazila*), puritanical literalists, and strict constructionists (*usulis*). Foer argues that the *usulis* favor a form of ethnical humanism and theological pluralism that is opposed to terrorism.

authorities. On the other hand, periods of politicized Islamism—a better word than the Christian import of "fundamentalism"—cannot be read as totally aberrant to Islam.[3]

Some may believe that violent struggles to "modernize" the West occurred long ago; but there are still millions of living victims of the West's atavistic opposition to the dislocations of modernization and liberalization (the victims of fascism and Stalinism). Paul Berman correctly locates some elective affinities between the vision that Muslim Brotherhood ideologist Sayyid Qutb (Berman's Islamist "totalitarian" theorist) has of a virtuous, postpolitical world and twentieth-century totalitarian ideologies. But Qutb aimed only to overthrow Nasser and other modernizing "infidel" secular rulers of the Arab world (Berman 2003a). Only in the Sudan, Iran, and Afghanistan (temporarily) have Islamist regimes come to power, regimes not comparable in their global destructive power to Nazi Germany or Stalin's Soviet Union.

The fascist, antimodernist movements in Germany, Italy, and Japan drew support from displaced middle strata, a struggling petty bourgeoisie, and displaced peasants—the same social base of Islamist political movements in Iran, Algeria, and Egypt. No doubt the civil war against the Christian and animist southern Sudanese has killed close to two million Sudanese over the past twenty years (with nary a peep from the West, which may be lax in its opposition to the fundamentalist regime because of the Sudan's massive potential oil reserves). And in the war between Islamist Iran and secular, Baathist Iraq (enemies of Qutb's Muslim Brotherhood) both Islamist Iran and authoritarian secular Iraq sent hundreds of thousands of soldiers to their death in massive human-wave attacks. The Reagan administration, of course, aided secular Iraq in its battle against religiously totalitarian Iran. Unless Berman projects the most extreme forms of Islamic fundamentalism gaining and sustaining state power in a powerful Islamic state (say, Pakistan), it would be hard to imagine the crimes of Islamist fundamentalism (real as they are) being comparable to the crimes of Stalinism and Nazism (Sciallaba 2003). And Iran may well be the exception to the rule; it is the only country with mass literacy and industrial development in which an Islamic fundamentalist regime came to power (courtesy of the vicious repression of the modernist, secular shah's regime). Yet younger, educated strata, women, and most urban middle-class and working-class strata long ago lost their initial enthusiasm for Iran's Islamist government. In Turkey, Pakistan, Jordan, Yemen, Indonesia, and elsewhere, when Islamist parties have gained mainstream political influence their political stance has evolved in a strikingly moderate and pragmatic direction.

3. Jihad, the Taliban, and Al Qaeda: The Saudi-Pakistani-U.S. Connection

The virulent antimodern opposition of the Afghani Taliban to any and all public visibility for women is an extreme within Islamist politics. The ultra-purism of the Taliban derived from the encounter in the 1980s between the three million Afghani refugees in Pakistan with the apolitical, but extremely socially conservative *deobands* (religious schools for male youths) and madrasas (seminaries) of Pakistan's Sunni Islamic community. The missionaries of the Tablighi Jama'at, a mass fundamentalist current originating from these South Asian religious educational institutions, conduct mass religious gatherings across the Islamic world (including the North American diaspora). But these apolitical gatherings focus exclusively upon the quest for a religiously pure, personal lifestyle, as well as on the conversion of individuals. Though a Tablighi Jama'at-inspired mosque in Marin County, California, spiritually recruited John Walker, it took the atypical, politicized offshoot, the Taliban (and eventually Al Qaeda), to train Walker in the arts of combat (Metcalf 2001).

The deoband religious schools of South Asia, whence the Taliban (*talib* means student in Urdu) emerged during the mass Afghan exile in Pakistan in the 1980s, inculcate a traditionalist Islam centering upon the rectitude of individual behavior (particularly with regard to the behavior of women). Many South Asian *ulama* (the South Asian equivalent of *mullah*, but without its sometimes political implications) of the Tablighi Jama'at movement pragmatically supported the Indian Congress Party during the independence struggles before World War II. In the 1930s and 1940s the ulama of South Asia mostly opposed the formation of an independent Islamic Pakistani state. And even the pro-Pakistani and Muslim League offshoot, the Jamiat Ulema-I-Islam, has often made pragmatic alliances with the major Pakistani secular parties, including the People's Progressive Party (PPP) under the notoriously Westernized political leadership of the landlord Bhutto clan. (Benazir Bhutto, the most powerful political woman in the Islamic world, is a Harvard and Oxford product known for her high 'Western' lifestyle.) The Jamiat Ulema-I-Islam never achieved more than minor party status in Pakistan until it recently participated in an Islamist coalition that won regional power in some of the Northwest Territories (in reaction to the U.S. invasion of Afghanistan).

Initially the Taliban regime adopted a pragmatic orientation to the United States. The Clinton administration originally believed that the Taliban promised to overcome the chaotic warlordism Afghanistan experienced after the 1991 Soviet withdrawal. The Sunni traditionalism of the Taliban attracted the U.S. government because it made them natural enemies of the Shi'ite Northern Alliance warlords, who were allied with Iran. This traditionalism also inclined the Taliban to work closely with the Sunni-majority Pakistani military regime. Pakistan has long been the United States' client partner in South Asia, ever since Henry Kissinger's famous 1970 "tilt" toward Pakistan in its conflicts with India. The rule of the Taliban (under their minders from the Pakistani secret service) both limited Iranian influence among the Shi'ites of northeast Afghanistan (whom the Taliban mercilessly persecuted) and held open possible cooperation in the transnational efforts of the United States to construct an oil pipeline from Central Asia to the Indian Ocean, a pipeline that could conveniently avoid crossing Iran (Metcalf 2001).

An irony of post-cold-war history is that U.S. support for an anti-Soviet, pan-Islamic mujahedin may have home to roost in the 1995 Taliban–Al Qaeda alliance in Afghanistan. The Taliban did not have a particular ideological or political agenda for Afghanistan other than quashing warlordism and restoring *shari'a*, ritual purity, and the subjugation of women. In fact, the Taliban seemed willing to be directed by the Pakistani secret service; the Taliban leadership preferred the spiritual life of Kandahar to worldly administrative duties in Kabul. The Taliban were also strongly backed by a Saudi government that consciously viewed the Taliban (and their foreign mujahedin supporters) as a means for expanding Saudi influence in South Asia and for continuing to export as mujahedin the disillusioned, underemployed Saudi youths who had been politicized by the Wahhabist morality of Saudi schools. The origins of the mujahadin and Al Qaeda are in Egyptian and Saudi circles that either participated in or ideologically supported the fall 1979 fundamentalist uprising in Mecca against the corrupt Saudi oligarchy—a regime that has long been the lynchpin of U.S. alliance politics in the Middle East.

During the 1970 India-Pakistan war, Kissinger tilted U.S. foreign policy against secular, religiously pluralist, Indian democracy in favor of a repressive, anti-Communist, Islamic Pakistan. India's sins were its strong nonaligned position and economic and military relations with the Soviet Union. This two-decade support in the "great game" of Soviet-U.S. contests in South Asia led the United States to subsidize and train many of the individuals who would eventually form Al Qaeda. This reality, combined with the neoconservative cabal in the Reagan administration (Cheney, Wolfowitz, and Rumsfeld) garnering administration support for the secular Baathist Iraqi war against the "more dangerous" Iranian Shi'ite regime, renders "chickens-coming-home-to-roost" analyses of 9/11 somewhat plausible (though the frequent insensitivity of U.S. scholars to the desires of their fellow citizens for security against further attacks has lessened the audience for such analyses). In fact, if we ever discover "weapons of mass destruction" (WMDs) in Iraq, they are likely to be chemical agents left over from the 1980s war against Iran (and used against the Kurds in 1988). Not surprisingly, the largest suppliers of chemical agents to Iraq were the Western powers—French, German, and, yes, U.S. transnational chemical corporations.

The origins of pan-Islamic global terror partly derived from U.S.-backed regimes suppressing their moderate Islamist political opposition. Then in the late 1970s, Sadat's brutal suppression of a fairly moderate Muslim Brotherhood, Saudi hostility to any religiously inspired dissent, and Algerian suppression of the Islamic Salvation Front engendered a pan-Islamic political sensibility, as nationally based Islamist parties were no longer viable. Despite the United States supplanting the Soviet Union as the patron of the Sadat regime after 1973, the United States never counseled Sadat against suppressing the Muslim Brotherhood. Sadat would die at the hands of its more militant offspring, Eygptian Jihad, an organization that has integral ties with Al Qaeda. Egyptian Jihad drew upon the pan-Islamic potential of Sayaab Al-Qud's ideology of the "lesser jihad" of the sword. But even here Al-Qud and the original Muslim Brotherhood focused almost exclusively upon eliminating corruption and Western cultural influences within post–World War II Egypt, Syria, and Iraq. There was little, if any, talk of a global war on the West. The struggle against the "*jihillya*" (Arabic for those who lived in ignorance before Islam) was limited to the fight against corrupt, pro-Western Arab rulers (Berman 2003a). But the suppression of Islamist politics by secularist, often pro-Western regimes and the failure of both Arab socialist and Arab nationalist projects helped introduce global and anti-American elements into the strategy of "lesser jihad." In the seminal first period of Islamist radicalization (1979–1981) the brute oppression of the Muslim Brotherhood simultaneously by the House of Saud, Sadat, and Syria's Hafaz Al-Assad did not yield one word of protest from the U.S. government. Egypt and Saudi Arabia were U.S allies, and Reagan and Bush Sr. were in the midst of attempting rapprochement with the formerly pro-Soviet Syrians.

Even among pro-terrorist tendencies within Islamist politics one must be careful not to create artificial uniformity. The Khomeini wing of the Iranian revolution (now under Supreme Council President Ayatollah Ali Khatamei) has clear ties to the Shi'ite-based Islamic Jihad and Hezbollah in southern Lebanon (both groups arose in reaction to U.S. and Israeli support of the Lebanese Christian militias). But those political, social, and terrorist movements have limited their armed attacks to Israeli targets and U.S. troops, business people, and diplomats in Lebanon. Neither group has been involved in any documented attacks beyond Lebanon and northern Israel. The politicized wing of Shi'ite Islam has been in conflict with the Sunni-based Muslim Brotherhood for generations. Only a U.S. foreign policy that demonizes an allegedly homogenous Islamic world could create "unholy" alliances between Shi'ite and Sunni Islamist politics. The recent joint mass Sunni-Shi'ite prayer meetings in Baghdad are unique in Islamic history.

4. Analyzing the New Global Terrorism: Is It Inexplicably "Irrational"?

What renders late modern, global terrorism distinct from prior, nationally based revolutionary and terrorist organizations is the openness of the global economy; the ability to travel and live abroad rather cheaply; and the ability to communicate secretly via satellite and computer networks. And the absence of specific geographic targets and feasible demands upon opposing states is also new. Recent global Islamist terror targets have been vacation resorts serving Israelis and Australians in Kenya and Indonesia; synagogues in Tunisia; U.S. military ships in Yemen; U.S. embassies in Tanzania and Kenya; and expatriate Protestant churches in Pakistan.

Hundreds of Muslims were killed in these bombings, in part because the global Islamist terrorist movement has no geographic home and, therefore, does not need to compete for the hearts and minds of a national populace that it potentially wishes to govern. Thus, it can be—and has been—extremely cavalier about civilian deaths, even Islamic ones. Suicide bombers are not easily deterred; and decentralized cells that hide themselves by integrating themselves into diaspora student and immigrant communities are not easy to penetrate. But the global intelligence and security cooperation necessary to combat such a diffuse global network must be politically and diplomatically sensitive in a manner that a dystopian global terrorist movement need not be. Governments do have to fight for the hearts and minds of people at home and abroad, particularly since terrorists need a sea in which to swim among Islamic communities across the globe. Thus, overt, indiscriminate targeting of Islamic diaspora communities for surveillance and harassment may well result in increased covert support for terrorists—even in recruitment—than would a discreet policy that focused on behavior rather than racial profiling.

Obviously, political grievances do not motivate most of the individuals who hold them to attack innocent civilians. But it is ludicrous to think that the Arab-Israeli conflict and the U.S. military presence in Saudi Arabia had nothing to do with the motivation of Al Qaeda operatives (Ignatieff 2003). The announcement by the United States that it will end most of its military presence in Saudi Arabia represents an implicit admission of this reality, though its continued support for the Saudi oligarchy will continue to fuel that grievance. The United States would be more likely to enhance its security through diplomatic and economic pressures in favor of liberalizing Middle Eastern and South Asian regimes—pressuring not just for more liberal treatment of secular dissidents but also for the expansion of political space for nonviolent Islamist movements. Such domestically rooted parties must win over a domestic public—and eventually share in the responsibility of governance. The pragmatic realities of governance have defanged many a terrorist or revolutionary movement—witness the experience of the Sandinistas in Nicaragua and the FDR/FMLN in El Salvador.

There remains, however, an inhumane fanaticism in Al Qaeda and a chilling totality in its Islamist ideology, sufficient to render the term *Islamic fascism* not a complete misnomer. Al Qaeda's tactics reflect the nihilistic rage of displaced middle-stratum *narodniks* and prior vanguardist, "substitutionist" terrorist movements. As Seyla Benhabib points out, if Al Qaeda militants really are universally committed to eliminating the infidel West, then anything short of mass conversion will not deter them (Benhabib 2001). But such movements are not simply the creation of warped, irrational minds. Terrorist rage, no matter how ineffective, often arises from totally comprehensible political grievances. To treat Al Qaeda as an irrationalist cult of slaughter is to ignore the potential rational logic behind its attack on the World Trade Center, a logic that the United States played into by subsequently attacking Afghanistan. As political scientist Michael Doran has argued, Al Qaeda hoped that an ensuing U.S. invasion of Afghanistan would drive the nuclear-armed Islamic nation of Pakistan into alliance with the Taliban and Al Qaeda (whom Pakistani security services had long nurtured). In addition, Al Qaeda believed that U.S. "overreaction" would render the Islamic world even more hostile to U.S. interests and presence abroad (Doran 2002). Pakistan did not join the side of overt Islamist rebellion, and it is allegedly cooperating with the United States in the "war on terrorism." But it is not clear if Pakistan's security agencies have broken all ties with the Taliban and Al Qaeda, both of which are making a comeback in the Northwest Territories of Pakistan and in southern Afghanistan. Al Qaeda's goals are not totally unfeasible; already the United States is being forced to withdraw much of its military presence from Saudi Arabia; how long will it be able to maintain bases in Turkey, Abu Dabi, Qatar, and Iraq without incurring further terrorist assaults?

Terrorists have memories. The "Black Hawk down" fiasco in Mogadishu in late 1992, which cost more than twenty American lives, and Hezbollah's suicide attack that killed two hundred and forty Marines in Lebanon in 1984 both led to rapid U.S. military withdrawals. American tolerance for loss of life in the "war" against terrorism may be greater; but already there seems little willingness upon the part of the Bush administration to mobilize the public in favor of the economic sacrifice, public investment, and troop commitment that true "reconstruction" and provision of basic security in Afghanistan and Iraq would entail.

The U.S. invasion of Iraq marked a dangerous transformation of the "war against terrorism" into a war against "terrorist states." The use of the "war" metaphor to describe the fight against terrorism has been unhelpful from the start, as the most effective tactics in combating decentralized networks of terrorists are not those of traditional warfare but, rather, interstate cooperation among police, intelligence,

war against terrorism vs. war gains terrorist states

and espionage agencies. Sleuthing aimed at rendering transparent covert financial networks is another crucial method, made difficult by the hostility of transnational banks and neoliberal governments to regulation. Terrorist financing is frequently tied to illegal drug trafficking and kidnapping, as well as the laundering of ostensibly legal "charitable" contributions. Treating terrorism as a form of international crime facilitates the cooperation of police networks across cultural and national lines. Dealing with terrorism through a military "war" polarizes nation-states in ways that will hamper effective antiterrorist efforts.

5. Can There Be a "Just War" against Terrorism?

The causes of terror are sociological and political, and they are more analogous to the origins of international criminal syndicates than to the causes of wars among states. Fighting wars against states with significant Islamic populations will curtail security cooperation with states in the Islamic world. And a war against a state—even a weak state that cannot (or is unwilling to) close terrorist bases—is likely only to drive terrorist operations into other weak states. As a result of the war in Afghanistan, Al Qaeda moved its bases and operations into the Northwest Territories of Pakistan, the Sudan, Kenya, Indonesia, the Philippines, and elsewhere. The post-9/11 spate of attacks—on the Saudi foreign-residents compound, Moroccan Jewish and Spanish cultural institutions, the Tunisian synagogue, the Mombassa resort and airport, and the Bali tourist disco—indicate that Islamic terrorist operations have not been noticeably curtailed. Winning a struggle against active terrorists means killing or apprehending them. The large number of civilian casualties caused by conventional wars between states are likely to be self-defeating, as they potentially enlarge the recruitment pool for terrorist groups. And such "collateral damage" can be ethically justified only if such attacks were absolutely necessary to curtail terrorism and if the casualties were unintended, as well as unavoidable in achieving a particular military objective (that is, in accord with the just-war doctrine of "double effects"). The civilian casualties from high-altitude bombing in Afghanistan were not absolutely necessary to uproot Al Qaeda and its Taliban-government hosts (the use of more ground troops would have been ethically preferable). And the Bush administration has yet to make a convincing case why killing perhaps more than five thousand Iraqi civilians and perhaps ten thousand or more Iraqi soldiers was necessary to curtail terrorism (Crawford 2003).

Only if it were extremely likely that a military attack on a nation-state would radically decrease the chances of an imminent terrorist attack would a preemptive military attack be justified by the doctrine of just war. Preemptive war is only justified if the threatened nation's attack is absolutely necessary to repel an imminent attack that would likely bring either large-scale loss of life or loss of territorial sovereignty in the absence of such a preemptive strike (Walzer 2000, 85). Thus, the doctrine of preemptive war enunciated in the September 2002 National Security Doctrine is, in reality, a "preventive-war" doctrine. Preventive war— which has never been recognized as moral by the just-war tradition— involves a nation attacking a regime that has the potential to develop into a threat to the attacker's "way of life" or a rival to its power status. Cheney himself said that "the risk" of WMDs falling into the hands of terrorists justified a unilateral preemptive attack on Saddam Hussein. The administration never claimed that there was an imminent threat of Saddam's delivering WMDs to terrorists or of his attacking the United States or its installations abroad (in a manner that could only be deterred by a first strike against Iraq). The administration admitted that it did not know for sure what types of WMDs Saddam possessed; nor was it demonstrated by the United States that his ties to terrorist groups were so strong that he would likely deliver WMDs to them.

Thus, Cheney's rationale for the war reflected the hypothetical logic of preventive-war doctrine rather than the more demanding logic of a preemptive strike: the existence of an imminent attack by an opponent that only can be successfully repelled by a "first strike." Cheney's preventive-war criteria used the name *preemptive war* but utilized the much less rigorous justificatory standards of "preventive war." Cheney's justificatory language spoke of potential, grave threats, rather than evidence of imminent use: "Deliverable weapons of mass destruction in the hands of a terror network or murderous dictator or the two working together constitutes as grave a threat as can be imagined. The risks of inaction are far greater than the risks of action" (Cheney 2002). The administration never advanced (or demonstrated) the traditional justificatory criteria for a preemptive war—of an imminent threat upon the territory and population of the United States (or any other nation) that could only be repulsed successfully by a preemptive U.S. military strike against Iraq. Rather, the administration implied that there was a high likelihood that somewhere down the road Iraq and its alleged cooperation with terrorist groups might pose a serious threat to U.S. (and global) security. But just-war theorists have traditionally objected to preventive wars against a hypothetical or alleged long-term threat because no nation can ever achieve total security. Any nation trying to do so will not only fail; it is likely to engage in massive, unjust violence in its quest for imperial certitude (Crawford, 15).

President Bush contends that an attack on any nation "who knowingly harbors or provides aid to terrorists" is morally justifiable. Yet this policy would justify any invasion of a state that does not readily and successfully apprehend terrorists in its midst. But what if such a state does not possess the capabilities to do so or disagrees with the United States' judgment of who constitutes a terrorist? A doctrine of preventive war against terrorism

preventive war

essentially disavows the doctrine of national sovereignty at the heart of just-war theory since the Treaty of Westphalia in 1648. The United States did not receive prior sanction from the Yemenite government for its attack on an alleged Al Qaeda jeep in the Yemen desert. Furthermore, the United States strongly implied to the governments of both the Philippines and Indonesia that if they did not "host" U.S. Special Forces units it would send them anyway. The United States also knew that the militaries of these countries longed to reestablish direct military cooperation with it, even though their civilian governments were disinclined to do so. Furthermore, the United States has used an anti-terrorist justification for increasing military aid to Colombia, even though such aid exacerbates the right-wing paramilitary oppression that drives peasants into the hands of a violent guerrilla movement that the United States claims (without any substantial proof) to be part of the international terrorist network.

Whereas the cause of preventing terrorist attacks on civilians is undoubtedly just, attacking sovereign states in the name of such action is not—unless it can be demonstrated that such an attack was necessary to deter a very likely and imminent attack that could not be deterred by more selective diplomatic, police, and security measures. The CIA admitted that Iraq was years away from developing a deliverable nuclear device; and the last time Iraq came close to producing fissionable material, the Israelis unilaterally destroyed that capacity by bombing a reactor in 1981.

As I mentioned earlier, if we find chemical weapons in Iraq they are likely to be very similar to the ones used in the Iraq-Iran war from 1980 to 1988 and against the Kurds in 1988. Not only did the French, with indirect help from U.S. transnationals, supply these weapons; at the time, the Reagan administration viewed Iraq as a deterrent against the Islamic revolution in Iran. Iraq does not have the means to deliver such weapons beyond its immediate regional neighborhood. And U.S. intelligence recognizes that both Syria and Iran have a chemical-weapons capacity that can readily deter this Iraqi capacity. No one outside the U.S. government believes there have been any ties of operative significance between the militantly secular Baathist regime and the Islamist Al Qaeda. Not to stoke the grounds for further misguided imperial overreach, but Iran is years closer to developing deliverable nuclear devices than was Iraq (the Iranian capacity being courtesy of Russian reactors and Pakistani know-how; the U.S. "ally" Pakistan also supplied North Korea with an intermediate-missile capacity). Iran and Syria have demonstrable ties to Islamic Jihad and Hezbollah. But neither Islamic Jihad nor Hezbollah has been accused of engaging in terrorist activity beyond Lebanon and Israel.

Traditional warfare against nation-states is such an obviously poor (and unjust) counterterrorism strategy that none of America's major

NATO allies, except the British, accepted the administration's rationale for the war against Iraq. The Bush administration's ex post facto justification of the war against Iraq has rested almost exclusively on the notion of a human-rights intervention against a horrid, genocidal regime. This demonstrates how weak the preemptive-war argument proved to be (as the United States scurries to find WMDs). The administration implicitly admits that its evidence for Iraqi possession of WMDs and ties to international terrorism is flimsy, as its predominant justificatory rhetoric after the invasion focused almost exclusively on the human-rights benefits for the Iraqi people of the overthrow of Saddam's regime. No doubt these benefits have been great; but, given the dangers unilateralism poses to the stability of the international order, traditional just-war theorists have only justified broad, multilateral invasions against genocidal regimes.

6. Just-War Theory and the Invasion of Afghanistan: A "Hard Case"

The U.S. invasion of Afghanistan could possibly be justified morally for having overthrown a Taliban government that permitted Al Qaeda to operate training bases within its territory. But many observers argue that the Taliban's alliance with Al Qaeda was purely tactical and that Al Qaeda's operations were more dependent on the support of the U.S.-backed Pakistani secret service than it was on the support of the Taliban government. American diplomatic and economic pressure might have been able to sever the links between America's Pakistani "allies" and Al Qaeda without engaging in major aerial bombardment of Afghan civilians. In part, the United States did not heavily pressure the Pakistanis because of the volatility of the situation in Kashmir and because of Pakistan's possession of nuclear weapons (and its wish to dissuade Pakistan from providing nuclear-related technologies across the globe). The lesson of U.S. coddling of the Pakistani regime—coupled with an understandable reluctance to take military action against North Korea—is that the United States is wary to engage in preemptive "regime change" against "rogue states" with nuclear weapons. Thus, current U.S. policy improves the chances of nuclear proliferation rather than deters it!

But even as great a military and economic power as the United States would not be able to deny any and all terrorist sanctuaries through the occupation of each and every weak state (not even the United States can really be "the cop of the world"). It is not even willing to spend the necessary tax dollars to reconstruct Afghanistan and Iraq and provide basic physical security for their populace. Even if it could guarantee basic security to the populations of Afghanistan and Iraq, would the United States succeed in radically decreasing terrorist threats to its own civilian population? The war in Afghanistan could be justified in just-war terms if and only if denying Al Qaeda terrorist bases in Afghanistan significantly decreased the threat to innocent civilian lives across the globe. In addition, civilian casualties in Afghanistan would have had to be consciously minimized, resulting only from unintended accidents in the course of attacks on strictly military targets (Crawford 2003, 18–19). The most cautious of "collateral-damage" estimates put the civilian deaths in Afghanistan at well over one thousand. Was the taking of these innocent lives (at least one-third of the total killed at the World Trade Center) absolutely necessary for enhancing global security against terrorism? Could not the expenditure of comparable tens of billions of dollars on nonmilitary forms of antiterrorist measures—such as securing U.S. ports and containerized shipping against vulnerability to terrorism—have been more prudential?

As in the subsequent Iraqi case, the Bush administration increasingly relied on the human-rights benefits that the overthrow of the Taliban regime wrought as its moral justification for the invasion of Afghanistan. It is ironic that a Republican government that appeals in domestic politics to patriarchal conceptions of state regulation of female sexuality has become the tribune for the oppressed women of Afghanistan. But outside the confines of Kabul, patriarchal warlord rule has returned, and both the Taliban and Al Qaeda are reemerging in southern Afghanistan. A case could have been made for multilateral military intervention against a Taliban regime that grossly violated human rights. But unilateral interventions (particularly against a nongenocidal regime) greatly threatens international stability (and thus human life), particularly when the invading country does not assume its moral and fiscal responsibility to repair the damage it caused to the civilian infrastructure, and does not provide security assistance beyond the capital city.

7. Forging New Ground: Just-War Theory and Global Terrorism

Just-war theory does not have a lengthy history of application to cases of military interventions allegedly aimed at global terrorist networks. Except for the Palestinian hijackings of the 1970s and some Kurdish attacks on West European targets, most terrorist activity has occurred within the boundaries of the state upon which the terrorist demands are focused. Al Qaeda is somewhat of a sui generis global terrorist network; its grievances are focused not upon the politics of one particular nation-state but against Judeo-Christian civilization itself.[4] Yet U.S. foreign policy is at

---

[4] Glib far-left analyses of Al Qaeda's actions contend that they were solely motivated by U.S. foreign-policy injustices, as if all that Al Qaeda represents is mass rage against U.S. imperialism and America's chickens coming home to roost. But this line of analysis denies the theocratic fascist elements in Al Qaeda ideology and also ignores the oppressive and patriarchal nature of fundamentalist antimodernist politics, including the "theocratic" totalism of extreme Islamism. For a sober analysis of the uniqueness of Al Qaeda (by an avowed left theorist) see Benhabib 2001.

the root of Al Qaeda's more immediate grievances—foreign troops in Saudi Arabia; economic sanctions against Iraq; and infidel control over the Muslim holy sites in East Jerusalem (Lewis 1998). The United States' withdrawal of troops from Saudi Arabia and its reengagement in the Middle East peace process is, in part, an implicit recognition that a change in Middle East policy might shrink the size of the aggrieved Islamic sea in which Al Qaeda swims (*The Economist* 2003).

Unlike previous terrorist groups, Al Qaeda acts not on alleged behalf of a particular, geographically specified constituency but in the name of the Islamic world. Nor does Al Qaeda have to worry about winning "hearts and minds," as it is not a revolutionary organization aiming to garner support from a particular populace in order to overthrow a specified government. The quest for popular, national support has always been a constraining influence on the actions of revolutionary and terrorist organizations. When these movements wantonly kill innocent people they invariably lose popular support and fail to achieve their ends. Thus, Sendero Luminoso utterly failed in Peru, even though mass poverty among indigenous peasants provided it an initial mass base of support. And the level of gratuitous violence used by the armed gangs operating in weak West African states today precludes any of them gaining secure state power.

Unlike the IRA, the Colombian FARC, Hamas, the PLO, or the Tamil Tigers, Al Qaeda does not recruit from a particular national or ethnic group. Rather, its operatives are recruited from among the disillusioned children of elite Saudi families; exiled Egyptian Islamist dissidents; former international mujahedin who fought in Afghanistan; and alienated, educated Islamic professionals in the European and American diaspora. Undoubtedly, U.S. foreign policy has played an integral role in sustaining a corrupt Saudi regime that alienated many of its educated youth. And the United States also financed the anti-Soviet Afghan foreign mujahedin from whom Al Qaeda would recruit. But whatever the historical etiology of Al Qaeda, it does not deny the United States and other nations the moral right to protect their population from terrorist attack. But the American public has not debated in an open and productive fashion after 9/11 what tactics will best (and justly) fulfill that legitimate government purpose.

The extent to which a network of some two thousand to three thousand Al Qaeda–influenced terrorists may exist around the globe—in loose alliance with Abu Sayef in the Philippines, Jamaah Islamiya in Indonesia, and Egyptian Jihad—provides the United States and other nations reason to intensify international police and intelligence cooperation. Those opposed to a military response to terrorism must have empathy with the day-to-day security concerns of our fellow citizens; we also have a moral and civic responsibility to say which security policies are likely to be an effective deterrent against terrorism. "No" is not a convincing moral or political program. Opponents of the Bush administration's "war" on terrorism must pose an alternative antiterrorist policy and speak to the fears of fellow residents of the United States, unless they view those who worked in the World Trade Center as "others" with whom they share no bonds of solidarity or vulnerability. On the other hand, the exaggeration of the terrorist threat abets the terrorist's aim of engendering external and internal repressive acts by the United States, particularly against Muslims. Domestic forms of oppression and racial and ethnic profiling countervene the very liberal values that Al Qaeda abhors. Certainly, individuals or groups with a demonstrable history of terrorist ties must be kept under surveillance; but democratic governments are justified only in profiling actual behavior, not ethnic, religious, or racial characteristics.

Necessary governmental action to detect and disrupt terrorist planning and operations is, of course, morally justifiable. But terrorism, historically, has been defeated more by containing it than completely obliterating it. This is the lesson one learns from the relatively successful British, German, Italian, and Spanish government policies toward their own domestic terrorist movements, ones that have caused as much—or more—fear among their citizenry as 9/11 has among residents of the United States. Terrorism cannot be totally destroyed by means of one massive military blow. And failure to address the political and sociological causes of terrorist recruitment will only lengthen the life of—and increase the effectiveness of—terrorist groups. If military power alone could end terrorism, the Israeli government's policies would have ended Palestinian terror long ago.

Just-war theory developed as a moral doctrine to govern conflict among sovereign nation-states. It is a utilitarian, consequentialist logic which holds that just wars must be a last resort, aimed at preserving the territorial integrity and security of a nation under attack (or under threat of an imminent attack that can only be successfully repulsed by a preemptive strike). Wars of aggression are unjust; national self-defense is the only unambiguously legitimate justification of the use of force. But not only must a just war have just cause (*jus ad bellum*); the means of warfare must also be just (*jus in bello*) (Crawford 2003, 6–8). Just wars must be carried out by competent state authorities who can be held responsible for decisions made in warfare. *Jus in bello* calls for proportionality of means to ends, as even a just war does harm to human beings. Thus, the overall good of war must outweigh the (absolutely necessary) harm caused by it. Force can only be used to preserve national sovereignty and must be proportionate to that purpose.

The aims of a just war must be limited to self-defense and cannot involve transforming the internal politics of other nation-states, except if so-called regime change is necessary to preventing future aggressive attacks. Of course, this "exception" potentially opens a Pandora's box, as the victor usually controls any international legal judgment following the war. After World War II, international tribunals found the German and Japanese regimes to be guilty of crimes against humanity and of being expansionist regimes that threatened world peace. Thus, the Allied powers, acting in the name of a new international organization, the United Nations, determined that only a regime transformation to democracy could eliminate the possibility of a revanchist Germany and Japan. There is a strong case to be made for truly international (or representative domestic) trials of the Baathist leadership for crimes against humanity. But it remains to be seen whether unilateral U.S. efforts to aid the Iraqi transition to a representative, democratic regime will garner legitimacy for that regime among its own people and in the eyes of world public opinion.

The doctrines of self-defense, proportionality, and limited aims govern *jus ad bellum*. Only absolutely necessary violence is justified; gratuitous violence must be avoided, including violence that threatens the prospect of postwar peace (such as assassination and breach of surrender). The doctrine of discrimination enjoins avoiding injury to noncombatants. The doctrine of "double effects" holds that injury to civilians can only be morally justified if both the military goal of the action was just and all efforts were made to avoid civilian casualties. Noncombatant injuries, to be just, must meet the double effects of being unintended and of the resulting saving of lives in warfare outweighing the unintended effects on noncombatants (for example, it would be morally justifiable to have attacked a nuclear-arms factory and killed innocent civilians that one did not know lived in the area; but to attack a storage area for conventional weapons that one knew was in a heavily populated area would be subject to moral and, if possible, international legal censure).

Just-war doctrine frequently must adjust to changes in military technology. Thus, with the emergence of aerial bombardment in World War II, the harm to civilians from the bombing of war-related industries located in urban centers emerged as an ambiguous question for traditional just-war theory. But despite the willingness of some consequentialist just-war theory to justify injuries to civilians living proximate to "legitimate" industrial targets, the fire bombings of Tokyo and Dresden by the allies at the end of World War II are frequently judged to have been unjust. According to some just-war theorists, these bombing raids (which killed more individuals in one week than did the Hiroshima and Nagasaki nuclear attacks) served no obvious military purpose other than demoralizing (and killing) the civilian population. Just-war doctrine condemns such action (even by a state engaged in a just war) because the moral doctrine of just war aims to sustain some degree of moral behavior amidst the amoral—if not immoral—world of a "just" war. That is, the killing of others, even in self-defense, should not be morally capricious (or unlawful).

Until now, just-war doctrine has not been applied to the actions of a state that is fighting terrorists who are not state-based or directly state-sponsored (or who are "hosted" by nations too weak to kick them out, even if they desired to do so). The Bush administration's new National Security Doctrine of preemptive war aims to apply the just-war tradition to the "war against terroism." The administration's arguments, however, seem oblivious to the doctrine that just wars can only be fought for the limited aim of national defense (or to aid a nation violated by external aggression). The goals of the National Security Doctrine implemented in fall 2002 are strikingly—and dangerously—unlimited: "The United States national security strategy will be based on a distinctly American internationalism that reflects the fusion of our values and our national interests" (National Security Council 2002). According to this dangerous, revolutionary change in foreign-policy doctrine, the United States is justified in intervening against regimes that oppose our "values." In an aggressive appropriation of the controversial doctrine that democracies do not war against one another, the new national-security doctrine implies that wars to install regimes that conform to U.S. norms of a "free and open" global market economy can be justified because regimes that do not conform to such norms pose a constant threat to global peace.

The administration's rationale for these limitless foreign-policy aims is that terrorist actors who threaten the United States have transformed modern warfare. No longer does the main threat to the security of the United States derive from states that must mobilize their citizens and resources for war in a lengthy, observable process. Given the covert nature of terrorist attacks, the United States is now justified in intervening against any regime that might aid terrorist organizations: "The only way to deal with the terrorist network is to take the battle to them. That is in fact what we're doing. That is in effect self-defense of a pre-emptive nature" (Rumsfeld 2001). The most recent Quadrennial Defense Review speaks of using military force to defend our "enduring national interest," of "contributing to economic well being" through the "vitality and productivity of the global economy" and "access to key markets and strategic resources" (Department of Defense 2001). Thus, according to official Defense Department doctrine, the United States has a right to go to war to preserve the global neoliberal economic order.

The fall 2002 National Security Doctrine also contends that in the "war against terrorism" both terrorist organizations and "terrorist" or "rogue" states are "imminent threats" to American citizens. Citizens can only be fully defended against these organizations if they are defeated by "pre-emptive" military attacks. As both terrorist organizations and rogue states mobilize in secret (and through deceit), and as they do not engage in the visible mobilization of state-governed armies, navies, and air forces, we must strike at them before a clandestine suitcase bomber (or other lone-rider suicide attacker) rains mass death upon innocent civilians. Thus, the Bush administration's assumption that there exists an imminent threat posed by (the unspecified possible acts of) rogue states, cooperating with terrorist organizations, overturns the traditional just-war logic of limited preemptive wars against imminent attackers. The Bush National Security Doctrine advocates a potentially unlimited series of preventive wars against anyone, any group, or any nation that at some point might threaten the United States (National Security Council 2002). Just-war theory only justifies truly preemptive wars against hostile nations on the verge of attack, against whom the victim would not be able to survive unless it struck first. But the doctrine of preventive war—which justifies a nation initiating a war against a potential enemy that might someday gain the ability to inflict harm upon the attacking state—has always been rejected by just-war theorists (Crawford 2003, 15).

Defense against terrorist organizations cannot neatly be subsumed under just-war doctrine, for terrorists are not responsible sovereign states whose purpose is to defend a specific territory and protect innocent civilians. Thus, terrorist organizations, particularly ones with no national political aims, are less constrained in the use of force than are nation-states. And a global network of terrorists—rather than a more traditional, nationally based terrorist or revolutionary organization—is less likely to make demands upon one nation-state that can (at least in theory) be met (Benhabib 2001). Integral to most revolutionary action (and even domestically based political terrorism) is a desire to garner popular support. But terrorist individuals or cults that have no realizable political agenda (such as Timothy McVeigh or Aum Shinrikyo or Al Qaeda, if its goal is truly the elimination of the "infidel" West) do not admit of political solutions to their grievances (unlike, say, the Tamil Tigers, who may end their terrorism in return for regional autonomy for the Tamils within a federated Sri Lanka, or an IRA that may destroy its arms in return for greater rights for Catholics within Northern Ireland) (Post 2001; Potoniere 2001).

The Bush administration's doctrine of wars against "rogue" states contends that such states are highly likely to use weapons of mass destruction to coerce other states, and that they willingly harbor terrorists. But who is the U.S. government to judge that North Korea or Iran is more likely to use its WMDs for either diplomatic coercion or military gain than is Pakistan, India, Israel, or China (or the United States, France, Russia, or Britain)? And how does the U.S. government know that diplomatic measures, nuclear deterrence, or economic sanctions could not dissuade nations from engaging in high-jinks nuclear threats or from actively supporting terrorist groups? Has not diplomacy worked to contain Iran, China, Pakistan, India, and North Korea thus far? And did it not work against the only other global military and nuclear power the United States has ever faced—the former Soviet Union? At present, the United States is sending a powerful message in favor of nuclear proliferation by responding to North Korea's possession of nuclear weapons through diplomatic means, while attacking an Iraq that clearly possessed no nuclear weapons and did not use its alleged chemical and biological weapons against an overpowering, conquering opponent.

If the U.S. invasion of Afghanistan contributes to a long-term decrease in Al Qaeda's effectiveness—and the civilian and military casualties incurred were absolutely necessary to end the use of Al Qaeda's bases—then that invasion may be deemed just. How indispensable were the Afghan training bases for the success of the 9/11 attacks? Only history can judge, though the United States' unwillingness to expend the necessary funds (and troop commitments) for reconstruction and security (particularly beyond Kabul) likely dooms the possibility of such judgment being retrospectively favorable. Could Al Qaeda bases elsewhere, such as those in the Northwest Territories of Pakistan (America's alleged ally in the "war against terrorism"), in Somalia, or in the outlying islands of Indonesia or the Philippines, not play a similar role? And would this justify the United States in occupying the entire planet—assuming it had the capacity to do so? And did not the operations aspect of 9/11 originate more in Saudi Arabia, Germany, Maine, and Florida than in the training camps of Afghanistan? Lax domestic security measures on the part of both the United States and its allies played a far greater role in the success of the 9/11 attacks than did the lessons learned in the training camps of Afghanistan (lessons easily taught elsewhere).

The Afghan case is unique in that the Taliban abdicated many security roles to Al Qaeda's foreign mujahedin. The Taliban leaders proved more interested in living the spiritual life in Kandahar than in exercising administrative and police powers from Kabul (Doran 2002). Al Qaeda provided many of the shock troops in the wars between the Taliban and the warlords of the Northern Alliance. But this may well have been a purely pragmatic alliance, as the Taliban also worked closely with the Pakistani Security Service (which also aided Al Qaeda), and the Taliban maintained relatively cordial relations with the United States until 1998. In the immediate run-up to the U.S. attack on Afghanistan, the United States never seriously investigated the Taliban's offer to turn over Osama bin-Laden to "neutral" third parties. Perhaps this was not a serious offer to turn over bin-Laden to a party that would cooperate in detaining him and his allies and prosecuting them before an effective international tribunal. But the United States never explored the option. Again, if the administration had truly followed the moral precepts of just-war theory it would have pursued all possible solutions short of armed conflict before using the deadly means of war.

The administration could have made a case for a humanitarian multilateral intervention against the gross violations of human rights committed by both the Taliban regime and the Iraqis. Developing such an international consensus would have been difficult (though the United Nations did, retroactively, endorse the belated NATO intervention in Bosnia). Sometimes unilateral humanitarian acts can be morally justified

without multilateral action, such as the Vietnamese invasion that overthrew the genocidal Khmer Rouge. But just as ten years of pro-
Vietnamese puppet rule in Cambodia tainted the humanitarian claims
of the Vietnamese, so will the United States' humanitarian justification of
the Iraqi invasion be tainted if it uses its occupation to pursue narrow
strategic and economic advantage, such as expanding bases in the Persian
Gulf and gaining greater control over Iraqi oil (not to mention massive
reconstruction contracts for U.S. firms). If Iraq did not play a crucial role
in the geopolitics of oil, would the United States have unilaterally
intervened on behalf of human rights? After all, the oil-less Sudan has
not witnessed a U.S. invasion on behalf of the close to two million
(predominantly Christian) victims of a war carried out by a brutal Islamic
fundamentalist regime.

Even if NATO's motives for the belated Bosnian and Kosovo intervention partly involved providing a post-Soviet justification for NATO, in
retrospect, if the intervention saved lives, then it may be justified by just-
war theory's moral consequentialism. Though the West was complicit in
the disastrous break-up of post-Tito Yugoslavia, only the most fundamentalist critics of U.S. "imperialism" would deny that the belated U.S.
intervention saved Bosnian Muslim and Kosovar lives. A unified multi-
ethnic government that respected minority rights in both Kosovo and
Bosnia may not be possible in the near future. This raises the provocative
question as to what the responsibility is of the international community
for providing basic security—the Hobbesian minimal right to life
itself—in ethnically riven, dysfunctional states. How long would foreign
peacekeeping forces have to remain in Bosnia and Kosovo, given the
likelihood that ethnic violence would return once they left?

In light of the unilateral U.S. attack on Iraq (with the junior partner,
Britain, in tow), the veneer is off any U.S. pretense to work through the
United Nations to disarm Iraq. The war against Iraq is an ideological
assertion of the right of the American Empire to use brutal force to
restructure the globe in its own image. The imperial vision of the Bush
administration conceives of the "free world" as regimes that follow
neoliberal economic-development policies and support U.S. foreign-
policy aims. Thus, such noted "democracies" as Saudi Arabia and
Pakistan remain in the U.S. camp of "freedom."

8. After the War on Iraq : Future Opposition to the Bush Doctrine

With the successful initial phase of the invasion of Iraq over, the relevant
question remains how best to restore international norms with regard to
the use of force and how best to promote greater autonomy for the Iraqi
people. The only legitimate aims for an occupying power (particularly one
that did not follow international law when invading and overthrowing an
admittedly despicable regime) would be to work multilaterally to restore

domestic security; to apprehend and try—by lawful domestic or international judicial institutions—those suspected of committing crimes
against humanity; and to facilitate, as expeditiously as possible, the
restoration of a representative Iraqi government. Not only should the
United States allow U.N. inspections to resume; it should invite nations
experienced in peacekeeping operations (Canada, India, Fiji, and so on)
to carry out these tasks in accordance with international law. It would be
particularly wise to bring in security forces and aid organizations from the
Arab and Islamic world. That the United States has refused to do this
bodes ill for the chances of any Iraqi constitution and government formed
under the U.S. occupation to garner popular legitimacy. Any truly
democratic regime must also be free to choose its own foreign policy; a
democratic Iraq would likely be highly critical of U.S. policy in the
Middle East. And a legitimate and stable Iraqi government would need
both to control the oil revenues of Iraq (including the right to have a
previously very competent state corporation continue to produce and
refine the oil) and to be free to take competitive bids from both domestic
and foreign corporations for reconstruction projects. U.S. pressure to
denationalize the Iraqi state oil industry clearly violates international law.

Despite some serious initial resistance in southern Iraq, the Anglo-
American invasion went sufficiently "smoothly" for people around the
globe to fear that the Bush doctrine may now be extended into armed
invasions of Syria and/or Iran. Only the international outcry that
preceded the Iraqi intervention and the present difficulties confronting
the occupying powers in restoring basic services and security in Iraq
preclude this possibility (plus the formidable nature of a unified Shi'ite
Iran of one hundred million people). The nuclear capacities of North
Korea and Pakistan have led the United States, thus far, to opt for
diplomatic and economic pressure as the means to influence these nations'
foreign and strategic policies. The Bush administration may realize that
the lesson developing nations may take from the Iraqi affair is that their
national autonomy is best secured by the possession of nuclear weapons.
Thus, some in the Bush administration advise that we must risk a military
confrontation with North Korea in order to curtail the threat of massive
nuclear proliferation.

Rather than continuing with a relatively successful multilateral exercise in the disarmament of Iraq, the Bush administration engaged in the
first unilateral war sanctioned by its arrogant and irrational national-
security doctrine of preemptive war. Beginning in 1996, a small group of
right-wing policy operatives, gathered under the name of the Project for a
New American Century (led by William Kristol, Richard Perle, and Paul
Wolfowitz), articulated the concept that the twenty-first century should
be an American century in which U.S. military and economic power
would dominate the world, making it safe for "free markets" and
"democracy." Globalization backed by American power would make

the world safe for "the American way of life." The influence of this group and their policy centers has been so profound and so obvious that Bush officials in key positions, such as Secretary of State Powell, have found it necessary to deny its influence (Lind 2003).

The new National Security Doctrine contends that the United States is justified in attacking preemptively any nation that it conceives of as a "long-run threat" to U.S. interests anywhere. It is a vision of imperial arrogance mirrored in the United States' disregard both for world public opinion and for the majority of states in the U.N. Security Council. It is a doctrine that threatens to negate the very principle of national sovereignty that underpins global stability. If Iraq is first, will Iran be next? What of North Korea? Pakistan? Venezuela? Colombia? Brazil? And how can a United States that has violated numerous international treaties (the Kyoto accords; the International Criminal Court; the ABM treaty) caution a Pakistan or an India (or an Egypt or an Israel) not to engage in preemptive strikes against one another?

The neoconservatives have long believed that brute military superiority is readily fungible for political change. They remain under the delusion that it was only massive U.S. military spending that led to the collapse of the Soviet Union. It is as if Gorbachev never existed. Only U.S. military might, and not the unproductive and oppressive nature of the Soviet socio-economic system, caused the Soviet collapse. Little mention is made of the crucial role played by Gorbachev's refusal to order Soviet troops to put down the massive peaceful revolts of Eastern Europeans against Soviet domination. Today, in an era when small, nonnational groups of terrorists can threaten the civilian population of any nation, the neoconservative faith in the omnipotence of traditional military power is as stunningly ignorant as was the cold-warrior belief that the military could win the "hearts and minds" of the third world.

It does not take a left-wing analyst, merely *The New York Times*, to illustrate how Al Qaeda is already using the U.S. threats against Islamic Iraq to step up recruitment across the Islamic world. Terrorism cannot be fought by traditional "wars" (hence the dangerous misnomer of "the war on terrorism"). It can only be fought by sophisticated police methods; by cooperation among national intelligence agencies; and by espionage and financial sleuthing. What are the chances that the intelligence agencies of nations with large Islamist opposition movements, such as Pakistan, Egypt, and Saudi Arabia, can continue to cooperate with the "great infidel" in its "war on terrorism"? There exits a blatant contradiction between effective multilateral cooperation against terrorism and a unilateral war on the "axis of evil." But a Bush regime that believes it can both balance the budget and hand tax giveaways to the rich long ago demonstrated that consistency is the hobgoblin of feeble minds.

Those who believe that the post-cold-war era poses the tenuous possibility of multilateral action on behalf of human rights should agitate for U.N. administration of postwar Iraqi economic, political, and military reconstruction. This is not yet an achievable demand, as there still does not exist a coalition of nations strong enough to take on U.S. hegemony. The United States has considerable economic leverage over the governments of China and Russia. However, in the case of North Korea, security concerns about an unbridled U.S. military response have led China, Russia, Japan, and South Korea to pressure the United States to abandon its opposition to unilateral negotiations with North Korea. Similar international pressure—from both civil society and democratic nation-states—may be sufficient to guarantee that a democratic Iraqi government would be able to utilize its national oil revenue for its own democratic development, rather than for paying the costs of the U.S. military expedition and occupation.

The unilateral attack on Iraq is part and parcel of the neoconservative worldview that conceives of the United States as the sole force for good in the world. In this parochial worldview, the city on the hill will bestow the benefits of its neoliberal economic model—and its military power—upon global humanity. The last time American imperial hubris reached this height it led to the disastrous overextension and defeat of the United States in Vietnam (not to mention more than three million Vietnamese and fifty thousand American deaths). Similar grave costs to global peace—and the United States' domestic well-being—could be visited upon us if domestic "regime change" does not occur in the near future. The neoconservative posture of permanent war abroad is part of the same ideology that calls for the gutting of the domestic public sector; redistribution of income and wealth upward to the rich; and deregulation of the global economy in the interests of transnational corporations. The economic crisis spawned by such policies may facilitate regime change at home.

Thus, the responsibility of the intellectual is to outline—as publicly and as accessibly as possible—the distinction between an intelligent multi-lateral effort to combat terrorism and a counterproductive, unilateral war on terrorism. In the early days of the Vietnam War, academic and student opposition laid the intellectual groundwork for the eventual public delegitimizing of U.S. foreign policy in Southeast Asia. Without a similar response by the academy today, it is conceivable that a Democratic presidential victory in 2004 would not yield any significant change in U.S. foreign policy. Without a regime change in post-cold-war U.S. foreign-policy doctrine, the prospects for global peace and justice will remain dim.

References

Atlas, James. 2003. "A Classicist's Legacy: New Empire Builders." *New York Times*, "Week in Review" (May 4): 1, 4.

Benhabib, Seyla. 2001. "Unholy Politics." In Social Science Research Council essays "After September 11," at www.ssrc.org/sept11/essays.

Berman, Paul. 2003a. "The Philosopher of Islamic Terror." *New York Times Magazine* (March 23): 24–29, 56, 58, 65–67.

———. 2003b. *Terror and Liberalism*. New York: Norton.

Cheney, Dick. 2002. "In Cheney's Words: The Administration Case for Removing Saddam Hussein." *New York Times* (August 27): A8.

Crawford, Neta C. 2003. "Just-War Theory and the U.S. Counterterror War." *Perspectives on Politics* 1, no. 1 (March): 5–25.

Department of Defense. 2001. "Quadrennial Defense Review Report." Washington, D.C.: U.S. Government Printing Office (September 30).

Doran, Michael. 2002. "The Pragmatic Fanaticism of Al Qaeda." *Political Science Quarterly* 117, no. 2 (summer): 177–90.

The Economist. 2003. "Ciao, Saudi." (May 3–9): 32–33.

Euben, Roxanne L. 2002. "Killing (for) Politics: *Jihad*, Martyrdom, and Political Action." *Political Theory* 30, no. 1 (February): 4–35.

Foer, Franklin. 2002. "Moral Hazard: The Life of a Liberal Muslim." *New Republic* (November 18): 21–25.

Geertz, Clifford. 2003a. "Which Way to Mecca?" *New York Review of Books* 50, no. 10 (June 12): 27–30.

———. 2003b. "Which Way to Mecca? Part II." *New York Review of Books* 50, no. 11 (July 3): 36–39.

Ghadbian, Najib. 2000. "Political Islam and Violence." *New Political Science* 22, no. 1: 77–88.

Hassan, Nasra. 2001. "An Arsenal of Believers." *New Yorker* (November 19): 36–41.

Hoffmann, Stanley. 2003a. "The High and Mighty." *American Prospect* (January 13): 28–31.

———. 2003b. "American Goes Backward." *New York Review of Books* 50, no. 10 (June 12): 74–80.

Ignatieff, Michael. 2003. "The American Empire: The Burden." *New York Times Magazine* (January 5): 22–27, 50–54.

Kepel, Gilles. 2002. *Jihad: The Trial of Political Islam*. Cambridge, Mass.: Harvard University Press.

Krueger, Alan, and Jitka Maleckova. 2002. "Does Poverty Cause Terrorism?" *New Republic* (June 24): 27–33.

Lewis, Bernard. 1998. "License to Kill: Osama Bin Laden's Declaration of Jihad." *Foreign Affairs* (Nov.–Dec.): 14–19.

Lind, Michael. 2003. "How Neoconservatives Conquered Washington— and Launched a War." *Salon* (April 9), at ⟨http://www.salon.com/opinion/feature/2003/04/09/neocons/index_np.html⟩.

Mann, Michael. 2001. "Globalization and September 11." *New Left Review* 12 (Nov./Dec.): 51–72.

Metcalf, Barbara. 2001. "'Traditionalist' Islamic Activism: Deoband, Tablighis, and Talibs." In Social Science Research Council symposium on 9/11, at www.ssrc.org/sept11.essays/metcalf.

Mortimer, Rex. 1974. *Indonesian Communism under Sukarno: Ideology and Politics, 1959–65.* Ithaca, N.Y.: Cornell University Press.

National Security Council. 2002. *The National Security Strategy of the United States of America.* Washington, D.C.: Office of the President (September).

Post, Jerrold. 2001. "Killing in the Name of God: Osama Bin Laden and Radical Islam." Talk to the New York Academy of Medicine (October 30), at www.theapm.org/cont/Posttext.html.

Potoniere, Paolo. 2001. "Al Qaeda—Call It a Cult." Pacific News Service, at ⟨http://news.pacificnews.org/news/view_article.html./article_id5fc2a 7b9f:983ea6bf61839d6da0968f4⟩.

Roy, Oliver. 1995. *Afghanistan: From Holy War to Civil War.* Princeton: Princeton University Press.

Rumsfeld, Donald. 2001. "Interview with Wolf Blitzer." *CNN* (October 28), at www.defenselinkl.mil/news/Oct2001.

Said, Edward. 2002. "Disunity and Factionalism." *Al Ahram* (August 15–21), at ⟨http://weekly.ahram.org.eg/2002/599/opl.htm⟩.

Scialabba, George. 2003. "The Clash of Visualizations." Review of Paul Berman, *Terror and Liberalism. The Nation* (April 28): 31–35.

Telhami, Shibley. 2002. *The Stakes: America and the Middle East: The Consequences of Power and the Choice for Peace.* Boulder, Colo.: Westview Press.

Walzer, Michael. 2000. *Just and Unjust Wars: A Moral Argument with Historical Illustrations.* Third edition. New York: Basic Books.

———. 2002. "No Strikes: Inspectors Yes, War No." *New Republic* (September 30): 19–22.

———. 2003. "The Right Way." *New York Review of Books* 50, no. 4 (March 13): 4.

5

OF POWER AND COMPASSION

SHIBLEY TELHAMI

When the U.S. military overthrew the Taliban regime in Afghanistan with apparent ease after the horror of 9/11 and the United States was able to act forcefully without the United Nations in toppling the regime of Saddam Hussein in Iraq, the power gap between the United States and any other state became more evident than at any other point since the end of the cold war. The United States will thus be constantly lured by an approach that relies primarily on its obvious advantages as the sole remaining superpower because a deeply pained public is hoping for quick and simple answers. This approach focuses largely on using U.S. military power to address the challenges America faces and on dealing with governments alone, through incentives and threats, without concern for world public opinion. It seeks to pursue American interests in the world, especially in the Middle East, with little regard for the vital interests of others and sees the war on terrorism as primarily an American issue — or at least one whose definition is a unilateral American right.

America remains strong and capable. When confronting other states militarily, it surely will prevail, even when it goes it alone. In exercising such power, it will inevitably reshape the priorities of other states and, as in the Middle East, even remake the regional political order.

But the dilemma of the exercise of power is that defeating others is not always the same as winning. There are many reasons to be concerned that such an approach applied to the Middle East will hurt not only America's enemies but also its friends and in the end may undermine the very interests that we are trying to defend. There are four main reasons for concern: understanding the limitations of power; motivating others to challenge America; mischaracterizing the nature of the challenge faced, and thus the nature of the necessary response; and overlooking the values at stake, what we stand for as a nation. Articulating these four concerns is the aim of this essay.

Limitations of Power

It is gratifying to be the most powerful nation on earth, deterring potential enemies and punishing those who attack us on our own soil. The ability to punish those who were behind the crimes of 9/11 has been not only cathartic but also necessary for preventing other attacks. Both the threat and the exercise of power are important in achieving national goals and securing global stability—and they are both sometimes unavoidable.

At the same time, it should be clear that although power is an important asset for prudent diplomacy, it is not a replacement for diplomacy. We have more power than anyone else, but this power is not unlimited. Others too wield power and have the potential to wield more. In exercising power, we must always calculate not only the likely short-term benefits but also the long-term consequences for our ability to exercise it again. Making more enemies than friends is inefficient and imprudent.

Consider the Iraq war launched in 2003, carried out with minimal support from others and in the face of opposition from many countries in the region and around the world. The United States succeeded in overthrowing the government in Iraq, even if its action was nearly unilateral. But to assure a favorable outcome in the long term, the United States needed to commit significant economic, military, and political resources for an extended period. The fact that the task required such resources at the same time that America was continuing its global war on terrorism, especially in central Asia, diminished America's ability to undertake additional campaigns elsewhere. It could undermine the coalition the United States needs for the success of its antiterrorism campaign. If the intent of a strategy of this sort was in part to exhibit America's overwhelming power and Washington's willingness to employ it so as to deter potential enemies, the result may in the end be overextension—the Achilles' heel of many empires. America's ability to deter new threats to its interests would be undermined. This is the dilemma of power: It is most effective when it is least used; the more one uses it, the fewer the remaining resources and the less credible the threat of its use.

It is also important to consider the effect of the war with Iraq on many around the world who were increasingly resentful of American unilateralism: they become more motivated to forge coalitions to reduce the impact of American power. States aspiring to acquire nuclear weapons, such as North Korea and Iran, have accelerated their efforts in an attempt to deter American unilateralism. If American unilateralism is replicated by other regional powers, the consequences for the global order will be even more challenging.

Motivating Others to Challenge America

Military strategists have long understood that a central issue in the outcome of any conflict is motivation, both one's own and the adversary's. The extent to which a cause is seen as more or less "legitimate" internationally affects the degree of parties' motivation. Military power is obviously central in the outcome, but in the long term the importance of motivation balances the importance of military power.

As a stronger party's will to fight or to accept even limited casualties decreases, the will of its weaker opponent increases and its threshold of pain rises. The contrast between Israel's experience in Lebanon on the one hand and its confrontations with Palestinians on the other may prove instructive.

Israel withdrew from Lebanon in 1999 after years of occupation. Although the lesson learned by some in the region was that guerrilla warfare works against Israel, because of the perception that Israel was militarily defeated by the Lebanese Hezbollah group, the outcome was in large part a function of each party's motivation. Militarily, Israel possessed overwhelming power vis-à-vis Hezbollah, the Lebanese state, and its domineering neighbor, Syria. Hezbollah forces numbered in the hundreds and had limited equipment. Israel not only had decisive military advantages but also inflicted considerably more pain on Hezbollah and on Lebanon (and sometimes on Syrian forces) than was inflicted on it. Because of Israeli actions, Lebanon faced the creation of tens of thousands of refugees; hundreds of casualties; and the serious undermining of its economy through such methods as the destruction of power stations, which paralyzed its capital, Beirut. In contrast, Israel's economy was minimally damaged by its presence in southern Lebanon, and the number of casualties it sustained was small by the measures of warfare (a few dozen a year). Israel could have afforded to continue its presence, and many within Israel's military establishment did not want to pull out of Lebanon without a peace agreement.

In the end, however, Israel did withdraw without such an agreement. Hezbollah members and others in the region interpreted this result as a military victory that could be replicated in the Palestinian areas. This conclusion was an erroneous and unfortunate interpretation. Israel's withdrawal and Hezbollah's success simply cannot be understood by the power equation alone, or by the usual measures of winning or losing a war. At issue was each side's motivation. More important, the degree of motivation was a function of two factors that are not directly related to power: the extent to which the conflict was seen by each side as vitally important to its existence and the extent to which the cause was perceived as legitimate in international eyes.

The fact that Israel occupied Lebanese lands and operated from them was seen by most Lebanese, including those who opposed Hezbollah, as a threat to their sovereignty that superseded any divisions among them. The fact that there was no imminent threat to Israel's existence from Lebanon and that the Hezbollah guerrillas largely focused their operations against Israeli troops on Lebanese soil raised questions in the minds of the Israeli public about the need to stay in Lebanon and about justifying even the smallest number of Israeli casualties. Had Hezbollah framed its objectives in terms of eradicating Israel rather than liberating Lebanon, and had it sent suicide bombers to kill Israeli civilians, Israel's motivation would have been significantly different. At a minimum, motivation affects each side's threshold of pain and its will to exercise power. To achieve independence, Lebanon could endure immense pain; for no obvious vital interests, Israel could endure little. This issue of motivation is also affected by outside notions of the legitimacy of each side's cause: the sense that Lebanon's drive to seek independence was in harmony with the principles of sovereignty that most around the world accept generated more international sympathy for Lebanon than for Israel—which in turn reinforced the determination of the Lebanese.

The Palestinian-Israeli confrontation in the West Bank and Gaza has been of a different nature. Here too Israel has had overwhelming power superiority. The Palestinians have had even more motivation than the Lebanese because they have no state at all and are under occupation. Their threshold of pain has thus been very high because the issue is ultimately about existence. For Israel, three issues have made the question of motivation significantly different from the situation in Lebanon. First, the proximity of the West Bank to the heart of Israel makes the outcome much more important. Second, a significant portion of the Israeli population has always wanted to claim the West Bank as part of Israel. Third, the suicide bombings of civilians inside Israel have made the issue more vital because the threat is more immediate. As a consequence, even though the Palestinians have inflicted many more casualties on Israel than Hezbollah has, Israeli motivation has increased rather than diminished. Thus, the balance of motivation on the Israeli-Palestinian front fuels the conflict even more than the actual distribution of military power and reduces the chance that the conflict can be won through Palestinian attacks or through Israel's military superiority. Israel can inflict far more pain on the Palestinians than it suffers, but that is not the same as winning or achieving peace.

For a powerful America, it is important to keep in mind when contemplating military options globally, as in the Middle East, that motivation is a factor affecting the utility of power and the will to use it. Those who live in the Middle East will care more deeply about its future than we will. No strategy to defend American interests in areas like Iraq and the rest of the Persian Gulf can succeed in the long run unless the United States ensures that it does not increase its deeply motivated enemies in the process.

The Nature of the Challenge and the Necessary Response

Understanding the Challenge

American power can fully address threats to vital U.S. interests emanating from any state or combination of states. Terrorism is a threat that emanates largely from nonstate actors. It is not surprising that none of the terrorists who attacked America came from countries that our State Department labels "terrorist states," or were evidently connected to any such countries. Our military capabilities are sufficient to deter the most ambitious governments around the world, and every state, including Iran and North Korea, is sensitive to the deterrence of more powerful parties.

U.S. military might is a primary reason why Saddam Hussein did not employ his chemical weapons in 1991, when our own military simulations showed that such an act would have resulted in thousands of American casualties. Deterrence worked: as former Secretary of State James Baker warned, the use of such weapons would have been the end of Saddam's government. However, it is much harder to deter motivated individuals and small groups that often thrive where central authority is weak and where deterrence is therefore less effective. In an era when states have less control of the flow of information and technology, it is increasingly easy for motivated groups and individuals who are willing to take risks to carry out terror attacks, and the threats they pose are likely to be increasingly lethal.

Certainly states cooperate to minimize the threat, which ultimately is a threat to them all; the very logic of sovereignty in the international system is built on governments' monopoly of the use of force. But because the problem is global, it cannot be addressed unilaterally. The strategy can succeed only through significant cooperation with other states in intelligence, finance, and direct confrontation of threatening groups. A policy that brings about regional instability—through a spillover of Iraqi instability and the inflammation of public opinion in the region—and with it a weakening of states on the one hand and a loss of their willful cooperation on the other, will fail to reduce the terrorist threat.

Consider, for example, the serious fear that terrorists may acquire weapons of mass destruction. In the past decade, the legitimate global concern was not that sovereign states would make such weapons available to terrorists but that the disintegration of the Soviet Union meant the loss of full control over these weapons in the former Soviet states. Even the reported discovery in 2002 that members of al-Qaeda or other groups were apparently experimenting with chemical weapons in northern Iraq was telling: such experimentation didn't take place in areas where the Iraqi government had control; it occurred in the semiautonomous Kurdish areas that were partly protected by U.S. air power. After the Iraq war, reports indicated that some terrorist groups were moving into Iraq. Where there is less sovereignty, there is more chance for terrorism.

It should also be apparent that terrorism has a "demand side" as well as a "supply side." A military strategy could erode the power of some of the suppliers, the organizations that tap into popular disaffection to recruit members and plan attacks. But the demand side would remain: the public anger, despair, and humiliation that motivate people to join such groups and that provide the suppliers of terror with a ready market for their horrible products. So long as that demand side remains or, even worse, increases, the vacuum created by the destruction of one supplier will quickly be filled by other aspirants. Not all, or even most, people who are desperate or feel a sense of deep humiliation are inclined to be recruited by groups engaged in terror. But when one looks at a society as a whole and finds that majorities are enraged, it is usually an indication that people on the margins of that society are being radicalized into sometimes brutal action.

Increasingly, public attitudes in the Arab world and much of the Muslim world have included not only strong resentment of American foreign policy but also a sense of deep despair and humiliation that people connect in their minds to that policy. Enhanced American dominance in the Gulf region is likely to add to that feeling. And despite the best of intentions after 9/11, the debates in America and in the Arab and Muslim worlds have increasingly portrayed the confrontation as involving America on the one hand and Arabs and Muslims on the other. This phenomenon is dangerous because it puts both sides on a slippery slope toward a long-term confrontation that benefits no one.

Although there are numerous issues accounting for the differences between the United States and many in the Arab and Muslim worlds, there is no escaping the fact that the Arab-Israeli conflict is the biggest source of anger and humiliation. Without this issue there would still be many differences, as there are between the United States and various parts of the world. But the depth of anger that motivates many people and creates ready recruits for terrorist organizers would be reduced. It would also become easier to work with regional actors to address common problems.

There can be no pretending that the structure of America's relationship with the Middle East is not centrally affected by the Arab-Israeli conflict; wars like the recent Iraq war would only stun the region into a temporary lull before the reality reappears: America *is* a central player in the Arab-Israeli issue. The American commitment to Israel, which often pits the United States against all others in international organizations, means that when Israel is threatened, the United States must respond. On the other hand, when Israel prevails and Arabs are on the losing side, America will inevitably receive much of the blame for providing Israel with military, economic, and political support. The anger toward Israel increasingly becomes anger toward America as well. In the long term, no reordering of regional politics can resolve that dilemma except the resolution of the Arab-Israeli conflict, especially the Palestinian issue. Only peace between Israelis and Arabs could significantly reduce the challenge to America's interests in the region. No other issue is as central to America's interest in the Middle East and to reducing the demand side of regional terrorism.

The Need to Build Bridges of Mutual Understanding

It is much easier to destroy bridges than to build them, but more bridges of understanding must be built between the United States and the people in Arab and Muslim countries. Invariably, public-opinion surveys indicate that a primary source of Arab and Muslim frustration and anger toward the United States is a perceived lack of empathy for their pain and hardship. Even aside from the rights and wrongs of policy on such issues as Iraq and the Palestinian-Israeli conflict, the prevalent perception is that America does not value the lives of Arabs and Muslims. Effective public diplomacy is an essential component of American foreign policy in the region.

Public diplomacy is not the same as propaganda, and there are limits to what can be achieved through this means. The United States needs to explain its policies and to disseminate information about American culture, values, and aims. But public diplomacy must be present at the inception of any policy and must include dialogue and feedback. If the aim of policy is to send messages to others or to generate particular responses, it cannot succeed without understanding those others' aims, aspirations, priorities, and sensitivities.

Sometimes a single word from the president or secretary of state can outweigh millions of dollars spent on a campaign of public diplomacy. Two examples from recent history are telling. The first is President Bush's inadvertent use of the term *crusade* in describing the global campaign against terrorism, because in the Muslim world that word evokes fears of a Christian crusade against Islam. It is as if the president of Egypt or Pakistan declared a new global policy aimed at America based on *jihad*, a term that is understood in the United States to mean Islamic holy war, though it is often used by Arabs and Muslims to mean simply struggle or campaign. Although the president later corrected the implication and began using different terms, his early statement continued to be used against him in the region as reflecting the true intent of U.S. policy.

A second example, of words that were *not* said, took place during the emotional period of destructive Israeli operations in Palestinian cities in the spring of 2002, ordered by Ariel Sharon after horrific suicide bombings that killed many Israeli civilians. While Israelis were under-standably focused on their own pain and tragedy, Arabs were moved by the deaths of so many Palestinian civilians, the damage to their cities, and their helplessness in the face of a powerful Israeli army as displayed live on their television screens. These images reinforced their association of Sharon with war, violence, and a 1982 massacre of Palestinians in Lebanon. They waited to hear from the White House, hoping for plans to put an end to violence or at least for words of empathy. President Bush, however, described Sharon as a "man of peace." These words were posted over pictures of death and destruction in the Arab press and undermined everything else the president said.

There is another important reason for building bridges and establishing dialogue with people in the region in the campaign against terrorism in particular. Terrorism is an immoral means employed by different groups for different ends. To reduce its occurrence, it must be delegitimized by societies wherever it takes place. If the war on terrorism is to succeed, it must be seen not as an American war against specific groups but as a campaign to render the use of terrorist methods illegitimate, to make it harder for groups to recruit, to gain points, to be accepted. Such a policy would mean building a coalition and projecting moral consistency, for legitimacy and illegitimacy are ultimately about consensus and cannot be created in isolation. An effective policy must strive to prevent the perception that the conflict is between "us" and "them" in the sense of Americans versus Muslims and Arabs, constituting a clash of civilizations. It must recognize the internal struggle over the fate of society in the Arab and Muslim worlds; significant, influential segments of these societies share many of our values, if not our policies. Empowering and helping these forces wage their own struggle for change is essential in winning the battle for hearts and minds.

Such empowerment cannot be addressed only through public diplomacy, which is about projecting information, images, and values to foreign publics. The ability of moderates to speak out in society— even in a free society—is limited in times of national crisis. When there is a sense of national pain, voices of dissent are often seen as unpatriotic, disloyal, or serving the interests of adventurers. Debate is muted, hard-liners play on public emotions, and moderates go on the defensive. It is an unfortunate phenomenon that appears everywhere, including in our own free country, but it is even more prevalent where society is less free. Although many in the Middle East reject the use of terrorism, few have spoken out as tension with the United States has grown over the Arab-Israeli issue. This silence is driven sometimes by self-censorship, sometimes by intimidation, and sometimes simply by anger: "If the United States cannot feel our pain, we will not feel its pain." Hence, American policy is very much a factor in affecting the prospects, shape, and outcome of such debates in the Middle East.

The role of governments and official policies in times of national crisis is essential for setting the tone of national debates and for helping mobilize moderates to confront those who support extreme options because they are blinded by fear or pain. Governments in the Middle East have a central role to play in the internal debate, and our own government has much influence in setting a tone of friendship and empathy that empowers and assists moderate forces. A policy that creates genuine peaceful alternatives is the best way to empower moderates, to rally them, to enable them to put forth a prospect of hope as they publicly debate the voices of militancy. Such policy alternatives need not always originate in Washington; the United States must find many ways to work with others in the region and elsewhere. American backing for efforts of the European Union, or for ideas like the Saudi peace proposals, could be used to enhance American interests as well as the prospects of peace in the Middle East.

The Values at Stake

I have argued that a compassionate approach, one that builds coalitions and considers the vital interests of other states, one that does not disregard the wishes of people around the globe, is also a prudent approach generally, and certainly toward the Middle East. It is as essential for a successful foreign policy as the measured exercise of power itself. But compassion is also an end in itself—especially for those powerful enough to afford it. In reaction to the horror that befell our nation, there were dual fears: a fear of the actual threat posed by terrorism in today's world, and the worry that our response to that fear will undermine the very values that make our nation great.

America's success in contemporary politics has certainly been bolstered by its superior military power. But that military power itself is a product of a successful economic and political system that reflects what America stands for. Those around the world who have sought change in their own political and economic systems have done so in large part on their own and not because America forced its ideas on them. Success is a model. Those who want to match it will have to emulate the model, and those who don't will likely fail. Powerful ideas are intentionally accepted or rejected by those who compete in the global market; ideas win by inspiring, not by threatening. Democracy is part of the success story of America. Even those who are reluctant to embrace it, such as Chinese leaders, have understood the need to emulate much of America's economic approach lest they be left further behind. In embracing a new economic approach, such nations have also unleashed a political process they will not be able fully to control.

Some believe that we can spread democracy through war, but it should be apparent that democracy is about the will of the people, about their right to choose. Ultimately, our role in that issue is to cooperate, to assist, and above all to inspire. Democracy, by definition, cannot be imposed. The thought would not be comforting to most Americans that because we have the power—and know what's best for others better than they do themselves—we should disregard the wishes of other people around the globe on issues that are often more vital to them than to us.

No other society has been as open, egalitarian, diverse, or hospitable to immigrants as America's. The openness is part of America's greatness and its political and economic success. A policy toward the Arab and Muslim worlds that has the effect of turning America into a fortress, building barriers between the United States and nations comprising more than a billion people, and allowing fear to compromise civil liberties even in our own land is not the stuff of greatness. We may succeed tactically in the short term, but only by losing ourselves, what we stand for. In the end, we become what we do.[1]

---

[1] This essay is based on chapter 6 of my *The Stakes: America and the Middle East* (Boulder, Colo.: Westview Press, 2003, updated 2004).

6

TERROR AND THE ATTACK ON CIVIL LIBERTIES

RONALD DWORKIN

Two years after the September 11 catastrophe Americans remain in great danger. The danger is of two kinds, of which the first—further terrorist attacks—is obvious. Well-financed terrorists, who live and undergo training in various foreign countries, are determined to kill Americans and are willing to die in order to do so. If they gain access to nuclear weapons, they would be able to inflict even more terrible harm.

The second, less obvious danger is self-inflicted. In its response to this great threat, the Bush administration has ignored or violated many fundamental individual rights and liberties, and we must now worry that the character of our society will change for the worse. The administration has greatly expanded both surveillance of private individuals and the collection of data about them. It has detained many hundreds of prisoners, some of them American citizens, indefinitely, in secret, and without charge or access to a lawyer. It threatens to execute some of these prisoners after trials before a special military tribunal where traditional safeguards to protect the innocent from conviction will not be available.

There has been much powerful criticism of these policies by civil liberties groups, journalists, conservatives who worry about liberty, and others. Many of these critics argue that the administration's policies are unconstitutional or illegal under international law. I believe they are right. But the administration has been surprisingly successful in persuading federal judges to uphold its policies against legal challenge,[1]

---

[1] Federal courts have held, for example, that the United States does not have sufficient control over Guantánamo Bay to force the government to allow habeas corpus petitions on behalf of the prisoners held there (see *Al Odah* v. *United States*, 321 F.3d 1 134, D.C. Cir. 2003, and *Ctr. for Nat'l Sec. Studies* v. *DOJ*, 331 F.3d 918, D.C. Cir. 2003), and have also upheld the administration's position that the courts do not have power to review the president's designation of individuals captured in a military zone as enemy combatants (see *Hamdi* v. *Rumsfeld*, 337 F.3d 335, 357, 4th Cir. 2003). These decisions are, in my view, wrong. Whether a territory is sufficiently subject to American sovereignty so that American authority must respect the writ of habeas corpus depends on whether sovereignty is effective, not whether it is permanent. So the fact that American control of the Guantánamo base is secured only by a long lease seems irrelevant. The court in its Hamdi decision cited the Constitution's designation of the president as commander in chief, but that designation hardly means that courts are deprived of their normal power to protect individuals from arbitrary government authority even in war. The government also relies on the Supreme Court's 1942 *Quirin* decision, which held that Nazi spies who had landed in America with

and international lawyers are divided over whether our practices violate any of our treaty obligations.[2] In any case, many of those who defend the government's policies argue that questions of legality are close to irrelevant in times of national emergency: they say that, as Chief Justice Rehnquist has put it, in war the laws "speak with a muted voice."[3] We must therefore take up a different and more basic issue: whether the

sabotage in mind, including one American citizen, could be tried by a military tribunal and executed without substantial judicial review. (See *Ex Pane Quirin et al.*; *US ex rel. Quirin et al.* v. *Cox*, Provost Marshal 317 US 1.) That decision was regrettable, even sordid. See my article "The Threat to Patriotism," *The New York Review*, February 28, 2002. In any case, the decision is inadequate precedent for the Bush administration's refusal to allow detainees to contest their status as enemy combatants and to allow them access to counsel. The Nazi saboteurs admitted that they acted as spies for a foreign enemy power, and they were represented by very skillful lawyers, including Kenneth Royal, who later became secretary of the army.

[2] The question whether America's treatment of prisoners at Guantánamo Bay, in Iraq, and elsewhere violates international law largely depends on the interpretation of the Geneva Conventions, which are a complex series of covenants and protocols each of which was ratified by at least 156 nations. (The United States is a party to some parts of the conventions but not others; one question about which international lawyers divide is whether, because so many other nations are party to all parts of the conventions, the United States must respect even those provisions it did not ratify because they all now represent customary international law.) The conventions distinguish two main classes of people a nation captures in military action: those who are acting as agents of another power with which the nation is at war, and those who are acting as civilians on their own. The latter may be prosecuted as criminals. The former must be treated as prisoners of war provided they meet other conditions: they must fight under a responsible command, carry their arms openly, wear a fixed and recognizable sign like a uniform, and themselves obey the laws of war. The Bush administration interprets these provisions to allow a third category, which it calls "unlawful combatants" (a term that nowhere occurs in the Geneva Conventions), by which it means those who are not entitled to prisoner-of-war status or treatment because they do not wear uniforms or do not obey the laws of war, for example, but who may nevertheless be detained without criminal charges because they have taken up arms as part of an organized group. That interpretation has been widely challenged. (See, e.g., Knut Dörmann, "The Legal Situation of Unlawful/Unprivileged Combatants," *The International Revue of the Red Cross* 84, no. 849, March 2003.) In any case, Article 5 of the Third Geneva Convention, to which the United States is a party, requires that parties convene tribunals to determine whether particular prisoners are entitled to prisoner-of-war status when there is doubt. The First Additional Protocol, which the United States signed but did not ratify, specifies that requirement in much greater detail: it requires that each prisoner be presumed eligible for prisoner-of-war status and allowed to contest any reclassification before a "competent" tribunal. The administration refuses to recognize those further requirements of the protocol, and insists that there is no doubt that those it has detained are not entitled to prisoner-of-war status.

[3] Chief Justice William H. Rehnquist, Remarks at the 100th Anniversary Celebration of the Norfolk and Portsmouth Bar Association, May 3, 2000 (transcript available at www.supremecourtus.gov/publicinfo/speeches/sp_05-03-00.html). But Rehnquist has also warned that "[it] is all too easy to slide from a case of genuine military necessity . . . to one where the threat is not critical and the power [sought to be exercised is] either dubious or nonexistent," and that it is "both desirable and likely that more careful attention will be paid by the courts to the . . . government's claims of necessity as a basis for curtailing civil liberty." See his *All the Laws but One* (Vintage, 2000), pp. 224–25.

*could be legal, maybe, but
still indefensible blamey
violate peoples fundamental
human rights*

TERROR AND THE ATTACK ON CIVIL LIBERTIES   83

administration's polices are indefensible even if they are legal because
they violate people's fundamental human rights—rights at the foundation of the international moral order that nations must respect even when
under threat. If so, then these policies are not only (wrong) but shameful.

1

The administration's USA Patriot Act, hurried through Congress almost
immediately after September 11, enacted a breathtakingly broad definition of terrorism, including, for example, violent acts "intended to
influence the policy of a government by intimidation or coercion," so that
someone is guilty of aiding terrorism if he contributes money to any
group with those aims. The act greatly expanded the power of government to conduct secret searches of private homes, permitted the attorney
general to detain aliens as security threats whenever he wanted, stipulated
new rules enabling the government to demand records of any person's
book purchases or borrowings from bookstores and libraries, and increased the government's surveillance authority in many other ways. A
recent report by an internal Justice Department inspector alleged "dozens"
of violations of civil rights in the enforcement of the act.[4]

More than 650 prisoners are now held in the administration's
detention camp at Guantánamo Bay, anonymously and under harsh
conditions.[5] Inmates at other U.S. detention camps, in Iraq, in Bagram in
Afghanistan, and on the British-owned island Diego Garcia in the Indian
Ocean, among other sites, are subjected to violent and coercive
interrogation, including beatings, withholding of pain medication, sleep
deprivation, and loud noise intended to be disorienting. There is good
reason to worry that these prisoners are tortured, and that recalcitrant
prisoners are "rendered" for questioning to foreign countries where such
torture is routine.[6]

The military tribunals the administration threatens to use to try some
of its detainees are appointed by the Defense Department, and have the
power to impose sentences, including the death penalty, without the
normal evidentiary safeguards of the criminal process—hearsay evidence
and involuntary confessions are admissible, for example, if they would

[4] See Philip Shenon, "Report on US Antiterrorism Law Alleges Violations of Civil
Rights, *The New York Times*, July 21, 2003.
[5] See Joseph Lelyveld, "In Guantánamo," *The New York Review*, November 7, 2002.
[6] See Dana Priest and Barton Gellman, "US Decries Abuse but Defends Interrogations;
'Stress and Duress' Tactics Used on Terrorism Suspects Held in Secret Overseas Facilities,"
The Washington Post, December 26, 2002; Rajiv Chandrasekaran and Peter Finn, "US
Behind Secret Transfer of Terror Suspects," *The Washington Post*, March 11, 2003; Peter
Finn, "Al Qaeda Recruiter Reportedly Tortured; Ex-Inmate in Syria Cites Others'
Accounts," *The Washington Post*, January 31, 2003.

have "probative value to a reasonable person." There is no appeal except to the secretary of defense and the president.[7] Defendants are provided with appointed military lawyers and permitted to hire, at their own expense, civilian lawyers who have security clearances, except that civilian lawyers may not attend hearings that the presiding officer declares closed. Legal associations have questioned whether American lawyers should participate in trials that so severely limit their power to defend their clients adequately.[8]

The government is now holding incommunicado at least three prisoners, Yasser Esam Hamdi, José Padilla, and Ali Saleh Kahlah al-Marri, in military prisons in the United States without charging them, and without allowing them access to a lawyer. Hamdi is an American citizen. The government says he was arrested by the Northern Alliance while fighting for the Taliban in Afghanistan, but it makes that claim in a cursory memorandum written by a minor official with no direct knowledge of the facts, and it refuses to support the claim with any further evidence. Padilla, also an American citizen, was arrested in Chicago as a "material witness" in the government's investigation of the September 11 attacks, but when a court-appointed lawyer challenged his detention, and a judge ordered a hearing, the president designated him an unlawful enemy combatant, and he was denied a hearing. Marri is a Qatari student who was arrested on a charge of lying to investigators about his travels and faced an ordinary criminal trial until the president announced, last June, with no supporting evidence or argument, that he too is an enemy combatant who may be held incommunicado without charge.[9]

Zacarias Moussaoui is a French national who was arrested in the United States before September 11: the administration claims that he was the "twentieth hijacker," who would have joined in the attacks had he not been arrested earlier. It has prosecuted him in a federal court, asking the death penalty. The government's principal evidence, apparently, is that he received money from al-Qaeda officials now in U.S. custody abroad who also sent money to the hijackers. But the government has refused court orders to allow Moussaoui's lawyers to interview those al-Qaeda officials, and has threatened that if these orders are not overridden

---

[7] The rules of the military tribunals were clarified in Department of Defense Military Commission Order No. 1 of March 21, 2002. The president's initial order was in certain ways even more severe: it provided, for example, that judges need not be convinced beyond a reasonable doubt to vote guilty, and that only a two-thirds vote of judges was necessary to impose the death penalty. The March 21 order requires proof beyond a reasonable doubt and requires a unanimous vote for death, though only a two-thirds vote for conviction.

[8] See Neil Lewis, "Rules Set Up for Terror Tribunals May Deter Some Defense Lawyers," *The New York Times*, July 13, 2003.

[9] See Eric Lichtblau, "Bush Declares Student an Enemy Combatant," *The New York Times*, June 24, 2003.

by the courts on appeal it will prosecute Moussaoui in a military tribunal where there will be no question of allowing his lawyers access to al-Qaeda officials.[10]

It would be a gross mistake to suppose that these powers and acts are justified because those whom they threaten are all guilty, as Donald Rumsfeld suggested in his amazing statement that the prisoners at Guantánamo Bay are all killers. It is itself a grave compromise of human rights to assume guilt before guilt is demonstrated by fair means. Of course Americans have used unconventional and apparently unfair legal tactics before, as many other nations have done, when we have been frightened by war or by real or imagined threats of subversion. In World War II, for example, the U.S. government herded Japanese Americans who posed no security risk into detention camps. But the Bush administration's policies threaten a more lasting corruption of our traditions because the danger it cites as justification will last not for a few years, as the other real or supposed crises did, but for at least a generation and perhaps longer.

Conservatives have for many years wanted government to have the powers that administration officials now claim are legitimate; September 11 may have served them only as an excuse. John Ashcroft's Justice Department has been using its new powers under the Patriot Act, which were defended as emergency provisions against terrorists, to investigate and prosecute a wide variety of more ordinary crimes, including theft and swindling.[11] The government's anti-terrorist policies may be an irreversible step to a new and much less liberal state. That makes the question I posed—do these policies violate fundamental human rights—even more urgent.

legal but do they violate moral norms

2

Many Americans believe that the Bush administration's security policies are a justified response to the terrorist threat.[12] They believe that the

---

[10] The government said it would consent to an order dismissing the prosecution so that it could appeal the ordered access to captured officials. See Philip Shenon, "In Maneuver, US Will Let Terror Charges Drop," *The New York Times*, September 26, 2003. But the judge, Leonie M. Brinkema, instead ordered the trial to continue, with the government not allowed either to allege Moussaoui's involvement in September 11 or to seek the death penalty. The government must now decide whether to appeal those orders or to transfer the case to a military tribunal immediately. See Kirk Semple, "In Setback to US, Judge Refuses to Drop Moussaoui Case," *The New York Times*, October 2, 2003.

[11] See Eric Lichtblau, "US Uses Terror Law to Pursue Crimes from Drugs to Swindling," *The New York Times*, September 28, 2003.

[12] A recent CNN/*USA Today*/Gallup Poll found that only 22 percent of Americans thought the administration had gone too far in restricting civil liberties. However, two-thirds said the government should not take any additional anti-terrorism steps if they further compromised civil liberties. See Dana Milbank, "President Asks for Expanded Patriot Act," *The Washington Post*, September 11, 2003.

attacks on September 11 require (as it is often put) "a new balance between liberty and security." That much-used expression suggests that we can properly judge the new policies by asking whether they are in our overall interest, as we might decide, for instance, whether to strike a new balance between road safety and the convenience of driving fast by lowering speed limits. But, with hardly any exceptions, no American who is not a Muslim and has no Muslim connections actually runs any risk of being labeled an enemy combatant and locked up in a military jail. The only balance in question is the balance between the majority's security and *other* people's rights, and we must think about that as a matter of moral principle, not of our own self-interest.

Among the most fundamental of all moral principles is the principle of shared humanity, that every human life has a distinct and equal inherent value. This principle is the indispensable premise of the idea of human rights, that is, the rights people have just in virtue of being human, and it is therefore an indispensable premise of an international moral order. Various international covenants like the Universal Declaration of Human Rights of the United Nations and the Geneva Conventions are statutory attempts to codify that basic moral principle into particular rules that can be made binding as a matter of domestic and international law. It may be a controversial question, as the Bush administration insists, whether its security measures violate the specific terms of any of the conventions to which the United States is a party.[13] But those measures do violate the basic principle of shared humanity that underlies them all.

They violate that fundamental principle because they follow a strategy of putting American safety *absolutely* first, a strategy that recommends any measure that improves American security against terrorism even marginally or speculatively, or that improves the cost-efficiency or convenience of America's anti-terrorism campaign, without counting the harm or unfairness of that measure to its victims.[14] America followed that strategy in interning Japanese Americans—the benefit to security of

---

[13] For a comprehensive study of the application of the international law of human rights to America's proclaimed war on terrorists, see Anthony Dworkin, "Military Necessity and Due Process: The Place of Human Rights in the War on Terror," forthcoming in *New Wars, New Laws?*, edited by Matthew Evangelista and David Wippman (Transnational Publishers).

[14] The government does not apply a comparable principle to its budget: it does not treat even evidently important security measures as having top financial priority. In the midst of its declared war on terror it has negotiated huge tax cuts mainly for the benefit of very rich taxpayers, and skimped on security expense. Federal funding for local organizations that would face the consequences of further terrorism has been grotesquely small, for example. See *Emergency Responders: Drastically Underfunded, Dangerously Unprepared*, Report of an Independent Task Force Sponsored by the Council on Foreign Relations, Warren B. Rudman, Chair (2003). This report is available at www.cfr.org.

that wholesale detention was minimal, and the damage it inflicted on its victims was enormous—and we look back on that episode with great national embarrassment.[15] Of course every government has a special responsibility to look after its own citizens' safety, and a nation may, when necessary, use violence in self-defense. But the harm it deliberately inflicts on others must be comparable to the harm it thereby prevents to its own people, and when our government shows itself ready to impose grave harm on foreigners or on suspected Americans for only speculative, marginal, or remote benefits to the rest of us, its action presupposes that their lives count for nothing compared to ours.

That contemptuous assumption is evident both in the policies I have described and in the justifications the Bush administration offers for them. It refuses to permit even minimal judicial, congressional, or other independent checks on its decisions. It places detention camps outside the United States to avoid habeas corpus petitions. It claims the exclusive right to decide who is an enemy combatant with no need to provide any substantial evidence to any court. It refuses to permit any judge to examine its opaque claims that security requires that it deny basic protections to people it accuses of crime. It keeps its detentions and its treatment of detainees as secret as possible to forestall any criticism by other parts of government, the press, private citizens, or international human rights organizations. It claims that wartime security demands this secrecy and immunity from judicial and other supervision. That is an argument made by every police state, and it may be the most self-serving and indefensible claim the Bush administration has made so far.

For though it is certainly more convenient for the administration to execute its policies in secret with no oversight from any other department of government, the suggestion that this secrecy benefits security begs the question, because that suggestion must itself be taken on trust. The alleged security benefits seem minimal in any case. Judges, senators, and representatives are American officials too; they can be trusted, and they have developed special procedures to protect classified information that have been used successfully both in legislative hearings and in terrorist trials held in ordinary courts in the past.[16] The administration may argue that in war it should take no risks, however small. But when the lives and freedom of those the government has arrested are at stake, taking absolutely no risks however small means valuing those lives and freedom as worthless. That is the strategy of putting American safety not only first but absolutely first, and it is morally impermissible.

[15] See Peter Irons, *Justice Delayed: The Record of the Japanese American Internment Cases* (Middletown, Conn.: Wesleyan University Press, 1989).

[16] See *United States* v. *Bin Laden*, 92 F. Supp. 2d 225, SDNY 2000 (1998 U.S. Embassy Bombings in Nairobi, Kenya, and Dar-es-Salaam, Tanzania) and *United States* v. *Salameh*, 261 F.3d 271, 2d 2(K)1 (1993 World Trade Center bombing).

When the government does try to explain why security requires the measures it has taken, its explanation confirms that impermissible strategy. It says, for example, that it must be allowed to monitor conversations between suspected terrorists and their lawyers because lawyers may pass orders to terrorists still at large. But that danger is remote, because suspected terrorists who have been imprisoned for any substantial time are unlikely to have useful information or authority, and the danger could in any case be minimized by requiring lawyers for suspected terrorists to undergo a security check. The government says it cannot release the names of prisoners because terrorist organizations may not know which of their members have been arrested and which are still available for assignments. But it seems most unlikely that effective terrorist organizations do not know, or cannot determine, which of their members who are important enough to matter have disappeared for months or years. The administration claims that secret military tribunals are better forums for trying suspected terrorists than courts that are independent of the military because important security secrets might possibly be exposed in ordinary trials. But, as I have said, the courts have developed methods, such as closed proceedings, for dealing with sensitive security matters in the past, and there is no reason why they cannot protect official secrets in future trials.

The government says it cannot allow Padilla to speak to his lawyers because that brief break in his questioning—which has now gone on for many months and is presumably interrupted for meals, sleep, and rest anyway—might possibly affect the success of the interrogation, which might depend on coercion and on disorienting the prisoner. It is better, the government says, to hold him indefinitely incommunicado. The prosecutors refuse to allow Moussaoui's lawyers to interview the captured al-Qaeda leaders because that might interrupt their interrogations, which have also gone on for months.[17] Better to execute him without the benefit of whatever exonerating information those leaders might supply. The government says it cannot provide actual evidence that Hamdi was in fact captured fighting for the Taliban on the battlefield because preparing the records would take time and money away from other counterterrorism activities. Better that he should languish for years in a military jail.

It is significant that the American-led invasion of Iraq in March 2003 was also defended by putting American safety absolutely first. The administration claimed that Iraq's clandestine development of terrible weapons threatened our security, and that it had discovered links between Saddam Hussein's government and al-Qaeda. It is now plain that the evidence for the first of these claims was thin and for the second

---

[17] See Neil Lewis, "Bush Officials Lose Round In Prosecuting Terror Suspect," *The New York Times*, June 27, 2003.

nonexistent.[18] But the administration says, as Deputy Defense Secretary Paul Wolfowitz has put it, that it was entitled to act on "murky" or speculative evidence to protect American security even at the cost of thousands of American, British, and Iraqi lives.[19]

The Justice Department has been almost explicit, moreover, in acknowledging that it ranks American safety absolutely first. In response to charges that it is overzealous in protecting security at the cost of liberty, the attorney general has said that the government makes "no apologies for finding every legal way possible to protect the American public from further attacks."[20] That is a particularly revealing statement, since the administration claims that the law permits almost anything in war, and that judges have little authority to review the administration's decisions anyway.

3

My suggestion that the Bush administration's strategy is immoral may seem open to an important objection. It is plainly legitimate in some circumstances for a government deliberately to inflict grave injuries on some people in order to lessen the risk of harm to others, even when that risk is only statistical or speculative. We do exactly that, after all, when we use the criminal law to punish convicted criminals. We deprive them of freedom in order to deter them and others from committing crimes; we do harm to them, that is, to make each of the rest of us statistically and marginally safer. We do much the same in conventional war: we try to kill the enemy's soldiers in order to protect our own soldiers and citizens from risks that are, for each of them, only speculative. So we cannot say, after all, that a government may never injure some people to protect others from a lesser or more speculative harm. If we can do that in combating ordinary crime and in conventional war, then why not in fighting terrorism?

This response assumes, however, that the principle of shared humanity is simply ignored or overridden in the criminal process or in conventional war. But that is not true. On the contrary, civilized nations have all

[18] The latter claim was particularly powerful in persuading the nation that war was necessary: CNN reported that in February of 2003, 76 percent of Americans thought that Iraq was involved in the September 11 massacres. See Bruce Morton, "Selling an Iraq–al-Qaeda Connection" (March 11, 2003), available at www.cnm.com/2003/WORLD/meast/03/11/Iraq.Qaeda.link. As of the date of this essay, according to preliminary reports of an inspection team, no banned weapons had been found in Iraq in spite of intensive searching. The administration has apparently abandoned its claim of a tie between Iraq and the September 11 massacres. See "Bush Reports No Evidence of Hussein Tie to 9/11," *The New York Times*, September 18, 2003.

[19] See Reuters dispatch, "Wolfowitz Says US Must Act Even on 'Murky' Data," *The New York Times*, July 27, 2003.

[20] See "Report on US Antiterrorism Law Alleges Violations of Civil Rights," *The New York Times*, July 21, 2003.

evolved rules to regulate both the criminal process in their countries and their conduct in wars, and these rules are designed specifically to recognize that a nation is not entitled to care only for the interests of citizens it tries to protect. It must also show concern and respect for the lives of those it injures in trying to protect those citizens, even when that means that the protection is somewhat less effective or complete.

Our criminal process imposes harm only when that harm can accurately be described as punishment. We do not select some people to put in jail because we think they are more likely than the average citizen to commit serious crimes, though we might indeed be safer if we did that. The people we punish have selected themselves by actually violating laws that they have a legal responsibility to respect. Our procedures insist on safeguards, moreover, to ensure that those we punish are indeed guilty, that is, that they have indeed made themselves liable to that punishment, because running any substantial risk that a criminal defendant may be punished though innocent, just to improve the efficiency of the process of deterrence, would be treating the defendant's life as expendable. Those are the safeguards that the administration now ignores.

In war we also often inflict terrible injury on some people—particularly on the soldiers of the enemy nation—in order to protect each of our own soldiers or citizens from lesser or more speculative harm. We cannot appeal to the criminal model to justify that practice because in ordinary wars we must kill soldiers who are not subject to our legal authority and who have not violated any canons of international law. We must therefore rely on a different set of arguments to show why our military operations do not violate the principle of shared humanity. In war we face massed armies who attack us, or defend themselves against us, as a single unified force. If we follow the ordinary principle of justified self-defense—if we kill particular soldiers only when killing them is the only means of preventing the certain death or serious injury of our own soldiers—then we will lose the war. We must aim to disable any enemy forces that we can strike.

But once again the laws of war forbid us from putting our own safety absolutely first. We may not target civilians, even though that might well save some of our soldiers' lives and end our war sooner. The bombing of Hiroshima and Nagasaki, in retrospect, seems monstrous, and in any case would be ruled out now by our international commitments. Moreover, the Geneva Conventions forbid treating prisoners of war according to a safety-first principle. Prisoners must not be coerced even by means that fall short of torture to answer any questions beyond those necessary to identify themselves, even though coercive interrogation would provide valuable military information. Their equal status as human beings must be recognized by providing them with the same level of accommodation and medical treatment as is provided for the soldiers who guard them, even though that, too, is costly.

These constraints of fair criminal procedure and these humane rules of war are important not just when a nation's constitution or its treaty obligations make them binding, but because a very large community of civilized nations thinks that either they or closely similar constraints are necessary to prevent criminal prosecution or war from becoming a crude sacrifice of some people for the sake of others, a sacrifice that would ravage rather than respect the idea of shared humanity.

However, America's campaign against organized international terror cannot be conducted wholly within the constraints of either the crime model or the war model I have described. We should indeed pursue terrorists through any police action that is practicable, not only in our own country but also through international police and intelligence networks and in collaboration with willing foreign governments. We should attempt to persuade any nation where terrorists are found to arrest them and either try them itself or extradite them to our country or to an international tribunal for trial.[21] If it were feasible to pursue and prosecute terrorists only in this way, the crime model would be fully appropriate.

But that is not feasible. Terrorist societies are spread throughout the world, and they command allegiances and resources far beyond those of even legendary criminal organizations like the mafia. They conspire to commit violence not for personal profit, as drug cartels do, but in service of an ideology that is shared by many people, often including members of the government, in the nations from which they operate. It is extremely difficult to distinguish individual terrorists from a substratum of supporting peoples and powers. It is therefore tempting to regard powerful terrorist groups like al-Qaeda as quasi nations or political powers, and to treat our actions against them as more in the character of a war than a police action.   *why war seems plausible*

The model of war is not fully appropriate either, however.[22] War is historically a matter of status, not means: we enter a state of conventional war on a date, like December 8, 1941, and we leave it on another date, like August 14, 1945. We fight conventional wars against nations that have boundaries, and leaders with whom we can negotiate truces and surrenders, not against loose organizations whose hierarchies are secret and indistinct and whose officers and soldiers do not wear uniforms. We can conquer Kabul and Baghdad, but there is no place called Terror where the terrorists live.

---

[21] It is a difficulty that the legal systems of many nations, and of the European Union, forbid extradition to countries that impose the death penalty.

[22] For an argument that it is counterproductive to designate our campaign against terrorism as a war, see Philip B. Heymann, *Terrorism, Freedom, and Security: Winning Without War* (Boston: MIT Press, 2003).

The Bush administration assumes that if neither of the traditional systems for dealing with crime and war fully fits America's campaign against terrorism, then anything goes: we can then pursue American safety first, without constraints. But that assumption is unwarranted and unprincipled. The fact that terrorism presents new challenges and dangers does not mean that the basic moral principles and human rights that the criminal law and the laws of war try to protect have been repealed or become moot. We must instead ask what different scheme—what third model—is appropriate to respect those principles while still effectively defending ourselves.

That immensely important project should now engage international lawyers, police specialists, military analysts, historians, politicians, and philosophers of different traditions and cultures. Perhaps reflection, debate, and experience will provide some consensus on a new legal system for terror that can one day be encoded in some new set of international conventions. In the meantime we must do the best we can, not by abandoning all of the constraints of the two traditional models but by trying to capture the principles those constraints serve in a new model that incorporates aspects of each of the others.

That new model might require a nation to pursue first international terrorist organizations that have harmed its people through police action, either on its own or in collaboration with international or foreign police units, unless such police action is, or becomes, inadequate. A terrorist organization might control territory of its own so that no local police action can reach it, for example, or a local government might be unwilling or unable to attack the organization effectively. In that event a nation may mount a military campaign against the organization even if it must invade a foreign country, such as Afghanistan, whose regime is protecting it.

But once a nation has taken prisoners in such a campaign, whether by capture on a foreign battlefield or by arrest at home or elsewhere, it must follow a different procedure. It must choose, case by case, which of the two models I described it then wishes to pursue. Within a reasonable time after capture—say, two months—it must decide whether a prisoner is to be treated as a prisoner of war or as a suspected criminal. (It may later revise its decision if new evidence requires.)

That decision must be made not in accordance with a defensive reading of the rules of the Geneva Conventions, which were written with more conventional wars in mind, but in the spirit of the principles behind those rules. Since terrorist organizations do not have national identities or uniforms, for example, it cannot be decisive, in determining whether a detainee is a criminal and not a prisoner of war, that he wears no uniform. If the government decides to treat any prisoner captured in battle as a criminal rather than as a prisoner of war, its decision must be reviewed by a "competent" tribunal as required by the provisions of the

Geneva Conventions that almost all civilized nations have accepted. If it decides to treat anyone it captures not on a battlefield but in an ordinary police action as a prisoner of war rather than as a criminal, then it must permit him to challenge that classification, whenever practicable, through a habeas corpus petition in a federal court.[23]

Those detainees the government designates as prisoners of war must be treated in accordance with the humane rules of those conventions. They must, for example, be given accommodation and medical care equal to that of the troops guarding them, and subjected to no form of interrogation beyond what those conventions permit. The conventions permit a nation to try a prisoner of war for war crimes, such as willful killing of civilians, that would presumably include terrorist attacks in the United States. But if any prisoner of war is charged with such a crime, the conventions require that he be tried in a military court whose rules give him all the procedural protections that members of the American military have who are court-martialed. (The rules of American courts-martial are much more protective of the accused than the military tribunals in which the Bush administration proposes to try foreigners. The former severely restrict the admissability into evidence of hearsay and involuntary confessions, for example, and provide for appeals to an appellate court that includes civilian judges, and then to the Supreme Court.) The conventions' rule that prisoners of war may be detained until the end of hostilities cannot be plausibly applied in these circumstances, however, because that rule plainly presumes that wars begin and end through discrete formal acts. The U.S. "war" against terrorism can have no formal end: it may last at least a generation. Congress must therefore stipulate a maximum period—say, three years—for which anyone designated a prisoner of war in the campaign against terrorism may be held, though Congress would retain the power, so long as organized international terrorism remains a serious threat, to extend the period, either in particular cases or in blanket extensions of a stipulated maximum period, on a showing of necessity and after suitable debate.

Those the government designates suspected criminals need not be treated as prisoners of war. But their treatment must be governed by the ordinary procedures and protections of our criminal practice, again modified as necessary to fit the special circumstances. Suspects must be informed of charges against them and given access to lawyers and the benefits of a judicial process. Ordinary federal courts, which, as I have said, have the power to protect classified information, should be sufficient. But Congress might, if it thought necessary, provide specialist courts for such trials in the exercise of its constitutional power to create courts and define their jurisdiction. Any specialist courts must, however, respect the crucial separation of judicial and executive power; their

---

[23] See *Schlesinger v. Councilman*, 420 U.S. 738 (1975).

decisions must be made subject to review by higher courts independent of the military and the executive branch. If the government claims that security requires that conversations between a suspect and his attorney must be monitored, a judge must review and approve that claim.

The specific cases I have mentioned earlier can be used to illustrate this new model. The government might declare Moussaoui a prisoner of war, citing his admission that he belongs to al-Qaeda. It might then detain him subject to the conditions of the Geneva Conventions, though he would have to be released in due course or tried for war crimes under rules similar to those used in American courts-martial, which would presumably permit his lawyers to interview any witnesses essential to his defense. Or the government might continue to declare him a criminal, and then subject him to the prosecution and protection of the familiar criminal law, which would also mean that he was permitted to interview essential witnesses. The government could continue to refuse to allow his lawyers access to the captured al-Qaeda officials, that is, only if it treated him as an ordinary prisoner of war and did not seek to try him for any offense that would make access to those officials necessary for his defense. It is not unreasonable to ask our government to make this choice. Criminal prosecutors must often decide whether to forgo prosecution of a particular suspect when prosecution might compromise continuing investigations, and Moussaoui could in any case be detained as a prisoner of war.

The administration would be forced to make similar choices about the other detainees I have mentioned. It may fear that it does not have sufficient evidence to convict Padilla of any crimes in an ordinary criminal court. If so, then it must release him unless it can show that he had sufficient contacts with al-Qaeda to be classified as a prisoner of war, in spite of the fact that he was arrested in Chicago and not on any foreign battlefield. If so, then it must detain him, not incommunicado in solitary confinement in a military brig, but in circumstances consistent with prisoner-of-war status.

The government must make that choice about Hamdi as well. True, military officers cannot be asked to prove in court that every person they capture on the battlefield is in fact an enemy soldier. (It would not be unrealistic, however, to make an exception for those whose presence on the battlefield might be thought surprising, like American citizens.) But even if we accept the principle that courts cannot scrutinize the capture of battlefield prisoners, it hardly follows that the government may lock up anyone it captures on a battlefield indefinitely, without charge, and keep him incommunicado. If the administration prosecutes Hamdi as a criminal, it must allow him access to counsel and the normal protections of the criminal process, and it must provide genuine evidence against him. If it does not, then it can detain him only in the different status of a protected prisoner of war.

The Guantánamo detainees are also being held indefinitely and in secret, with no access to lawyers, under circumstances that would be intolerable even if they were convicted criminals. But they have not been charged with crimes or given the benefit of legal advice or process. If the detainees are prisoners of war, they must be treated as such. If they are suspected criminals, they must be treated as such. The government must choose, once again, not because it is required to do so by treaties but because its failure to do so treats the lives of the detainees with impermissible contempt.[24]

Rights would be worthless—and the idea of a right incomprehensible—unless respecting rights meant taking some risk. We can and must try to limit those risks, but some risk will remain. It may be that we would be marginally more secure if we decided to care nothing for the human rights of anyone else. That is true in domestic policy as well. We run a marginally increased risk of violent death at the hands of murderers every day by insisting on rights for accused criminals in order to keep faith with our own humanity. For the same reason we must run a marginally increased risk of terrorism as well. Of course we must sharpen our vigilance, but we must also discipline our fear. The government says that only our own safety matters. That is a counsel of shame: we are braver than that, and have more self-respect.[25]

—October 7, 2003

---

[24] This new regime of principle may be open to exceptions in truly extraordinary situations: cases, for example, in which the U.S. military has some special and urgent reason for coercive interrogation of a prisoner whom it cannot in good faith accuse of a crime and treat as a criminal. But in such cases the threat that requires that treatment—the proverbial example of the ticking bomb and a prisoner who knows where it is—will be sufficiently grave and imminent so that coercion can be justified without appealing to any principle that would justify imposing serious harm for marginal benefit. In such a case we must accept that we are acting unjustly out of necessity, and try to limit the injustice in any way possible. See Dworkin, "The Threat to Patriotism."

[25] My thanks to James Cockayne, Anthony Dworkin, Philip B. Heymann, Gayle M. Horn, and Stephen Schulhofer for written comments on a draft of this essay and other help.

7

CIVILIZATIONAL IMPRISONMENTS

AMARTYA SEN

1

Conflict between civilizations has been a popular topic for a long time—well before the dreadful events of September 11 ushered in a period of open confrontation and pervasive distrust in the world. Yet these terrible happenings have had the effect of magnifying the ongoing interest in the so-called clash of civilizations, of which the classic statement can be found in Samuel Huntington's famous and ambitiously impressive book *The Clash of Civilizations and the Remaking of World Order*, which appeared five years before the World Trade Center was targeted. Indeed, many leading commentators have tended to see a firm connection between global conflicts and civilizational confrontations—most notably, between "Western" and "Islamic" civilizations. The intellectual basis of that thesis and related ideas requires a close examination, both for its obvious epistemic interest and—more immediately—for its far-reaching relevance to practical politics in the contemporary world. The need for that critical scrutiny is now greater than it has ever been.

The thesis of a civilizational clash can be ideologically linked with a more general idea that provides the methodological foundation of the "clash thesis." This concerns the program of categorizing people of the world according to some single—and allegedly commanding—system of classification. To see any person wholly, or even primarily, as a member of a so-called civilization (in Huntington's categorization, as a member of "the Western world," "the Islamic world," "the Hindu world," or "the Buddhist world") is already to reduce people into this one dimension. The deficiency of the clash thesis, I would argue, begins well before we get to the point of asking whether the disparate civilizations (among which the population of the world is forcefully partitioned out) must necessarily—or even typically—clash. No matter what answer we give to this question, by even pursuing the question in this restrictive form we implicitly give credibility to the allegedly unique importance of one categorization over all the other ways in which people of the world may be classified.

Opponents of the "clash theory" can actually contribute to its intellectual foundation if they accept the same singular classification of the world population. The same impoverished vision of the world—divided into boxes of civilizations—is shared by those who preach amity among discrete and disjunctive civilizations and those who see them as clashing. In disputing the obtuse and gross generalization that members of the Islamic civilization have an essentially belligerent culture, for example, it is common enough to argue that they actually share a culture of peace. But this simply replaces one stereotype with another; and it involves accepting an implicit presumption that people who happen to be Muslim by religion would be much the same in other ways as well.

Aside from all the difficulties in defining civilizational categories as disparate units (on which more presently), the arguments on both sides suffer from a shared faith in the presumption that seeing people exclusively, or primarily, in terms of religion-based civilizations to which they are assumed to belong is a good way of understanding human beings. Civilizational partitioning is a pervasively intrusive phenomenon in social analysis (stifling other ways of seeing people) even without its being supplemented by the incendiary belief in the particular thesis of a civilizational clash.

If "the clash of civilizations" is the grand thesis about the divisions of the contemporary world, there are lesser but still influential claims that relate contrasts of cultures and identities to the conflicts—and the profusion of atrocities—that we see in different parts of the world today. Instead of one majestically momentous partition, as in Huntington's world, that splits the world's population into contending civilizations, the lesser variants of the approach view local populations as being respectively split into clashing groups, with divergent cultures and disparate histories that tend, in an almost "natural" way, to breed enmity toward each other. Conflicts involving Hutus and Tutsis in Rwanda, and Serbs and Albanians in the former Yugoslavia, and Hindus and Muslims in the subcontinent, and so on, are then re-interpreted in lofty historical terms, reading into them much more than contemporary polities. Modern conflicts that call for analysis in terms of contemporary events and machinations are then interpreted as ancient feuds—real or imagined—that place today's players in pre-ordained roles in an allegedly ancestral play. The "civilizational" approach to contemporary conflicts (in grander or lesser versions) serves as a major obstacle to focusing more fully on the actual prevailing politics and the dynamics of contemporary events.

It is not hard to understand why the civilizational approach is so appealing to so many people. It invokes the richness of history, and it seems to call upon the depth and the gravity of cultural analysis, seeking profundity of understanding in a way that an immediate political analysis of the "here and now" would seem to lack. If I am disputing the civilizational approach, it is not because I do not see its attractions and intellectual temptations. Indeed, I am reminded of an event nearly fifty years ago, shortly after I first arrived in England from India as a student at Cambridge. A kindly fellow student took me to see the recently released film *Rear Window*, in which I encountered James Stewart looking at some very suspicious events in the house opposite his own. Like the James Stewart character, I too, in my naïve way, became convinced that a gruesome murder had been committed in the apartment across the courtyard; but my intellectual friend went on explaining to me (amid whispered requests from neighbors urging him to shut up) that he was quite certain that there was no murder at all, no basis in reality for James Stewart's (and my own) suspicion, and that the whole film was really an indictment of McCarthyism in America, which encouraged everyone to watch the activities of other people with great suspicion. "This film is a critique," my friend informed the novice from the Third World, "of the growing Western culture of snooping." Such a film, I had to agree, would have been in many ways a much more penetrating and solemn work, but 1 kept wondering whether it was, in fact, the film that we were watching. What must be similarly asked is whether what we are watching in the world in which we live is actually a clash of civilizations, or something much more mundane that merely looks like a civilizational clash to determined seekers of profundity.

The depth that civilizational analysis seeks is not exclusive, though, to the high road of intellectual analysis. In some ways, civilizational analysis mirrors and magnifies common beliefs that flourish in not particularly intellectual circles. The invoking of, say, "Western" values against "non-Western" values is rather commonplace in public discussions, and it makes regular headlines in tabloids as well as figuring in political rhetoric and anti-immigrant oratory (from the United States and Canada to Germany, France, and the Netherlands). In the aftermath of September 11, the stereotyping of Muslims came often enough from people who are no great specialists in civilizational categories (to say the least). But theories of civilizational clash have often provided allegedly dispassionate and sophisticated foundations for coarse popular beliefs. Complicated theory can sometimes bolster uncomplicated bigotry and can make the world a much more flammable place than it needs to be.

2

What, then, are the difficulties of civilizational analysis? I shall begin by discussing a little more the problem that I claimed was its most basic weakness: the presumption that a person can be regarded preeminently not as an individual with many affiliations, nor as a member of many different groups, but as a member merely of one particular group, which gives her a uniquely important identity. The implicit belief in the over-arching power of a singular classification is not only gross, it is also

[handwritten margin notes: "divisive strict classification diminishes hope for shared humanity"]

grossly confrontational in form and in implication. Such a divisive view goes not only against the old-fashioned belief (which tends to be ridiculed these days as much too soft-headed) that "we are all basically just human beings," but also against the important understanding that we are *diversely* different. Indeed, I would argue that the main hope of harmony in the contemporary world lies in the plurality of our identities, which cut across each other and work against sharp divisions around one single hardened line of impenetrable identity. Our shared humanity gets savagely challenged when the confrontation is unified into a solitary —and allegedly dominant—system of classification; this is much more divisive than the universe of plural and diverse categorizations that shape the world in which we actually live.

The realization that we each have multiple identities may sound like a much grander idea than it is. Indeed, it is a very elementary recognition. In our normal lives, we see ourselves as members of a variety of groups: we belong to all of them. The same person can be an American citizen of Malaysian origin with Chinese racial characteristics, a Christian, a libertarian, a political activist, a woman, a poet, a vegetarian, an asthmatic, a historian, a schoolteacher, a bird-watcher, a baseball fan, a lover of jazz, a heterosexual, a supporter of gay and lesbian rights, and a person deeply committed to the view that creatures from outer space regularly visit Earth in colorful vehicles and sing tantalizing songs. Each of these collectivities, to all of which this individual belongs, gives her a particular identity, which—depending on the context—can be quite important; but none of them has a unique and pre-ordained role in defining this person.

[handwritten margin note: "person not defined by a potential identity"]

The relative importance of the different groups to which any person belongs can vary, depending on the context and the person's priorities. Being a teetotaler, for example, can be a more important identity when one is invited to a wine-tasting party than the same person's identity as, say, a poet or an American or a Protestant. It need not cause any problem for action choice, either, especially when the demands associated with different identities do not, in fact, conflict. In many contexts, however, the different components of one's identity may well compete in one's decision regarding what to do. One may have to choose the relative importance to attach to one's activism as a citizen over one's love of baseball if a citizens' meeting clashes with a promising game. One has to decide how to deal with alternative claims on one's attention and loyalties that compete with one another.

Identity, then, cannot be only a matter of "discovery" (as communitarian philosophers often claim); it is a matter of choice as well. It is possible that the often-repeated belief that identity is a matter of "discovery" is encouraged by the fact that the choices we can make are constrained by feasibility, and sometimes the constraints are very exacting. The feasibilities will certainly depend on particular circumstances. The constraints may be especially strict in defining the extent to which we can persuade others to take us to be different from what they take us to be. A Jewish person in Nazi Germany could not easily choose a different identity from the one with which others marked him or her. The freedom in choosing the importance to attach to our different identities is always constrained, and in some cases very sharply so.

This point is not in dispute. The fact that we always choose within particular constraints is a standard feature of every choice. As any theorist of choice knows, choices of all kinds are always made within particular feasibility restrictions. As students of elementary economics all have to learn, the theory of consumer choice does not deny the existence of a budget that restrains the consumer's purchasing ability. The presence of the budget constraint does not imply that there is no choice to be made, but only that the choice has to be made within that constraint. What is true in elementary economics is also true in complex political and social decisions. While the Jewish person in Nazi Germany may have had difficulty in paying attention to her other identities, there are many other contexts that give more room for effective choice, in which the competing claims of other affiliations (varying from nationality, language, and literature to profession and political belief) will demand serious attention and require a reflective resolution.

There is also the ethical issue regarding the status of identity-based claims of any kind vis-à-vis arguments that do not turn on any identity whatsoever. Our duty to other human beings may not necessarily be linked only to the fact that we share a common human identity, but rather to our sense of concern for them irrespective of any sharing of identity. Moreover, the reach of our concern may apply to other species as well, despite the lack of a shared human identity and the non-invoking of any other identity that would try to translate a general ethical argument into a specialized identity-centered morality.

While religious categories have received much airing in recent years, they cannot be presumed to obliterate other distinctions and other concerns, and even less be taken to be the only relevant system of classifying people across the globe. It is the plurality of our identities, and our right to choose how we see ourselves (with what emphases and what priorities), that the civilizational classifications tend to overlook, in a largely implicit—rather than transparent—way.

The civilizational classifications have often closely followed religious divisions. Huntington contrasts "Western civilization" with "Islamic civilization," "Hindu civilization," "Buddhist civilization," and so on; and while hybrid categories are accommodated (such as "Sinic civilization" or "Japanese civilization"), the alleged battlefronts of religious differences are incorporated into a carpentered vision of one dominant and hardened divisiveness. By categorizing all people into those belonging to "the Islamic world," "the Christian world," "the Hindu world," "the Buddhist world," and so on, the divisive power of classificatory priority is implicitly used to place people firmly inside a unique set of rigid boxes. Other divisions (say, between the rich and the poor, between members of different classes and occupations, between people of different politics, between distinct nationalities and residential locations, between language groups, and so on) are all submerged by this allegedly preeminent way of seeing the differences between people.

The belief in a unique categorization is both a serious descriptive mistake and an ethical and political hazard. People do see themselves in very many different ways. A Bangladeshi Muslim is not only a Muslim but also a Bengali and a Bangladeshi, possibly quite proud of Bengali literature. The separation of Bangladesh from Pakistan was driven not by religion, but by language, literature, and politics. A Nepalese Hindu is not only a Hindu, but also has political and ethnic characteristics that have their own relevance, and that allow Nepal to be, unlike India, an officially Hindu state (indeed, the only one in the world). Poverty, too, can be a great source of solidarity across other boundaries. The kind of division highlighted by the so-called anti-globalization protesters (one of the most globalized movements in the world) tries to unite the underdogs of the world economy, cutting across religious or national or civilizational lines of division. The multiplicity of categories works against rigid separation and its ignitable implications.

3

Aside from being morally and politically destructive, the epistemic content of the classification according to so-called civilizations is highly dubious. It could not but be so, since in focusing on one exclusive way of dividing the people of the world, the approach has to cut many corners. In describing India as a "Hindu civilization," for example, Huntington's exposition of the alleged "clash of civilizations" has to downplay the fact that India has more Muslims than any other country in the world, with the exception of Indonesia and marginally Pakistan. India may or may not be placed within the arbitrary definition of "the Muslim world," but it is still the case that India (with its 130 million Muslims—more than the entire populations of Britain and France put together) has a great many more Muslims than nearly every country in the so-called Muslim world.

It is impossible to think of "Indian civilization" without taking note of the major role of Muslims in the history of India. Indeed, it is futile to try to have an understanding of the nature and the range of Indian art, literature, music, or food without seeing the extensive interactions that were not deterred by barriers of religious communities. And Muslims are not, of course, the only non-Hindu group that helps to constitute India. The Sikhs are a major presence, as are the Jains. Not only is India the country of origin of Buddhism, but Buddhism was the dominant religion of India for more than a millennium. Atheistic schools of thought—the

Charvaka and the Lokayata—have also flourished in the country from at
least the sixth century B.C.E. to the present day. There have been Christian
communities in India from the fourth century C.E.—two hundred years
before there were Christian communities in Britain. Jews came to India
shortly after the fall of Jerusalem; Parsees started coming in the eighth
century.

Given all this, Huntington's description of India as a "Hindu
civilization" is an epistemic and historical absurdity. It is also politically
combustible. It tends to add a superficial and highly deceptive credibility
to the extraordinary neglect of history—and of present realities—that
some Hindu fundamentalists have tried to champion, most recently in an
exceptionally barbaric way in Gujarat. Even though these political
groups seem to be trying their best to overturn Indian secularism, the
secular constitution of India as well as the large majority of Indians who
are committed to secularism will make it hard to achieve this. The fact
that the poison of sectarian violence so far has not spread beyond the
limits of one state—Gujarat, with a ruling government that is at best
grossly incompetent but most likely a great deal worse—is perhaps
ground for some cautious optimism about the future of India. But the
human costs of violent extremism have been truly monumental.

The portrayal of India as a Hindu civilization may be a simple-minded
mistake, but crudity of one kind or another is present in the
characterizations of other civilizations as well. Consider what is called
"Western civilization." Indeed, the champions of "the clash of
civilizations," in line with their belief in the profundity of this singular
line of division, tend to see tolerance as a special and perennial feature of
Western civilization, extending way back into history. Huntington insists
that the "West was West long before it was modern," and cites (among
other allegedly special features, such as "social pluralism") "a sense of
individualism and a tradition of individual rights and liberties unique
among civilized societies." This, too, is at best a gross oversimplification.

Tolerance and liberty are certainly among the important achievements
of modern Europe (leaving out such aberrations as Nazi Germany or the
intolerant governance of British or French or Portuguese empires in Asia
and Africa). But to see a unique line of historical division there—going
back over the millennia—is quite fanciful. The championing of political
liberty and religious tolerance, in its full contemporary form, is not an old
historical feature in any country or any civilization in the world. Plato
and Augustine were not less authoritarian in their thinking than was
Confucius. This is not to deny that there were champions of tolerance in
classical European thought, but if this is taken to give credit to the whole
Western world (from the ancient Greeks to the Ostrogoths and the
Visigoths), there are similar examples in other cultures.

The Indian emperor Ashoka's dedicated championing of religious and
other kinds of tolerance in the third century B.C.E. (arguing that "the sects

of other people all deserve reverence for one reason or another") is certainly among the earliest political defenses of tolerance anywhere. The recent Bollywood movie *Ashoka* (made, as it happens, by a Muslim director) may or may not be accurate in all its details, but it rightly emphasizes the importance of secularism in Ashoka's thinking two and a half millennia ago and indicates its continuing relevance in contemporary India. While a later Indian emperor, Akbar, the Great Mughal, was making similar pronouncements on religious tolerance in Agra at the end of the sixteenth century ("No one should be interfered with on account of religion, and anyone is to be allowed to go over to a religion that pleases him"), the Inquisitions were active in Europe and Giordano Bruno was being burned in the Campo dei Fiori in Rome.

Similarly, what is often called "Western science" draws on a world heritage. There is a chain of intellectual relations that links Western mathematics and science to a collection of distinctly non-Western practitioners. Even today, when a modern mathematician at, say, Princeton invokes an "algorithm" to solve a difficult computational problem, she helps to commemorate the contributions of the ninth-century Arab mathematician Al-Khwarizmi, from whose name the term *algorithm* is derived. (The term *algebra* comes from his book *Al-Jabrwa-al-Muqabilah*.) The decimal system, which evolved in India in the early centuries of the first millennium, arrived in Europe at the end of that millennium, transmitted by the Arabs. A large group of contributors from different non-Western societies—Chinese, Arab, Iranian, Indian, and others—influenced the science, the mathematics, and the philosophy that played a major part in the European Renaissance and, later, in the European Enlightenment.

In his *Critical and Miscellaneous Essays*, Thomas Carlyle claimed that "the three great elements of modern civilization" are "Gunpowder, Printing, and the Protestant Religion." While the Chinese cannot be held responsible for Protestantism, their contribution to Carlyle's list of civilizational ingredients is not insignificant, though it is less total than it is in the case of Francis Bacon's earlier list, in *Novum Organum*, of "printing, gunpowder, and the magnet." The West must get full credit for the remarkable achievements that occurred in Europe during the Renaissance, the Enlightenment, and the Industrial Revolution, but the idea of an immaculate Western conception would require a genuinely miraculous devotion to parochialism.

Not only is the flowering of global science and technology not an exclusively West-led phenomenon, there were major global advances in the world that took the form of international encounters far away from Europe. Consider printing, which features in Carlyle's list, and which Bacon put among the developments that "have changed the whole face and state of things throughout the world." The technology of printing was a great Chinese achievement, but the use to which the Chinese put this new method was not confined merely to local or parochial pursuits. Indeed, the first printed book was a Sanskrit treatise in Buddhist philosophy, *Vajracchedika-prajñāpāramitā sutra* (sometimes referred to as the "Diamond Sutra"), translated into Chinese from Sanskrit in the early fifth century and printed four centuries later in 868 C.E. The translator of the Diamond Sutra, Kumārajīva, was half Indian and half Turkish. He lived in a part of eastern Turkistan called Kucha, traveled extensively in India, and later moved to China, where he headed the newly established institute of foreign languages in Xi'an in the early fifth century. The West figured not at all in the first stirring of what came to be a mainstay of Western civilization.

4

The narrowness of the civilizational mode of thinking has many far-reaching effects. It fuels alienation among people from different parts of the world, and it encourages a distanced and possibly confrontational view of others. Even the resistance to so-called Westernization by non-Western activists frequently takes the form of shunning "Western" (or what some Western spokesmen have claimed to be "exclusively Western") objects, even though they are among the historical products of diverse global interactions.

Indeed, in a West-dominated world, many non-Western people tend to think of themselves quintessentially as "the other," in contra-distinction to the West. (This phenomenon has been beautifully analyzed by Akeel Bilgrami in an essay called "What Is a Muslim?" in *Identities*, edited by Kwame Anthony Appiah and Henry Louis Gates Jr.) The political force of this phenomenon makes the effects of Western expropriation of a global heritage even more disastrous. It plays a regressive role in the self-identification of the colonial and postcolonial world, and in parts of the "anti-globalization" movement. It takes a heavy toll by inciting parochial tendencies and needless confrontations; it tends to undermine the possibility of objectivity in science and knowledge; and it deflects attention from the real issues to be faced in contemporary globalization (including the ways and means of reducing massive inequality of opportunities without losing the technological and economic rewards of global interaction).

To focus just on the grand religious classification, in its civilizational garb, is not only to miss many significant concerns and ideas that can move people. Such a focus also has the effect of lessening the importance of other priorities by artificially magnifying the voice of religious authority. The clerics are then treated as the *ex officio* spokesmen for the so-called Muslim world, even though a great many Muslims have profound differences with what is proposed by one mullah or another. The same would apply to other religious leaders' being seen as the spokespeople for their "flocks." The singular classification not only makes one distinction among many into a uniquely inflexible barrier, it also gives a commanding voice to the "establishment" figures in the respective religious and sectarian hierarchy, while other voices are muffled.

A person's religious or civilizational identity may well be very important for her, but it is one membership among many. The question we have to ask is not, say, whether Islam (or Hinduism or Christianity) is a peace-loving religion or a combative one, but how a religious Muslim (or Hindu or Christian) may combine his or her religious beliefs or practices with other commitments and values, with other features of personal identity. To see one's religious—or civilizational—affiliation as an all-engulfing identity would be a deeply problematic diagnosis. There have been fierce warriors as well as great champions of peace among devoted members of each religion; and rather than asking which one is the "true believer" and which one a "mere imposter," we should accept that our religious faith does not in itself resolve all the decisions that we must make in our lives, including those concerning our political and social priorities and the corresponding issues of conduct and action. Both the proponents of peace and tolerance and the patrons of war and intolerance can belong to the same religion (and may be, in their own ways, true believers) without this being seen as a contradiction. The domain of one's religious identity does not vanquish all other aspects of one's understanding and affiliation.

The increasing use of a religion-based singular civilizational classification also makes the Western response to global terrorism and conflict oddly counterproductive. Respect for other civilizations is shown by praising the religious books of "other people," rather than by taking note of the many-sided involvements and achievements of different peoples in a globally interactive world. As Britain goes down the slippery slope of intensifying faith-based schools (Islamic and Sikh schools are already established, and Hindu ones may come soon), the focus is on what divides people rather than what unites them. The cultivation of analytical and critical reasoning, which Western chauvinists usurp as being quintessentially Western, has to take a back seat to religious education, in which the children of new immigrants are expected to find their "own culture." The sad effect of narrowing the intellectual horizon of young children is further compounded by the gross confusion of civilization with religion.

There is no historical reason, for example, why the championing of the Arab or Muslim heritage has to concentrate only on religion and not also on science and mathematics, to which Arab and Muslim scholars have contributed so much in the past. But crude civilizational classifications have tended to put the latter in the basket of "Western science," leaving other civilizations to mine their pride only in religious depths. The non-Western activists, then, focus on those issues that divide them from the

West (religious beliefs, local customs, and cultural specificities) rather than on those things that reflect global interactions (science, mathematics, literature, and so on). The dialectics of the "negation of negation" then extracts a heavy price in fomenting more confrontations in the world.

Moreover, the chosen method of giving each "community" its "own culture" makes the respective religious and theological authorities much more powerful in the schooling of immigrants to Britain, when they are sent to the "faith-based" schools. Religion-based divisions are intensified not only by the efforts of anti-Western religious fundamentalists but also by the West's own arrangements related to seeing "other people" simply in terms of religion, ignoring the many-sided civilizations from which the immigrants come.

5

The reliance on civilizational partitioning fails badly, then, for a number of distinct reasons. First, the classifications are often based on an extraordinary epistemic crudeness and an extreme historical innocence. The diversity of traditions *within* distinct civilizations is effectively ignored, and major global interactions in science, technology, mathematics, and literature over millennia are made to disappear so as to construct a parochial view of the uniqueness of Western civilization.

Second, there is a basic methodological problem involved in the implicit presumption that a civilizational partitioning is the uniquely relevant distinction, and must swamp other ways of identifying people. It is bad enough that those who foment global confrontations or local sectarian violence try to impose a pre-chosen unitary and divisive identity on people who are to be recruited as the "foot soldiers" of political brutality, but that task gets indirectly yet significantly aided by the implicit support that the warriors get from Western theories of singular categorization of the people of the world.

Third, there is a remarkable neglect of the role of choice and reasoning in decisions regarding what importance to attach to the membership of any particular group, or to any particular identity (among many others). By adopting a unique and allegedly predominant way of categorizing people, civilizational partitioning can materially contribute to the conflicts in the world. To deny choice when it does exist is not only an epistemic failure (a misunderstanding of what the world is like); it is also an ethical delinquency and a political dereliction of responsibility. There is a critical need to recognize the plurality of our identities, and also to acknowledge the fact that, as responsible human beings, we have to choose (rather than inertly "discover") what priorities to give to our diverse associations and affiliations. In contrast, the theorists of inescapable "clashes" try to deny strenuously—or to ignore implicitly—the multiplicity of classifications that compete with each other, and the related need for us all to take decisional responsibilities about our priorities. People are seen as belonging to rigid prisons of allegedly decisive identities.

In a well-known interview, Peter Sellers once remarked: "There used to be a 'me,' but I had it surgically removed." In their respective attempts to impose a single and unique identity on us, the surgical removal of the actual "me" is done by others—the religious fundamentalist, the nationalist extremist, the Western chauvinist, the sectarian provocateur. We have to resist such an imprisonment. We must insist upon the liberty to see ourselves as we would choose to see ourselves, deciding on the relative importance that we would like to attach to our membership in the different groups to which we belong. The central issue, in sum, is freedom. To make our identity into a prison is not social wisdom. It is intellectual surrender.

8

THE NEW POLITICAL INFAMY AND THE SACRILEGE OF FEMINISM

DRUCILLA CORNELL

I

On April 20, 2002, the Revolutionary Association of the Women of Afghanistan (RAWA) assailed the feminist majority of the United States, represented as it was in an article in *Ms.* magazine called "A Coalition of Hopes," for ignoring the horrible atrocities committed by the Northern Alliance and for erasing RAWA's historical role—twenty-five years of relentless struggle against the Taliban's inhumanity toward women. Most of the members of RAWA—at least those who were not executed or forcibly exiled—remain in Afghanistan, seeking support for their own program of secular democracy, women's rights, and the re-establishment of a working infrastructure, which is utterly necessary for anything resembling a democratic society to thrive.

In its response to the *Ms.* magazine article, RAWA posed a set of penetrating questions to U.S. feminists:

> Are they merely smearing the U.S. government and Western press who find it easier to present the Taliban as evil and the forces that the U.S. supported against them as good? Or have they joined with our government in a concerted effort to ignore these crimes and once again forfeit the lives and rights of women for our current national self-interest? Perhaps the feminist majority, in their push for U.S. economic and political power, are being careful not to anger the political powers in the U.S. who still deny and make apologies for the human rights abuses done by the likes of Massoud, Rabinni, Dostum, Hekmatyar, and others who were trained, armed, and supported by the U.S. during the Cold War years in Afghanistan, and then left in a power vacuum to destroy their people and their country. (RAWA 2002)

RAWA does not here cite the innovative philosophical work of Giorgio Agamben, who has tried to show the contemporary political relevance of the ancient Roman category of *homo sacer* by claiming that "[w]hen their rights are no longer the rights of the citizen, that is when human beings are truly *sacred*, in the sense that this term used to have in Roman law of the archaic period: doomed to death" (Agamben 2000, 22). But for the members of RAWA, their erasure is inseparable from our American "war which was not a war" against the Afghan people, in which the innumerable deaths of Afghan citizens did not count, could not be counted, either in a moral or in a mathematical sense. For we still do not know how many people have died as a result of our militaristic effrontery, people who were killed with impunity as *homines sacri*, people who looked up at our planes not knowing whether packages of aid or bombs were about to fall on their heads.

A careful thinker and committed antimilitarist like Richard Falk, who defended the necessity of expanding the right to self-defense for the U.S. in the case of the megaterrorism of al-Qaeda, insisted that the military action against Afghanistan should be criticized because the war was conducted with discredited weaponry. According to Falk,

> Especially controversial was the American reliance on discredited weaponry used in the Vietnam War—B-52 carpet bombing, cluster bombs, and huge daisy-cutter bombs containing 2,000 tons of explosives. The U.S. also depended on targeting guidance from intelligence sources on the ground, which turned out to be deliberately misleading on several occasions, as local military leaders sought to use American military power in unresolved ethnic struggles between antagonistic warlords. Criticism also arose because the Pentagon admitted that it was keeping no record of civilian casualties, and there were scattered, but unverified, reports that the American media was being encouraged by government officials to downplay the issue. (Falk 2003, 68)

Falk's greater concern, however, was that humanitarian intervention should proceed through the legal procedures and protocols of the United Nations, particularly when it is done in the name of human rights. Yet he has pointed out that only retrospectively did the U.S. appeal to humanitarian intervention as its motivation. Of course, humanitarian intervention should never proceed by unilateral action. But RAWA's political gesture goes much deeper than this: it forces us to question whether the humanitarian-intervention discourse of the U.S. government was not a particularly cynical effort to enlist U.S. feminists in an attempt to circumscribe the definition of what constitutes human-rights violations—to turn the feminist majority into an ideological prop that delegitimates the political need for redressing human-rights violations. RAWA members were never against the wearing of the burqua or other forms of veiling that certain Muslim women adopt voluntarily. They were against violent state action against women who did not wear the burqua. The identification in the U.S. media of freedom with unveiling reinforced the simplistic view that the Muslim religion and freedom were radically at odds.

The question of what role feminism should play in the growing peace movement grows increasingly more urgent to address, especially in the wake of thousands of Iraqis being doomed to death in Agamben's sense. We do not know how many Iraqis were killed in the U.S. and British invasion of March 2003, and we probably never will. Instead of giving us an accurate numerical account of Iraqi casualties, the Bush administration chooses to discount all Iraqi lives that have been lost as a result of our cruise-missile and aerial-bombing attacks. It lets us know, though, about whole divisions "being taken out," a gleeful hint that at least a thousand of "them" died, while all of our troops survived. Some reporters in the European press have suggested that there were ten thousand civilian casualties, while people in the devastated country of Iraq itself report to friends and relatives that the number was much higher than that. Those of us outside Iraq can only imagine the full extent of the causalities. Baghdad is in ruins. The "cradle of civilization" has been looted. Great treasures have been plundered, and museums have been turned into tombs—a most tragic irony, since it is usually museums, with their cultural artifacts, that offer us a record of what has been lost. All this destruction is claimed to be the result of the freedom we have given to the Iraqi people. We have righted the wrong of Saddam Hussein's brutal dictatorial regime. Or so we are told. The regime change has taken place, and we have won. Who will be next?

The overzealous hankering for global military and political dominance is by no means new in the history of U.S. imperialism; nor is the cynical justification that we pursue our aims in the name of humanitarian interests. In the recent case of the Taliban, the U.S. long ignored RAWA's call for international support for their efforts to bring to justice the Taliban leaders who had committed inhuman crimes against women. RAWA is a grass-roots organization seeking real democracy in Afghanistan, and for years there was no strategic value to the U.S. taking action against the Taliban. Indeed, not only was there no U.S. support for RAWA; the organization itself was seen as having a political agenda completely hostile to U.S. interests, considering RAWA's Marxist feminist commitments.

In much of her Marxist feminist work over the years, Gayatri Spivak has shown that the long and brutal history of Western imperialism was able to survive, ideologically and otherwise, because the liberation of the poorest of the poor among women also helped promote a program of systematic economic domination. But recently, in an essay called "Righting Wrongs," she has shifted her theoretical focus, arguing that we must revisit the classical liberal distinction between natural and civil rights if we are to understand how it is that unjustified conceptions of natural right are used to encroach upon the civil rights recognized by nation-states in the global south and by delegitimated social institutions and structures that grass-roots activists are trying to relegitimate. Her point is that only once these institutions and structures receive new legitimacy can the nation-states in which they function overcome the human-rights dependency that endlessly reproduces the figure of 'wronged victim'—a dependency that Spivak says "can be particularly vicious in its neo-colonial consequences, if it is the state that is the agency of terror and . . . [Europe and the United States] that is the savior" (Spivak 2003, 205–6). This self-permission for continuing to right wrongs is, for Spivak, premised on the idea that 'wronged victims' will never be able to help themselves, and indeed will always need to be politically buttressed from the outside, because of their necessarily inferior political status, which renders them at once unwilling and unable to participate in what the likes of Bernard Lewis and Samuel Huntington would call the modern civilized culture of democracy.

Spivak goes on to suggest that the notoriously shaky philosophical foundation of natural rights—the idea that our rights as "men" are anterior to our civil rights as citizens—often goes unnoticed in human-rights discourse. The reason for this, she claims, is that a decidedly Darwinian assumption underwrites much of that discourse—namely, that those who are naturally the most human must shoulder the burden of righting the wrongs of those less-than-human peoples who do not fit into our modern conception, as well as the classical liberal conception, of the rights-bearing individual being protected under the law. Nevertheless, Spivak fully endorses what I would like to call, following Immanuel Kant, the ideal of humanity. But she does so by admonishing those of us who are citizens of the U.S. and of Europe to unlearn our cultural absolutism, which is in fact our own cultural relativism, and which includes our hegemonic conception of modernity, our conception of ourselves as the natural saviors of the world, the ones who are the most truly human and who are thus in a position to name what counts, and especially what does not count, as human.

It is important to note that Spivak is not against human rights, that, believe it or not, she thinks such rights are necessary and sufficient, in particular historical contexts, for achieving the ethical goal of righting wrongs. But it is perhaps even more important to emphasize that central to her recent thinking no less than to her political activism in India and elsewhere is the idea that human-rights activists must constantly be cognizant of the fundamental inequality that allows them to right the wrongs perpetrated against so many others in this world, particularly women. With her conception of worlding, she forces those of us residing in the so-called first world to accept that we inhabit an imaginary world that is only too real, a world in which doing the right thing is horribly bound up with Social Darwinist assumptions about the natural power to name the human, the inhuman, the animal, the beastly. Spivak's sincerest hope is that we can salvage human-rights discourse by suturing it to "a future to come when the reasonable righting of wrongs will not inevitably be the manifest destiny of groups that remain poised to right them; when wrongs will not proliferate with unsurprising regularity" (Spivak 2003, 227). Anything less than this suturing would merely return us time and again to justifications of natural rights founded upon some or other avatar of Social Darwinism.

In view of Spivak's critique of Darwinian liberalism, consider Martha Nussbaum's attempt to name basic human capabilities—a forthright attempt to solve the dilemma of how natural rights conceived precisely as human rights could manage to trump civil rights and, indeed, justify overriding the sovereignty of nation-states. Although Nussbaum wishes to leave space for cultural interpretation of the basic capabilities, she believes it is possible to describe in normative terms the proper contents and functions of these capabilities, and therefore how exactly one who is not yet human ought to become human. Amartya Sen, in both implicit and explicit critiques of Nussbaum, expresses his disagreement with this kind of hierarchical value system of natural human rights over and against civil rights by insisting that the means and end of development is freedom—freedom to protect not only civil rights but also what the Marxist Spivak would call the social production and circulation of capital and value. At his most radical, Sen contemplates articulating Marxist economic claims from a politically liberal standpoint. But that is as far as he goes: he backs down from Spivak's far more daring project of raising questions about how we might suture a new ethics of responsibility to the figure of the other, to its imagined agency in a world that cannot count the other—in all its *sacred* forms and incarnations—among its sovereign agents.

Sen does, however, offer a potential solution to some of the ethical problems Spivak finds attendant upon human-rights discourse. In *Development as Freedom*, Sen claims that

> it is best to see human rights as a set of ethical claims, which must not be identified with legislated legal rights. But this normative interpretation need not obliterate the usefulness of the idea of human rights in the kind of context in which they are typically invoked. The freedoms that are associated with particular rights may be the appropriate focal point for debate. We have to judge the plausibility of human rights as a system of ethical reasoning and as the basis of political demands. (Sen 2000, 229–30)

I think there can be a feminist alliance between Sen's endorsement of the centrality of freedom in development and Spivak's own endorsement of humanist education. Indeed, I want to assert that feminism must be thought inextricably linked to an uncoercive political process of suturing the habits and values of radical democracy onto the cultural and ritual formations of the subaltern. Such is the theory-driven feminist practice that Spivak herself has undertaken so painstakingly by helping to establish schools for aboriginal children in rural India, and by working with grass-roots women's and antidevelopment groups who seek to weave together gender politics, the struggle to survive, and the actual formation of democratic organizations. But we cannot undertake this kind of work in our own countries and throughout the world without creating feminist ethics anew, without refashioning human-rights discourse so that at its core there is an ethical moment of reflexivity—our own vigilant self-reflection on the dangers of any individual, nation-state, transnational institution, or even nongovernmental organization (NGO) claiming that it is in a position to turn the ideal of humanity into something that can be given hierarchical and hence nonideal shape, something that those who usurp the sovereignty of others, subsuming it into their own, will use to render some *homines sacri* and others into people whose lives will always count among those who are living as politically legitimate human beings.

II

I have left in abeyance a question that only now is it possible for me to address directly—the question concerning the relationship of feminist political theory and activism to what I have claimed so far about the appropriation of the so-called feminist majority by Bush's war against terror. In answering it, I want to look more deeply into how women and symbolic articulations of the feminine lie at the heart of many efforts to consolidate nationalist projects, whether in the sense of imagining and creating a people or in organizing that people as a nation to develop a territorially bounded and legally established state.

Let us first acknowledge that the struggle for national consolidation and the establishment of a state can be radically at variance with each other. A famous example of the founding of a state that fragmented national identity is Lebanon. In Lebanon, citizens only belong to the state through their position in a religious community. The state institutionalized a national identity that was in religious fragments, and these fragments used women and the protection of patrilineage to maintain the existence of proscribed identities. On the other hand, women also often identify with both the national community in Lebanon (which includes Syrians, Palestinians, and Lebanese) as well as a supranational community (which includes Arabs, Pan-Christians, and Pan-Muslims). Even though proposals to change these identifications are now being circulated, the reality is that the religiously bound and patrilineally contained religious identities do not allow women to confer Lebanese citizenship on their children. The reason is that, given the religious institutionalization of citizenship as a series of competing and, for many years, warring sects, such recognition of women's ability as citizens of Lebanon to bequeath national identity as a matter of political belonging would completely disrupt the masculine genealogy upon which the state has organized the nation.

This is an obvious example of women being used to perpetuate the purity of religious identities. For women are the reproducers of the children of those identities but without the power to have rights over their own children and to allow their children, or indeed themselves, to pass from one religious sect to another. But there are more subtle examples of how women are crucial to the constitution of the state and the construction of the ideal of the nation. Certain strands of Chicana feminism, for example, have brilliantly shown that the role of actual women as reproducers of the nation and as iconic representations of mythological figures ensconced at the forefront of the nation-building project are bound up with what Jacques Lacan would have called the psychical fantasy of woman. These are the good women, the mothers of the nation who reproduce its citizens and mourn for their fallen children in times of war. To be sure, their mourning as good mothers of a particular state must have a proper object—namely, heroes and ordinary foot soldiers who fall in the course of defending their country and, of course, who are idealized in their role as protective patriarchs for good women and children.

We all know Benedict Anderson's famous argument that nations are imagined communities. In the case of the Chicana nation Aztlan, however, the organization of the nation is currently imagined without a political movement to claim territory, although in its initial proclamation of the imagined home of the Chicanas there were some within the movement who sought to territorialize Aztlan by reclaiming the Southwest of the U.S. and thereby disrupting the articulated unity of the U.S. as a coherent territory. Some Chicana feminists have even argued not only that national desire territorializes itself through the putative naturalness of the people to which the land belongs but also that it uses the imagined possession of women and their reproductive patrilineal line as the basis for a cultural group or identity being able to assert, "This land is ours." These feminists have sought to challenge the masculine and hegemonic roots of Aztlan by insisting that it remain, in Laura Elisa Pérez's words, "a utopic model of the homeland in that no-place that is everywhere embodied in discursive and other cultural practices" (Pérez 1999, 16).

This insistence, however, is inseparable from the work of Chicana artists, writers, and literary critics that, in different yet related ways, reimagines the figures of Aztlan. These figures are borrowed from the long history of Mexico and its fight for independence, and they include the famous figure of the good mother—the virgin of Guadalupe (*la virgen de Guadalupe*), the imaginary mother who, in her purity, devotes herself to the nation. The Chicana artist Ester Hernandez has transformed this figure from weeping mother and warrior's sidekick into a defender of the Chicana woman as a warrior in her own right, struggling for her political rights as well as for those of the constantly reimagined nation of Aztlan. "In this representation," writes Pérez,

> the central image of the Virgin (along with the metonymic chain of her attendant "virtues" central to the reproduction of patriarchy and colonialism) is displaced by that of a Chicana warrior in karate garb. The mark of the sacred, the enveloping aureola, is appropriated and transgressed in one

gesture, for the new female image is marked as a new ideal through its familiar signs of venerability, while its received construction is pierced, as by a warrior's side kick. (Pérez 1999, 28)

So on the other side of Lacan's psychical fantasy of woman, there is the indigenous woman, often imagined as the dark or beastly woman who disrupts the quest for national unity. The most infamous among such women is Malinche, purportedly Cortez's translator and mistress, who sullied the "purity" of the people by creating mestizas. Because of its connection to disrupting the purity of indigenous people, mestiza has been reappropriated by Chicana feminists to demonstrate how that name can be inverted as a symbol of resistance. This inversion, it is claimed, produces cultural and political multiplicity that allows mestiza consciousness to reimagine Aztlan as irreducible to an exclusionary nationalism that rests its claim to legitimacy on an ostensibly pure people. As Norma Alarcón argues,

> The native woman has many names . . . .[But] the point is not so much to recover a lost "utopia" or the "true" essence of our being, although, of course, there are those among us who long for the "lost origins," as well as those who feel a profound spiritual kinship with the "lost"—a spirituality whose resistant political implications must not be underestimated, but refocused for feminist challenge. . . . The most relevant point in the present is to understand how a pivotal indigenous portion of the mestiza past may represent a collective female experience as well as "the mark of the Beast within us"—the maligned and abused indigenous woman. (Alarcón 1999, 66–67)

Mestiza consciousness is therefore inseparable from how the feminine is deployed in projects of nation building. For such projects inevitably entail the imagination. But it also inseparable from the project of reclaiming the nation from the political imaginaries that resolutely separate women into the good, silent woman and the "whoring" woman (as in the myth of Malinche), who insists that women must be able to reimagine themselves.

If feminine sexual difference is not to suffer abjection in exactly this figure of "the beast within us," then the state must protect the symbolic space in which the meaning of women can be reimagined and redefined without reserve. I continue to call this space "the imaginary domain." Feminine sexual difference is undoubtedly a product of the imagination and of fantasy. But the political and cultural discourses that give it meaning and the materialization of that meaning constrain the bodies and minds of actual women. Chicana feminists have been exemplary in showing us that the reimagining of the feminine through actual images and icons as well as through changing the imagined idealizations of the good woman and her proper role in the nation are crucial to how nations consolidate themselves, and to the different forms of nation-ness they adopt in imagining how the state will be constituted and what it will embody.

This kind of imaginative feminist political theory is indispensable to those of us who are now seeking to challenge Bush's attempt to bolster a nationalism that reimagines America separately from the ideals of the American constitution. For women as idealized good women who mourn their proper objects—the fallen soldiers of the war against terrorism —are already being deployed to support Bush's infinite war on terror and the continuing curtailment of our civil rights. It is because the good woman mourns her proper object that she reinforces the us/them divide that pits the good nation against the evil enemy. This makes mourning and its connection to imaginary figures of women important politically. Thus, public mourning for the other—the 'enemy'—can disrupt precisely that deployment of the psychical fantasy of woman which occurs in the name of horrific nationalist aggression.

III

In January 1988, only one month after the first Palestinian *intifada*, a small group of Israeli women, deeply disturbed by Israeli aggression against Palestinian resistance, decided to take action. Once a week, at the same hour and in the same location, a major traffic intersection, they donned black clothing and raised a black sign in the shape of a hand with white lettering that read, "Stop the Occupation." Week after week, they stood there in silence, cars zipping by them in every direction. The sight of women so boldly ignoring traffic regulations and making a display of themselves in public streets caused traffic jams. As is often the case in grass-roots women's movements, the message of this first vigil in Israel spread by word of mouth, women telling other women about what they had seen and its powerful effect on them. By the spring of 1988, there were more than a dozen vigils organized in Israel that practiced, albeit in different ways, the form of bodily expression adopted by the first women who stood in black in the intersection. In Israel and Palestine, Women in Black continue to demand the complete evacuation of Israeli troops from Palestine and, at the very least, the acceptance of the creation of a Palestinian state based on the pre-1967 war borders between Israel and the Palestinian territories.

Women in Black emerged in a nation engaged in militaristic aggression against a so-called enemy people, the Palestinians. It was the refusal of the traditional national boundaries—the distinction between enemy and patriotic loyalty—that fueled the Women in Black vigils from the beginning. News about these vigils quickly spread to other women residing in aggressor nations whose governments were engaging in nationalist and ethnic violence. Women in Black committed themselves to the belief that an alternative feminist politics was strong enough to militate against governments bent on war-mongering foreign policy. In Serbia, for example, Women in Black stood bravely in public plazas in Belgrade as the Serbian government disseminated racist propaganda about Serbian ethnic superiority, which fueled Serbia's nationalist campaign of "ethnic cleansing." These Serbian Women in Black engaged in the very form of vigil practiced in Israel: they stood silently with signs and protested all forms of Serbian national aggression. Yet they also engaged in much more explicitly performative acts, including singing and dancing. During their performances, the women embraced the very names they had been called by their "good" nationalist men—traitors, sluts, lesbians, and whores; in so doing, they refused the abjection the names otherwise seemed to imply.

Today, Women in Black groups can be found throughout the world. In Germany, Women in Black demonstrate against neo-Nazism, demand full citizenship for guest workers, and relentlessly insist that Germany be fully disarmed. In India, Women in Black hold vigils that call for an end to the ill-treatment of women by religious fundamentalists; they also unite with their sisters in Pakistan and thus bridge the many political, religious, and ethnic divides between India and Pakistan. So the question arises: How have Women in Black been able to unite women all over the world, including precisely those women whose respective nations are embroiled in aggressive military campaigns against each other? Quite simply, the power of Women in Black lies in their ability to assume the stereotypical positions of women and to reimagine them in public and hence visible places. "The streets are ours": for years, this has remained the political platform of Serbian Women in Black, since the streets are where women, according to the conservative Serbian nationalists, are not supposed to "hang out," unless they are prostitutes. Good women stay at home, taking care of their families, not performing graphic demonstrations of their opposition to ethnic nationalism.

Yet Women in Black challenge the classical liberal distinction between public and private in an unusual and daring way: they take their politics into places where women traditionally conduct the day-to-day business of life—the supermarkets, the post offices, and the schools. They show that these so-called women's places are potentially radical places of political protest and symbolic expression. In one of their most famous performances, Serbian Women in Black unrolled two long scrolls in a public shopping area in the center of Belgrade. One scroll read, "I confess"; the other, "I accuse." They encouraged people to stop and write on the scrolls their views concerning Serbian militarism and the brutal war against republics of the former Yugoslavia. Unaccustomed to being treated as though their voices mattered, many women stopped shopping and took the opportunity to articulate in writing their deepest political and ethical convictions.

The very idea of Women in Black dressing in black is meant to convey the profound sense of resistance to a globalization that does not allow the demand for perpetual peace to be heard. Indeed, as the very first vigils tried to make clear, Women in Black are imitating two seemingly polarized aspects of the globalized world: Manhattan black, the color of the eminently fashionable woman, and the black that throughout the Balkans and in many other parts of the world continues to represent women's duty to mourn. Representing these contradictory elements of femininity *as* contradictory, Women in Black demonstrate how women's place in the nation-state as stereotypically defined by nationalism and militarism can be undermined through the aesthetics of representation. As one woman from Belgrade Women in Black described it,

> [S]tanding still mute with transparencies as a specific form of body art which together with a political message recalls . . . the fact that the woman's body is the direct use and impact of the feminine principle. For the first time, after the big democratic vote that was realized in Yugoslavia, Serbia and the first multi-party elections in 1990, the resistance of women became visible. (Zajovic 2001, 13)

Women in Black have increased the visibility of women, putting into question the traditional notion of political space by turning women's places into places of political expression and at the same time turning mourning rites into public displays of political protest against aggression. They have accomplished all this by mobilizing the stereotypes of femininity against their use in the perpetuation of nationalist aggression. Indeed, Women in Black have been brave enough to challenge any exclusionary notion of who should count as a woman for the purposes of their struggle against militarism. Straight men, gay men, lesbians, and even the transgendered are welcomed *as* women so long as they have the courage to engage in what Women in Black call the body thought of their politics and ethics. It would be a mistake, then, to think that Women in Black do nothing but mourn, as that would simply reinforce the stereotype of the feminine mother who has lost her children in war. The embodied politics of women, which includes the endless struggle to find new ways for the feminine body to present itself in public, also involves joyous celebrations that completely undermine the place of the good woman as the reproducer of the nation. Serbian Women in Black often quote Cassandra as her myth is retold by German feminist novelist Christa Wolf.

Women in Black are disloyal to their nations of aggression and militarism. No longer will they stand behind their husbands, fathers, and brothers if these men choose to engage in horrifying militaristic aggression against other human beings. Most Women in Black take part in ritual mourning, it is true; but many of their international meetings have included celebrations of disloyalty to traditional patriarchal formulations of women's proper place that make lesbian marriages between women of warring nations the very heart of what is being celebrated. A Woman in Black from Belgrade recently described such a celebration:

> The best example of these embodied activities and ideas are the international annual meetings of Women in Black: until now six encounters have been in Vojvodina, in different places, on a lake, in woods, under tents. . . . These three days were actually a rapture of joy and tears that through little sleep, much talk, music and wine brought to a catharsis. In 1996, in Novi Sad, a first public lesbian marriage, between an Albanian woman and an English woman, was celebrated with female/feminine rituals of dancing and singing. (Zajovic 2001, 17)

Joy and mourning, marriage of the unmarriable, celebration of a peaceful relationship to nature—all this is part of the body art and embodied politics of Women in Black. Because Women in Black all over the world practice a unique form of public mourning meant to disrupt the very idea and image of the good woman who mourns only for the lost soldiers of her own people, the infamy of their public mourning is inseparable from the way it performs the very disruption between woman and nation that is used in ethnic or patriotic feasts (as they are called by Women in Black) that devour actual people through a violent war machine. Both the politics and the ethics of Women in Black can be found in their mourning and their celebrations of women's powerful lives, both of which explode the traditional stereotypes of femininity. Such explosiveness is coupled with the full acceptance of the burden imposed by a belief in the idea that we cannot escape our humanity. That they heed the human call of political and ethical responsibility makes Women in Black one of the most important sources of wisdom, empowerment, and hope for all who desire a peaceful tomorrow and a better world.

The production of affect called forth in their mourning is inseparable from what Martha Nussbaum has recently called the judgment contained within the content of emotions; here the judgment is that those who are enemy 'others' are not cast outside the realm of the human, and that, therefore, their lives matter. Nussbaum distinguishes between emotion and affect because for her affect, unlike emotion, does not involve "highly selective patterns of vision and interpretation" (Nussbaum 2001, 510). The distinction Nussbaum draws between affect and emotion undoubtedly turns on her suspicion of some of the deepest insights of psychoanalysis about drives and the unconscious. But if we fail to acknowledge the role of the unconscious, it will continue to dominate us and thereby prevent us from making sound judgments and evaluations about it. Yet despite that weakness in Nussbaum, her broad understanding of the cognitive basis of emotion entailing an imagined world is crucial for understanding how Women in Black can challenge a vision of the nation-state mobilized around ethnic superiority as a justification for wars of aggression. In Serbia, for example, Women in Black publicly mourned the victims of Bosnia, Kosovo, and Croatia and, in doing so, demanded that people challenge the nationalist imaginary that had reduced such victims to enemies fated for slaughter because of their supposed ethnic inferiority. The public display of emotion was certainly part of a highly selective pattern of vision and interpretation that challenged the Serbian nation and its claim to be the true Yugoslavia. Nussbaum helps us understand not only that public displays of emotion have cognitive content in this broad sense but also that there is political and ethical power at stake in Women in Black enacting all the conditions of a wake, including the shedding of tears over those who are considered unworthy of their weeping.

Although Nussbaum understands the importance of the imagination in making the judgment that allows the emotion to be evoked in the first place, she nevertheless fails to see that there is no easy analytic divide between the imaginary and the imagination, and that, moreover, we cannot be absolved of our responsibility to reflect on how we might be captured by a psychoanalytic imaginary (in Lacan's sense) that dwarfs our own ability to imagine and reimagine. This failure becomes particularly important because Nussbaum insists that emotions simply attempt to fit the world. Women in Black publicly express emotions that do not fit their world but that seek to transform the vision and interpretation of the need for war that certain nationalist imaginaries promote. They use public expressions of emotion to transform these imaginaries and rekindle the imaginations of the very people who have been captured by fantasies of their ethnic superiority or, in the case of the U.S., their political exceptionalism. Thus, this distinction between imaginary and imagination is crucial for understanding the political and ethical power of Women in Black, because they invite us to judge human beings reduced to the figure of the enemy as just that, human beings, not Agamben's *homines sacri*.

When Israeli women bravely march into the West Bank and stand in silent vigil for fallen Palestinian men and women; when in New York Jewish women hold up a sign tragically reminding us that, in the past five years, 62 percent of the Palestinians killed were under the age of twelve, and weep for them and for their mothers, they are called traitors, whores, and lesbians because they refuse to treat those enemies as the worst beasts imaginable—because they mourn for them as human beings. The very image of the mother as the protector and reproducer of the nation is profoundly disrupted, and with it, the legitimacy of the aggressive acts that women are supposed to endure in the name of their proper place in the nation-state. Thus, the simple act of mourning is inseparable from recognizing what Kant called the ideal of humanity. For the death of every single human being in war is a tragedy, and one for which we must mourn.

Mourning is a political and ethical performance among Women in Black because it not only involves participating in wakes for actual victims but also is an act of what they simply call tenderness toward all others who can be mourned in their singularity, their infinite worth, their pricelessness. This performance acts out Derrida's recent claim that "dignity is of the order of what is called the *priceless*. What is absolutely precious, the other in his or her dignity, has no price . . . two human beings . . . have an equal moral, juridical, political *dignity* whatever their differences in all other respects" (Derrida 2002, 324–25). The lesson here is that there is a deep and profound psychoanalytic connection between the imagined good woman and the imagined nation. This takes us back to my opening discussion of RAWA's attack on the U.S. feminist majority. For the connection between woman and nation enabled the feminist majority to represent all good American women against the bad revolutionary outsiders RAWA, and, moreover, to legitimate the patently unnecessary bombing of Afghanistan in the name of feminist nationalism, which was in fact a sacrilege of feminism. Radical feminists who are citizens of the U.S. must, then, dare to be politically infamous; they must be vigilant in insisting that psychical fantasies of women not be turned into a justification for preemptive U.S. military aggression against other nations—that preemptive strikes can never be justified in the name of saving women, especially when bombs fall on the heads of women whom U.S. military men are supposedly saving. As a member of Women in Black from Serbia eloquently put it, "I do not see why we should not worry about 'our people' and 'their people' in the same way, because this exclusion of the other is at the roots of fascism, in the divisions between ours and theirs, me and the others and normal and abnormal" (Zajovic 2001, 148).

IV

Women in Black is just one of many women's anti-militarist organizations. Although some Women in Black are explicitly pacifist and, indeed, have been criticized for an unrealistic pacifism, the real issue is that because any three women who stand in black count as a vigil within Women in Black there are many different positions, some explicitly and generally pacifist, others with more specifically focused strategies of resistance. The power of Women in Black is that they refuse traditional definitions of the good woman supporting her men in time of war. Not only do they challenge limited articulations of feminine sexual difference within the constraints of normative heterosexuality and its corresponding kinship systems. They also seek forms of solidarity with the so-called enemy in the name of trying to develop a more sweeping program of anti-militarism. In this sense, they have moved toward something like a universalizable principle for anti-militarist and anti-nuclear political organizing.

In Japan, members of an organization called Okinawa Women Act Against Military Violence (OWAAMV) have explicitly developed a program and a new paradigm for security, which has four main principles:

1. The environment in which we live must be able to sustain human and natural life.
2. People's basic survival needs for food, clothing, shelter, health care, and education must be met.
3. People's fundamental human dignity and respect for cultural identities must be honored.
4. People and the natural environment must be protected from avoidable harm.

Women began organizing around the tragic rapes that have been a constant occurrence ever since the U.S. military established its base in Okinawa after World War II. Although the official U.S. occupation of Japan ended in 1952, Okinawa remained under direct U.S. military control until 1972. To this day it is one of the largest military bases of the U.S. So even though the U.S. no longer directly controls Okinawa, its military presence there dominates the entire island. The cost of this military base to women and children is not only continuous rapes and sexual assaults by U.S. military men but also environmental poisoning. This is why part of OWAAMV's new program for security entails environmental testing and cleanup. Although the U.S. and Japan have agreed to start transferring military facilities to civilian control, many NGOs remain concerned about the responsibility the U.S. must take for environmental cleanup before these facilities can be safely transferred.

Okinawa feminists have also worked to create the East Asia–U.S. network against militarism, which requires U.S. women to take responsibility for what the U.S. has done in Okinawa and to struggle with East Asian women for the new paradigm of security that OWAAMV believes can be a universalizable program. The move from traditional issues of women's concern—such as rape and sexual violence—to the question of building a transnational network and new paradigm of security demonstrates that because feminism challenges basic kinship arrangements that ground nationalist and militarist institutions, it opens up space for universalizability in the very course of its struggle. In other words, an Okinawan feminism that sees the connection between certain fantasies about women, particularly Asian women, and the way U.S. soldiers treat them cannot be about getting a square deal with the men (in the sense of fair and equal opportunity), since all the people in Okinawa suffer from the presence of the U.S. military base. Thus, Okinawan feminism moves beyond formal equality in the very definition of how it sees its struggle against rape as integral to the demilitarization of Okinawa itself. Women can only be safe if Okinawa is freed from U.S. military presence: this is the insight that led to an alternative anti-militarist program for security.

Of course, the word *security* is bandied about a great deal these days. It is politically important for feminists to answer the call for security, especially when we are told by the Bush administration that we must give up our basic constitutional rights in its name. The Okinawan feminist program for security, with its insistence on the connection of security to demilitarization and anti-nuclear struggle, is an alternative to the current rhetoric of security that has made us so insecure as the U.S. becomes increasingly responsible for undermining nuclear-nonproliferation efforts. But both Women in Black and OWAAMV have shown us that feminism must ally itself with a symbolic universality that sometimes may be expressed in explicit calls for universalizable programs like the Okinawan security program but at other times goes one step farther, questioning current representations of humanity informed by fantasies about women's place in the nation and their relationship to militarism. By interrogating such representations of humanity and the normative heterosexual kinship structures connected to them, radical feminism can challenge the construction of woman as a subordinate object in the name of a symbolic universality that opens up new spaces for rethinking how we can be human together, including how we might find something like lasting security and invest in the dream—the ideal—of perpetual peace.

References

Agamben, Giorgio. 2000. *Means Without End: Notes on Politics*, translated by Cesare Cesarino. Minneapolis: University of Minnesota Press.

Alarcón, Norma. 1999. "Chicana Feminism: In the Tracks of the 'Native' Woman." In *Between Woman and Nation: Nationalisms, Feminisms, and the State*, edited by Caren Kaplan, Norma Alarcón, and Minoo Moallem, 63–71. Durham and London: Duke University Press.

Anderson, Benedict. 1983. *Imagined Communities*. London: Verso.

Brown, Janelle. "Coalition of Hope." *Ms.* magazine (spring): 65–76.

Derrida, Jacques. 2002. *Negotiations*, translated by Peggy Kamuf. Stanford: Stanford University Press.

Falk, Richard. 2003. *The Great Terror War*. New York: Olive Branch Press.

Joseph, Suad. 1999. "Women Between Nation and State in Lebanon." In *Between Woman and Nation: Nationalisms, Feminisms, and the State*, edited by Caren Kaplan, Norma Alarcón, and Minoo Moallem, 162–81. Durham and London: Duke University Press.

Nussbaum, Martha. 2001. *Upheavals of Thought: The Intelligence of the Emotions*. New York: Cambridge University Press.

Pérez, Laura Elisa. 1999. "El desorden, Nationalism, and Chicano/a Aesthetics." In *Between Woman and Nation: Nationalisms, Feminisms, and the State*, edited by Caren Kaplan, Norma Alarcón, and Minoo Moallem, 19–46. Durham and London: Duke University Press.

RAWA. 2002. "Open Letter to Feminist Majority." http://www.rawa. org. April 20.

Sen, Amartya. 2000. *Development as Freedom*. New York: Anchor Books.

Spivak, Gayatri. 2003. "Righting Wrongs." In *Human Rights, Human Wrongs*, edited by Nicholas Owen, 168–227. New York: Oxford University Press.

Zajovic, Stasa, ed. 2001. *Women for Peace*. Belgrade: Women in Black.

9

REASONS FOR CONFLICT:
POLITICAL IMPLICATIONS OF A DEFINITION OF TERRORISM

ANGELICA NUZZO

Reasons for Conflict

Historically, in the United States dissent depended neither upon political representation nor upon the guidance of a political party. Its vitality always needed the charismatic presence of an individual leader able to propose strong ideals and feasible programs of action. This holds true now more than ever.[1] In the United States protest has always been social rather than political, unlike, for example, in many European countries: in France and Italy during the Resistance against the Nazi occupation or in Germany and Italy in the 1960s and then in the 1970s and 1980s—the years of "terrorism" (see Merleau-Ponty 1947; Arendt 1972 and 1973; Marcuse 1965; Sartre 1974). In the United States protest has served to aggregate a social representation of civil society rather than to unify people ideologically under the name and program of a political party.

The practice of "civil disobedience" was born in the United States. Intellectuals like David Henry Thoreau and Martin Luther King Jr. voiced dissent at crucial moments of American history and indicated, with "civil disobedience," the path to be followed. In his famous address at Riverside Church in New York on April 4, 1967—exactly a year before he was assassinated—King for the first time linked his opposition to the Vietnam War with his struggle in the civil-rights movement. Forty-six years later, on April 4, 2003, another meeting was held at Riverside Church, both to commemorate Martin Luther King Jr.'s legacy and to express the strong popular protest against yet another aggressive American war. Although King's words and vision still provided inspirational guidance (see King 1991), everybody at the Riverside Church meeting was aware that the situation at home and in the world at large had changed in relevant ways, and that the opposition had to find new paths to follow in order to respond effectively to the challenges of the present.

Today Lenin's question "What is to be done?" resonates more dramatically than ever. Any strategy for action requires comprehension

---

[1] This essay was written in New York City during the weeks that immediately preceded and the days that immediately followed the declaration of war against Iraq in March 2003. This fact lends a time-specific tone to the more general philosophical discussion of the issue of terrorism addressed here.

of the historical reality of the present in which all action necessarily must take place. Comprehension, in turn, requires information as well as a successful method of analysis. Unbiased information, however, has proved to be something extremely difficult—if not impossible—to obtain from the American media, which function rather as official channels of the government's propaganda. On the other hand, the analysis that intellectuals have been providing of the current situation has either supported the aims of U.S. imperialism or concentrated on issues that, I believe, do not effectively unveil—let alone sufficiently oppose—the dangers of the ideological construction supporting the government's war on Iraq. Discussions on what constitutes a "just war," for example, are certainly important and worth pursuing. But they do not question the very root of the ideological strategy of George W. Bush's administration—a strategy that seems to defy any traditional idea of "justice" in the first place.

Thus, the issue of "praxis" leads to the issue of "theory." The question, What is to be done? leads to another question: Who are the philosophers who can speak today to the people's dissent, who can illuminate a present more dark and confused than ever—a present in which information is censored and almost nonexistent? Who are the philosophers able to offer key concepts for the comprehension of a reality that seems to dissolve into fiction the closer we try to get to it? Indeed, the tendency of transforming reality into "fiction"—into Hollywood scenarios—is a deeply troubling tendency that is often viewed as typical of the United States (see Sontag 2003, 109). Even the March 2003 invasion of Iraq was immediately translated into the simulation of a video game that provides the illusion of an "active" and patriotic participation in the "real" war, and into the fiction of a new Hollywood movie called *Gulf War II*. It is difficult to understand whether these are examples of jokes in bad taste or the tragic sign that we are losing touch with reality.[2] Maybe we could fancy that philosophers may, in some way, contribute to bring us back to "reality"?

In this essay I offer a *philosophical* approach to the problem of isolating the sources from which governments officially and unofficially provide the public (on both sides of the conflict line) with "reasons," "justifications," and "grounds" for war and, more generally, for the political use of violence. My analysis takes place at the level of the *principles* that inform moral and political reasoning and judgment, and it

---

[2] We recall the words of film director Michael Moore when he accepted the 2003 Oscar award for the documentary *Bowling for Columbine*: In the United States, the work of nonfiction is more necessary than anywhere else precisely because in this country one always lives in fiction. See also Zizek 2002. Relevant to my observation is the behavior of the Pentagon toward Saddam Hussein's televised speeches to the Iraqi people. There are never analyses of *what* Saddam actually says. Instead, the discussion exclusively focuses on the claim that it is not the "real" Saddam who is speaking but rather his double.

evaluates the type of reasoning that leads to and supports different justifications of war.[3] From this perspective, I shall ask how we can account for the ideological grounds that in a democratic society motivate governments, in the eyes of public opinion, to unleash war. What is the logic that will allow us to discern, behind false or illusory reasons, the true grounds of conflicts, the true "causes" of conflicts?

The question that I discuss in this essay is not the ethical question of the just war, namely, On what grounds (assuming that there are indeed such grounds) can a war be justly waged? Instead, I want to address the different issue concerning the ways in which those grounds or justifications are first produced. My question is not, What are the reasons that can be recognized as legitimate (or even as moral) reasons for conflict? Rather, I ask: Where do those reasons come from, how are they fabricated, and according to what type of (moral and political) discourse? What is the logic that first creates or institutes official reasons for war? Can we, as philosophers, isolate principles and patterns that will allow us to understand how the story of a conflict is woven from the point of its outbreak on, beyond the historical and geographical particularities of different conflicts? My suggestion is that "reasons" are never just there, simply to be "found" and brought to light. They are the product of the logic and the ideology that first generate them and impose them on public opinion. "Facts" only follow.

My contention is that the "reasons" which the U.S. government offers in support of its latest acts of war, because of the way in which they are produced, ultimately inform the collective consciousness of a people and determine the moral response to war—including the phenomena of patriotism and resistance. My analysis entails a discussion of how collective memory of events and collective production of meaning shape the direction of our response to traumatic acts of war in times of crisis. I conclude with a more general argument in favor of the relevance of historical reconstruction and dialectical (and antigenetic) inquiry in identifying the reasons for which war is waged.

Dialectic as Method of Analysis

The philosopher who offers an indispensable—and new—tool for my present analysis is Hegel, with his *dialectical method*. In particular, two important aspects of Hegel's method are brought to bear on my present discussion. On the one hand, I make use of the idea of the intrinsic *historical* nature of the reality in which we live, which leads to the task of gaining a historical comprehension of our present. At stake is the

---

[3] What is the "logic" behind Mr. Bush's dangerously alogical argument, "If Saddam Hussein starts destroying his missiles we need to bomb Iraq because this means he is indeed in possession of weapons of mass destruction; if he does not destroy them, we need to bomb Iraq because this means that he is hiding weapons of mass destruction"?

understanding of what brought us to the present point, what the historical basis—or "cause"—is of Bush's declaration of "war on terrorism." On the other hand, I want to think of this problem *dialectically*. To this end, we must draw attention to the categories in which the discourse of the so-called war on terrorism is articulated, and question the rigidity of those categories and of the dualisms that support them—the fixed division, for example, between "good" and "evil," between "us" and "them," between "cause" and "effect." This dialectical analysis will allow me to expose here the flaw of a link which is essential to the logic of Bush's war on terrorism: the link between 9/11 and the war on Iraq.

Thus, I propose a *dialectical* reading of the relation between "cause" and "effect," or between the "ground" (*Grund*) and what is grounded, once war is seen as the allegedly necessary effect of, or response to, the occurrence of events that, under the designation *terrorism*, are regarded as primal "causes." Our usual linear and nondialectical logic holds that once the cause is given, its determinate effect *must* follow. By means of Hegel's dialectic, I want to expose the flaws of the linear logic of causality as well as the dangers that arise when this logic is applied to the reconstruction of historical events and to the political response that these events receive (and, it is claimed, deserve to receive). I take the case of Bush's war against terrorism as the chief example of this. Dialectic unmasks the illusion of the linear and apparently genetic logic of causality. Using Hegel's logic of essence (to which I can here only allude), I show how the effect truly (and logically) *precedes* the cause from which it seems to follow. For it is the effect that first institutes the cause as cause. The cause is individuated—or "posited"—on the ground of the effect, not the other way round. Hence, what appears as cause (terrorism) is in truth itself an effect; it is the true effect that follows from that which is instead presented as a subsequent and necessary effect (war). The conclusion of my dialectical argument is that although terrorism is presented as the indisputable cause of the war waged against it, terrorism is truly the effect of a strategy of war that extends far beyond the objective of fighting terrorism.

Before discussing this thesis, however, we need to respond to two intertwined questions: Why is the rhetoric of "terrorism" so central in Bush's politics? And why is it so important today, for the voice of dissent, to expose the logic on which the discourse of terrorism is based?

The "War on Terrorism" and the Impasse of Dissent

Political dissent in the United States has been paralyzed by the events of September 11, 2001. Almost two years after that terrible date, it still has to come to terms with this fracture in American history. The accusation of anti-Americanism that reduces opposition to silence has recently been repeated in the charge of antipatriotism with which antiwar protests are silenced. To be against the war in Iraq is to be against the American soldiers that are fighting it. This inference is as immediate as it is wrong. But it silences opposition. Such an inference is accompanied by a series of analogous—and analogously wrong—conclusions construed according to the same logic. To be against the war is to be in favor of Saddam Hussein; even worse, it is to reject the dogma according to which Saddam Hussein is the obscure power behind Al Qaeda and consequently responsible for the attacks of 9/11 (the specter of Osama bin-Laden has meanwhile been forgotten). This is a dogma that, against all evidence, the large majority of the American population has been induced to believe.[4] Hence, to be against the war is reason enough to be labeled a "terrorist." However, once we accept this "illogical" (and "ideological") connection between the war launched in March 2003 against Iraq and the events of 9/11, we can be confident that the propaganda of the Bush administration has won and that public opinion, along with any voice that the opposition may find, has already been defeated. For the program of a war against terrorism with which Bush immediately responded to 9/11 already took into account, as one of its successive stages, the attack on Iraq.

The weakness of the current opposition to the Bush administration in the United States is due, among other things, to a failure in debunking the false connection between the war on Iraq and the "terrorist" attacks of 9/11. It is due to the failure to expose the false logic according to which the phenomenon of terrorism was immediately defined—and the response to it inexorably sanctioned—by the Bush administration.

George W. Bush's rhetoric of the war against terrorism (a rhetoric employed already by Ronald Reagan) requires a fundamental clarification of the meaning of the term *terrorism*. It is all too well known that this is one of the most difficult terms to *define*. "The term"—we read in a communication of the American State Department on "global terrorism" dating back to 1992—"does not have a unanimous definition because the United Nations has been incapable of agreeing on its definition. . . . No definition has been unanimously accepted." Indeed, in 1987 the General Assembly of the United Nations had proposed a definition of terrorism that was not "unanimously accepted," but only because of the contrary votes of the United States under Reagan and of Israel. The reasons these two countries offered for their negative votes are significant. For the United States and Israel the fundamental flaw of the proposed definition was concentrated in the clause on self-

---

[4] The most recent—and almost the only—piece of evidence of a connection between Osama bin-Laden and Saddam Hussein (properly speaking, though, not really Saddam Hussein) is the involvement of the bin-Laden family in the fortunes of the Bechtel Group of San Francisco, the most substantial beneficiary in the enterprise of reconstructing Iraq after the war (see the *New Yorker*, May 5, 2003).

determination that the United Nations had inserted in order to rescue it from being labeled "terrorist": "The right to self-determination, freedom, and independence, as derived from the Charter of the United Nations, of people forcibly deprived of that right . . . , particularly peoples under colonial and racist regimes and foreign occupation." This was understood as applying to the struggle of the African National Congress against the apartheid regime in South Africa (a regime that was a U.S. ally, while the ANC was officially labeled a "terrorist organization"), and to the struggle of the Palestinians under Israeli military occupation (another occupation fully sustained by the United States) (see Chomsky 2002).

It is not my direct aim here to attempt a definition of the term *terrorism*. What I shall discuss instead is a concrete case of instrumental and ideological definition of it. More precisely, by means of dialectic I expose the general (ideo)logical mechanism according to which the definition is first construed. Dialectic allows us to explain why terrorism is defined by the U.S. government in such a way as to create the normative dilemma according to which one cannot not be either against or for terrorism—*tertium non datur*; or, to consider a variation dear to Mr. Bush, one must be either with America or against it, that is, with the terrorists (see Roy 2002).

Terrorism as Cause: "Absolute Evil"

What is the ideological procedure that allows the Bush administration to construe "terrorism" as the necessary target of a new type of "war"—the unconventional war that promises to dominate "the American century" as permanent war? As the target of this new type of war, terrorism *must* be defined as "absolute evil," must be located beyond and without all legal jurisdiction, all international order—indeed, without any order as such. Terrorism *must* be construed as the radical opposite of, and the radical threat to, Western democracy and its values of freedom. For it is only under this condition that terrorism gains the effective power to terrorize without needing any further proof, explanation, or evidence.[5]

At the level of the logic of essence, the second division of his *Science of Logic*, Hegel teaches us that the absolute beginning of the dialectical process—"being, pure being," which is identical with "nothing"—is the *real* beginning of the dialectical movement of thought's self-determination only because this beginning has been posited as absolute.[6] The beginning, as the absolute origin of the logical movement, is all but

---

[5] For a discussion of the connection between propaganda and terror in totalitarian regimes, see Arendt 1973, 341ff.

[6] The logic of essence is the second division of the "Objective Logic," the first part of Hegel's 1816 *Science of Logic* (as well as the "Logic" of his 1830 *Encyclopedia of Philosophical Sciences*).

absolute (if anything can be said to be absolute; for Hegel, only the end of the process as result can be said to be absolute, never the beginning). Moreover, it is a true beginning only when it is *regressively* and *retroactively* constituted from the very end of the whole process. In other words, the beginning is the true beginning of something only once this something has been completely brought to light, that is, construed in its full development. The past (the logical past as well as the temporal past of history and memory) is not a given, indisputable reality already formed and always presupposed. It is instead the product of a *regressive* construction, that is, a construction that, while stretching toward the future, determines, at the same time, that which counts as its past (see Nuzzo forthcoming). Collective memory is not a bare fact but a stipulation, a "collective instruction" (Sontag 2003, 85).

In opposition to a simplistic reconstruction of historical processes on the basis of the linear, deterministic, and nondialectical logic of causality, which assumes causes as originally given, and in opposition to a merely extrinsic teleology, which justifies the means on the basis of the ends, I suggest a different idea of historical development, articulated by the dialectical notion of a regressive constitution of reality as *historical* reality.

On this basis, my conclusion is that terrorism is not the first, original cause of the so-called war against terrorism formulated and declared by Bush (a first cause that would justify this war precisely as war against terrorism); nor does anti-American terrorism *precede* the war that has been waged against it as a response to it. Terrorism (as well as its symbol, 9/11) is instead the *true effect* or the *real consequence* of the war against terrorism that the United States has been waging for decades in numerous parts of the world. In other words, war is the true cause of that which it declares it is fighting—namely, terrorism. To expose this logic, to uncover the dialectic and antigenetic mechanism of the relations that constitute the reality of historical events (as opposed to their fictional and ideological packaging), is essential for any opposition to American imperialism. It is essential if we want to reach a nonideological and noninstrumental definition of terrorism. It is essential if we want to regain the historical—and oppose the fictional—sense of the reality in which we live.

Immediately labeled as a terrorist act, 9/11 has gained for the Bush administration and for American public opinion the status of an original event without cause and without ground. From the outset, the logic of the Bush administration has aimed at presenting 9/11 as an event with no cause, certainly not as an effect of some (hidden or yet unknown but still discoverable) cause. By uncovering the conceptual structure that supports the official definition of terrorism insistently circulated by the media, we discover that terrorism is presented as that which has no ground and is beyond all law. Terrorism is not the effect of a cause; it is not grounded in a ground. And 9/11 is the cause of all evil that, in turn, has no cause and stands at the origin of the causal chain with no possible explanation. Any inquiry or search for the ground, any attempt to explain 9/11 *a parte ante* (*why* did it happen?) is in principle forbidden and reduced to a meaningless enterprise. (The question, Why do *they* hate *us* so much? is truly a rhetorical question. It does not reveal an intent to find out the why, to uncover the cause, of that hate; rather, it simply affirms the sheer absurdity of a hate that is unquestionably assumed as groundless and unmotivated.)

Thus, 9/11 is presented as the Nietzschean "monument" that has lost any connection with its causal explanation—a monument placed outside any causal chain of explanation, a hypostatized event placed outside history (see Nietzsche 1980, 1:258ff.). The Nietzschean monument is, paradoxically and dangerously, the consecration of history outside (and against) history. According to Nietzsche, what is rendered "monumental" in the monument is the *effectus*, and this operation always takes place "at the expense of the cause." Removed from its connection with a cause, the event is thus transformed into an "effect-in-itself," namely, into an event that has been abstracted from time and history and thereby has also lost the status of a real "effect" (Nietzsche 1980, 1:261f.; see also 6:90ff.). In accordance with Nietzsche's suggestion, the monument of 9/11 claims the status of the Kantian inaccessible "thing in itself"—for the effect has been transformed into the cause, that is, into the cause of all appearance that itself never appears. It is open to discussion whether this cause really exists or is only a fiction (or propaganda)—a mere *Gedankending* (*ens rationis*). Obviously, as brute event, 9/11 is painfully and dramatically *real*. Its painful reality, however, is not the same as the reality of 9/11 construed by the Bush administration as the original *cause* of all so-called evil. It is only the reality of a brute, naked—and to that extent not interpreted—"fact" of human history. Here we can follow Hume's critique of the idea of causality: experience itself never yields the causality of a cause. And yet, only if 9/11 is presented as utterly uncaused—as the absolute origin or cause of all evil—can America appear as the absolute victim—a victim by definition absolutely innocent.

The Bush administration *had to construe* 9/11 as uncaused, original evil, because 9/11 had to become the absolute ground of all responses that would follow. This ground could not be presented, in turn, as the effect of a determinate cause that one could investigate, nor could it be the deed of a rational agent who acted from comprehensible motives (albeit wrong or illegitimate ones) and who in consequence could be prosecuted. The definition of terrorism as the ungrounded original evil is from the outset a form of political expediency. For, if the terrorist did have a ground, he or she would possibly have a grievance that ought to be investigated and addressed. This would be the appropriate response to the terrorist's act. But this is precisely the response that those who present the necessity of the war on terrorism do not want, cannot want, and utterly forbid. To label an enemy a terrorist is to forbid the search for the ground or reason for action. The label merely makes the claim that there is no such ground or reason. This is the difference between the representation of the political opponent (*Gegner*), by whom one is confronted for comprehensible reasons, and the representation of the terrorist enemy (*Feind*), whom one has simply to liquidate as a subject lacking any reason or comprehensible ground for action. While one fights the political opponent and his or her motives, one must utterly destroy the terrorist enemy.

Thus, terrorism is construed by the official definition of the Bush administration as a phenomenon lying outside and beyond any law—civil law as well as moral law, international law, the law of peace, as well as the law of war.[7] Terrorism terrorizes precisely because it is outside all law and all order. It follows (by the logic to which propaganda forces public opinion) that the only response to terrorism can be war, that is, the total annihilation of the enemy. It follows also that war against terrorism will not abide any law and will simply consecrate terrorism's absolute lawlessness. Bush's war against terrorism must present terrorism in these terms if it wants to gain the necessity that is supposed to justify it in the eyes of the nation and the international community. However, dialectically and paradoxically, it is precisely the war against terrorism that first posits—that *must* posit—terrorism as outside all law and rationality in order to fight it as such. The "presupposition," Hegel teaches us in the logic of essence, to the extent that it functions as a presupposition, reveals itself as something posited—that is, as something construed and manipulated; as mere presupposition it is a mere *Schein*, an illusion that we cultivate, removed from the search for the real ground, in order to exempt ourselves from taking responsibility for its consequences. Dialectically and paradoxically, terrorism reveals itself as the chief product and true effect of the war waged against terrorism viewed as the principal cause of that war. Hence, dialectic shows that terrorism is an effect, not a cause; an effect never justifiable but certainly historically and rationally comprehensible. It is immediately clear that as soon as terrorism is recognized as an effect, the politics aimed at opposing it will have to endorse a strategy totally different from Bush's war on terror. Politics will have to look at the reasons that lead to the exercise of violence and will have to fight the effect along with the causes that produce it.[8]

---

[7] In 1984, fighting "terrorism" in Nicaragua, Ronald Reagan proclaimed that without law only "chaos and disorder" could be sovereign. However, the day before this declaration he had announced that the United States would completely disregard the decisions of the International Court of Justice condemning his own administration's "unlawful use of force" and ordering the immediate halt of its acts of "international terrorism" (see Chomsky 2002).

[8] One should consider, in this context, the proposal advocated in response to 9/11 by the Vatican. It is a proposal for a "police operation conducted under the auspices of the United Nations . . . against a criminal conspiracy whose members should be hunted down and brought before an international court, where they would receive a fair trial and, if found guilty, be awarded an appropriate sentence." (Quoted by the military historian Michael Howard in *Foreign Affairs*, Jan./Feb. 2002). It should be noted that this proposal speaks of a "*criminal* conspiracy," not simply of terrorism.

Thus have we reached the conclusion of my dialectical argument. The American war (against terrorism) constitutes the true initial act of terrorism that for decades has been menacing the unstable world situation. For, according to dialectical logic, it is the American war that posits itself beyond any law and any international recognition (outside the legitimization of the United Nations as well as outside the International Criminal Court). It is the American war that escapes any rational justification, which, following Kant's suggestion, in order to be "rational" ought to subject itself to the "principle of publicity," that is, ought to make its reasons and grounds publicly recognized (Kant 1795, appendix 2). Instead, what is offered as the official justification of the March 2003 attack against Iraq? Bush and his administration have presented to the public the least plausible and least rational of reasons for it—the existence of an entity (fictitious at the time of the attack) called "weapons of mass destruction" that Saddam Hussein putatively possessed, directly and immediately threatening the territory and people of the United States. The line that separates fiction from outright lie is here extremely precarious. The point is that the war on terrorism is placed beyond any justification—and even any need for justification. Such a war does not need reasons—least of all *public* reasons—in order to be waged. The designation "war on terrorism" is meant to justify itself—provided one has strategically *defined* what one is fighting. This war is justified by that which it declares it is fighting—namely, terrorism. This is the danger of this type of definition.

And yet in the course of the attack on Iraq we have reached the tragic point in which the very reality of the war eventually uncovers the dialectical circle that keeps America in check. It is difficult even for the American media not to recognize that terrorism is the most authentic *product* of American aggressive politics. Thus, we are constantly reminded that soon terrorist attacks on American soil *will follow as a consequence of* the unleashing of war on Iraq. These attacks, the media project, will be conducted according to the terrorist procedure of using "suicide bombers"—an echo that replicates the unrepeatable monument of 9/11. But whereas 9/11 was an original cause, not a response to anything preceding it, the terrorist attacks that scare the American public in time of war are explicitly construed as the *effect* of the war on terrorism. Here truth finally seems timidly to surface. New York, the media predict, will be more and more like Tel Aviv. Indeed, the U.S. media are responsible for a campaign of "terror" injected deeper and deeper into American public opinion. The effect of this campaign is the figure of the new, "virtual" terrorist.

Moreover, because the war waged on Iraq is a war on terrorism, we should not be surprised to find the desperate and technologically disadvantaged Iraqi soldiers fighting it with the unconventional weapons of "terrorism," not with the highly sophisticated weapons of mass destruction that the media, during the conflict, tried with all possible means to make us forget about. The American war machine is met with responses like Sergeant Ali Jaffar Moussa Hamadi al-Nomani's suicide attack at the beginning of April 2003. An American spokesman immediately commented that al-Nomani's suicide attack "looks and feels like terrorism" (Fisk 2003). Yet al-Nomani's objective was a military one, carried out against an army of occupation. American and British television reports contemptuously label Iraqi soldiers "militia," and one BBC correspondent even reached the point of defining them as "quasi-terrorists." In other words, while American soldiers are fighting a war, the Iraqis are only terrorists (and do not even have the *right* to be treated as soldiers of a regular army). Analogously, the Nazis occupying France used the expression *terrorism* to typify the actions of the Resistance against the Vichy regime; and they even applied the term to the victims of the Warsaw ghetto during the Final Solution.[9]

What should be said, then, of the tragic "mistake" in which the unfortunate passengers (all children and women) of the bus at the Najaf checkpoint lost their lives? Who are here the terrorists? It is clear that the thin line separating "war" from "terrorism"—the cause from the effect or the effect from the cause—becomes increasingly faint. Only the highly problematic division between "us" and "them"—or Bush's theological Manichaeism of good and evil—gives the illusion that war and terrorism are separate. It becomes ever more evident, however, that terrorism is a dead end, a dangerous circle that cannot be broken by violence—in whichever way and by whichever name this violence is defined or justified.

History and the Definition of Terrorism

Having uncovered by means of dialectic the logic according to which the phenomenon of terrorism was officially defined and construed by the Bush administration from 9/11 to the March 2003 invasion of Iraq, we can now conclude that this logic betrays a more general character of American culture that opponents of Bush's policy must be able to respond to in order to be effective. At stake are America's general lack of historical sense and its rejection of a culture—and of a philosophy—that aims at investigating the historical grounds of human action, human thought, and human reality.[10]

[9] See Herman and O'Sullivan 1989, 39 and 261, quoting the Nazi *Stroop Report*, which states that "the real terrorists are being struck down" and that "subhumanity—bandits and terrorists—remains in bunkers."

[10] I am well aware that the following all-too-general considerations entail the risk of simplification proper to all generalizations. However, I think that the central point I am making does maintain its full validity despite the simplification it entails. Moreover, in referring to "American culture" I intend that which common sense, in Europe in particular, takes to be "proper" to America.

While the construction of 9/11 as absolute origin of terror had to abstract this event from all geographical characterization (viewing Saudi Arabia, Palestine, Afghanistan, and Iraq as constituting one and the same undifferentiated continuum), it also had to place 9/11 beyond any possible historical connection and any possible memory. According to the official construction that we have been analyzing, the terror of 9/11 came literally from nowhere—it must have come from nowhere, because if it came from somewhere its point of origin would be its point of destination, namely, the United States.[11] In no other place in the world does the horror of 9/11 stand outside history as it does in the United States. In South America, for example, the solidarity with the United States expressed for the atrocities of 9/11 immediately associated the condemnation of the act with the memory of another September 11—that of 1973 and the coup d'état by Augusto Pinochet supported by the United States. Around the world it has been stressed that the atrocities of 9/11, precisely in their devastating, all too "real" atrocity, are nothing new; other peoples suffered from them in a not so distant past.

In America, on the contrary, 9/11 yields no possible memory and no possible comparison. It cannot be related to any other historical event. Rather, it is the absolute beginning of all memory; it is, indeed, the beginning of a new history, of a new America (set, as it were, at the beginning of the "American century"). On September 11, 2001, America was born again. As terrorist act, 9/11 is the founding myth of a new America. Nothing of real import has preceded it; neither Thomas Jefferson nor George Washington, neither Abraham Lincoln nor Martin Luther King Jr. means anything anymore. The American flag has nothing to do with them. The flag is now about 9/11. The flag is associated with Osama bin-Laden and Saddam Hussein. In this way, American patriotism recognizes new—albeit negative—founding fathers. The gains of the civil-rights movement and the constitutional values of American democracy have been canceled in one stroke. The Patriot Act, now in its second, much more serious edition, will soon replace them. Paradoxically, the American flag no longer suggests George Washington, democracy, and civil liberties. If one points this out to Americans, however, one risks being considered antipatriotic and anti-American.

In this reborn America, the value of history is rejected and sent back to that "old"—and as old also irrelevant—Europe whence it originally came. American consensus does not need history. It is self-grounding and completely self-referential, as it works in a present with no time and no roots. The memory of a society based on immigration is removed. In America there is a museum of the Jewish Holocaust and plans for a museum of the

---

[11] Edward Said observes in astonishment that "it is surprising that the horrible Twin Towers–Pentagon attacks are treated as if they had come from nowhere, rather than from a world across the seas driven crazy by US intervention and presence" (Said 2003).

Armenian genocide but nothing similar for the African American and the Native American holocausts (Said 2003; Sontag 2003, 87f.).

Edward Said (2003) associates the American rejection of history with the typically American belief that "pragmatism" is "the right philosophy to deal with reality." The other philosophy that is admitted precisely because it programmatically does not deal with reality is "analytic philosophy" (see McCumber 2001, chapter 2 in particular). In this tradition, philosophical problems are all absolute beginnings, with no real cause and no relevant history. More important, truth is by definition ahistorical, set beyond any social, political, individual connection. This American "philosophy," comments Said, "is anti-metaphysical, anti-historical and, curiously, anti-philosophical. Postmodern anti-nominalism, which reduces everything to sentence structure and linguistic context, is allied with this." He concludes with a remark concerning his own institution, Columbia University, where "Hegel and Heidegger are taught in literature or art history departments, rarely in philosophy" (Said 2003).[12]

We have come full circle. American "official" culture and philosophy programmatically rejects history and systematically refuses to ask itself what the historical causes are of the reality in which we live—it even refuses to reflect on its own historical origins (see McCumber 2001). This is the ground on which the ideology of the "war on terrorism" flourishes; this is the voice of Bush's consensus.

References

Arendt, Hannah. 1972. "On Violence." In *Crises of the Republic*, 103–84. New York: Harvest Books.

———. 1973. *The Origins of Totalitarianism*. New York: Harvest Books.

Bloom, Allan. 1987. *The Closing of the American Mind*. New York: Simon and Schuster.

Chomsky, Noam. 2002. "Who Are the Global Terrorists?" In *Worlds in Collision: Terror and the Future of Global Order*, edited by K. Booth and T. Dunne, 128–37. London: Macmillan.

Fisk, Robert. 2003. "Al-Nomani." *The Independent* (April 2).

Hegel, Georg Wilhelm Friedrich. 1986. *Werke in zwanzig Bänden*, edited by E. Moldenhauer and H. M. Michel. Frankfurt a. M.: Suhrkamp.

Herman, Edward H., and Gerry O'Sullivan. 1989. *The "Terrorism" Industry*. New York: Pantheon.

---

[12] See also McCumber's claim, in discussing Bloom 1987 (McCumber 2001, 110f.): Hegel, Heidegger, and Marx are "thinkers who, because of their attitude toward sentential truth [i.e., truth is historical for those thinkers], are missing from most American philosophy departments."

Kant, Immanuel. 1795. *Zum ewigen Frieden*. Königsberg: Friedrich Nocolovius.

King, Martin Luther, Jr. 1991. "A Time to Break Silence." In *A Testament of Hope*, edited by M. James Washington, 231–44. New York: HarperCollins. Original 1967.

Marcuse, Herbert, Robert Paul Wolff, and Moore Barrington Jr. 1965. *A Critique of Pure Tolerance*. Boston: Beacon Press.

McCumber, John. 2001. *Time in the Ditch: American Philosophy and the McCarthy Era*. Evanston, Ill.: Northwestern University Press.

Merleau-Ponty, Maurice. 1947. *Humanisme et terreur*. Paris: Gallimard.

Nietzsche, Friedrich Wilhelm. 1980. *Vom Nutzen und Nachteil der Historie für das Leben, Unzeitgemässe Betrachtungen*. In *Sämmtliche Werke: Kritische Studienausgabe in 15 Bänden*, edited by G. Colli and M. Montinari, vol. 1. Berlin: DeGruyter.

———. 1980. *Götzen-Dämmerung*. In *Sämmtliche Werke*, vol. 6.

Nuzzo, Angelica. 1997. "Logica." In *Hegel*, edited by C. Cesa, 38–42. Bari: Laterza.

———. Forthcoming. "Pensiero e memoria: Logica e psicologia nella filosofia di Hegel." *Quaderni di filosofia* 2.

Roy, Arundhati. 2002. "Not Again." *The Guardian* (September 27).

Said, Edward. 2003. "Global Crisis." *Z-net* (March 17).

Sontag, Susan. 2003. *Regarding the Pain of Others*. New York: Farrar, Straus and Giroux.

Sartre, Jean-Paul, Philippe Gavi, and Pierre Victor. 1974. *On a raison de se révolter*. Paris: Gallimard.

The Stroop Report. 1979. New York: Pantheon.

Zizek, Slavoj. 2002. "Welcome to the Desert of the Real." *The Symptom: On-Line Journal for Lacan* 1, no. 2.

10

LOSING TO TERRORISM:
AN AMERICAN WORK IN PROGRESS

DAVIS B. BOBROW

As I write in late March 2003, a war with Iraq of more than a decade enters a phase of large-scale American invasion and occupation. That urges caution in declaring results from what the Bush II administration labels the "war on terrorism". In addition, it is always less than cautious for someone outside a particular discipline to enter into dialogue with the community served by a disciplinary publication. Nevertheless, I shall proceed with this essay of opinion for several reasons beyond the hard-to-resist invitation to contribute to this collection.

The first of these reasons is that some patterns of U.S. policy declared to be in response to 9/11 were to be expected, and they are likely in the short run to be intensified by general war on Iraq. The second is that my field, international relations and (in)security policy, offers pertinent standards of evaluation beyond those commonplace in discussions among philosophers. By those criteria the United States is losing to terrorism by pursuing the very means Washington has chosen to win against it. Losing refers to an unfinished process conceivably open to reversal. At this time, the grounds for expecting an actual, prompt reversal are slim, for the very reasons that made the American response predictable. In sum, I believe that, wittingly or unwittingly, the 9/11 terrorists sprung a trap, and Washington has jumped right into it.[1]

The section that follows states my definition of terrorism and some of its implications. Those suggest some general questions to ask about courses of action as counters to terrorism in terms of their relative merit. The subsequent section draws on major social-science and public-policy bodies of work for suggestions about likely decision making by an American administration in the face of dramatic terrorism like the events of 9/11. In my view, those expectations have been borne out by U.S. policies and will be met to an increasing degree so long as the war on terrorism as framed by the current U.S. administration stays at the center of national attention. The final section offers some criteria of evaluation from the international-relations and (in)security-policy literatures, and it

---

[1] I do not assume that an America-centered perspective is the only valid way to appraise 9/11 and the war on terrorism, only that it is one important way to do so and challenge enough for the space available here.

suggests that the policies in use offer at most very marginal gains and at worst highly negative consequences.

Terrorism

By "terrorism" I choose to mean inflicting severe physical and psychological harms on noncombatants without giving them practical opportunities to avoid those harms. What physical harms involve is obvious, but attention to them should not come at the expense of attention to psychological harms (instilling fear). The counter terrorism challenge is then one of reducing the incidence and severity of such actions, whoever takes them and whatever their motives. Given the extent to which uncertainties mount as nations and persons move from the present into the future, special weight should go to reductions in the near future that are less dependent on numerous conditionalities about long-term effects.

These positions have many implications, which include the following. Actions by official organs of a state (that is, a nation) or coalition of states can be terroristic, as can those by nonstate groups and individuals. Governments can engage in terrorism against their own or other populations. State terrorism can be physical or psychological, as in Stalin's or Saddam Hussein's reign of terror. Moralistic crusaders, even those with a grand, humanity-encompassing vision, can be terrorists, as can venal thugs. Use of military means which by their nature cannot limit their victims to combatants (most obviously weapons of mass destruction, or WMD) inherently involves committing substantial terrorism. Indeed, it is hard to find an instance of war or armed violence in the past century free of terrorism by all sides. A final implication of my definition is that terrorism and thus appropriate counterterrorism should be seen as a collective security problem of reducing bad actions, rather than as a collective defense problem of containing or eliminating specified bad actors.[2]

With reference to winning over or losing to terrorism, one can of course take a position that no terrorism is permissible, and thus that any engagement in modern war or armed violence or preventive policing is wrong and unacceptable. My position is a more relativist one, under which any particular war, campaign of armed violence, or domestic security program is justified only as it meets three tests. Do systematically and rigorously estimated expected consequences warrant confidence that the terrorism inherent in such actions will be substantially less than the terrorism it reduces? Does a specific war, campaign of armed violence, or domestic security measure offer the best available ratio of terrorism reduced or avoided to terrorism inflicted? Do specific variants of each

---

[2] For the general distinction, see Wolfers 1952.

underline more than they blur a clear distinction between terrorism and defense against it?

Phrasing key questions in this way is of course not even handed. It is easier to foresee with confidence what harms to noncombatants will follow from initiating a war or campaign of armed violence than what reductions it will produce in terrorism, and when it will do so. The burden of proof lies with those who would wage war and campaigns of armed violence, not with those who would avoid them. That burden of proof needs to be met for the specific situations on which policy focuses. And it needs to be especially well met for relatively immediate consequences as contrasted with far into the future ones based on "wouldn't it be nice" aspirations for a particular future predicated on inherently tenuous conjectures.

Decision-Making Tendencies and Policy Expectations

How a nation or individual political leader responds when faced with terrorism is a matter of choice based on estimates of anticipated reactions to and consequences of available policies. This section notes in brief and over-simplified fashion four sets of reasonably well-established general tendencies in policy decision-making: (1) receptivity by power holders to cause and effect estimates about the future; (2) the treatment of the risks of possible responses to losses and payoffs from candidate policies; (3) the self-interest calculus of elected politicians and established bureaucracies; and (4) the role of pre-existing beliefs in strategic anticipation. Individually and synergistically, these well-established tendencies imply what the Bush II administration (or perhaps any other) would be likely to do, and to leave undone, in response to 9/11. If the respective tendencies compatibly favor the same policy line, we expect a relatively high degree of policy consistency, clarity, and sustained pursuit. If their implications clash, we expect far more muddled and erratic policy.

Anticipated reactions are central considerations, and historical experience and expert analysis give us some substantial insight into what goes on in their calculation in public-policy systems. First, individual holders of power, and national governments, who see themselves as especially powerful favor estimates that support their doing what they want to and assuming that others will accommodate to it. "To possess power is to be in a position where it is less necessary to learn in order to act — it is others without power that have to do so. . . . Officials with power can brush aside information . . . can order . . . things done anyway . . . can refuse to learn . . . can reject warnings . . . can concentrate on their own plans . . . that is what having power means." They are not into reopening 'cans of worms' but instead have a "stake in continuing with decisions and policies the elaboration of which required a heavy investment in time, political resources, emotional considerations . . . " (Knorr and Morgan

1983, 234–35). Political power holders favor estimates that buttress their
sense of power, already chosen policies, and policy inclinations by
holding out prospects for successful action. Their appetite is much
less for evidence and interpretations that if taken seriously would run
counter to those tastes. And that appetite gets reduced further in the face
of a flow of evidence and interpretations that confirm previously made
policy bets.[3]

When leaders face terrorism against their administration and their
society, the dice are loaded in favor of forecasts that fit well with a sense
of power and an appetite for action, and take prior decisions as givens not
subject to critical review. These patterns suggest a tension with my
previous recommendation to place the burden of proof on those who
would proclaim the counter terrorism efficacy of war, armed violence,
and preventive policing. They set the odds to give an advantage to
forecasts that embrace one's powerful status and commend strongly
assertive actions against those who have challenged it. That is even
more so once a course is set. The door is then open to underestimates of
the terror inflicted by one's own actions and to overestimates of the
reduction in terror by others that will result.

With respect to counterterrorism, the bias in estimates about the
consequences of war, armed violence, and preventive policing is also fueled
by some decision tendencies associated with prospect theory (Levy 1996).
In brief, those tendencies are to be more prone to engage in risky behavior
if what is it stake is held to be retaining or regaining 'goods' which one still
has (or had, or expects to have) possession of. Avoiding or reversing losses
posed by a terrorist challenge can then distort judgments in ways that
reduce expectations about the magnitude of the first term in the ratio of
terrorism inflicted to terrorism reduced, and inflate expectations about the
second term. The probability and magnitude of these distortions are
greatest when the 'loss' to be avoided or recouped involves holdings seen
as in hand or within reach, of great value and obvious entitlement in their
own right, and highly correlated with continued possession of other
holdings. Arguments against particular loss-reversing or future loss-avoid-
ing policies based on the risks involved become less persuasive.

There is little doubt that at least since the early 1990s important
elements of several American presidential administrations have believed
that the U.S. had become the 'pole' in a unipolar international system.
The U.S. could (and should) maintain and entrench that position
militarily and economically and further the emergence of a world in our
image through the export of institutions (democratization and market-

---

[3] With regard to invasion and occupation of Iraq, absent unusual self-discipline, favor
would go to estimates predicting that the Iraqi regime would fight in ways that would
advantage American strategy and forces, and indigenous revolt against Saddam's regime.

ization) and lifestyles (Bobrow 2002b, 2001; President of the United States 2002, 1998). Major differences of opinion were and continue to be about more specific emphases, in effect priorities concerning means on two dimensions. The first dimension is that running from multilateralism to unilateralism; the second is that from exclusively military to exclusively nonmilitary actions. There is substantial evidence that for American publics and elites the events of 9/11 involved major losses—to a sense of safety at home, of global primacy, and of dominance in instruments of war and armed violence central to national pride and international order and progress (Bobrow and Boyer forthcoming). In effect, those events presented a potential loss-imposing domino effect, and responses to them would be justification advantaged as inherently defensive. A warranted response would be proportional to the envisaged chain of losses, rather than to the actual casualties of 9/11 and its direct economic costs. Normal prudence and risk-aversion considerations and their advocates in the policy process would be disadvantaged, and the terrorism likely to be inflicted by a particular response would be discounted. The jump in losses incurred and anticipated shifted the appeal of means toward the unilateral and military ends of the dimensions of means just mentioned. To hark back to our earlier discussion, multilateralism and nonmilitary means are inferior in their aura of power to unilateralism and military, coercive means.

Prospect theory also suggests a tendency to project onto the later steps in a course of action the expectations (probabilities) that the earlier steps can be accomplished successfully at tolerable cost. That advantages counterterrorism lines of policy whose initial steps look very feasible and effective by exaggerating the likely success of later steps, and it disadvantages courses of action for which the opposite seems to be the case.[4] With regard to American responses to 9/11 and hostile terrorists, advantaged responses are ones that involve readily available means against which their targets lack an immediately effective counter capability, for example, warfare abroad and internal security at home using modern technologies. Responses that instead involve hard-to-muster means and for which opponents have immediate troublesome counters are disadvantaged even if, once those difficulties are overcome, such responses arguably might well do more to erode the root causes of hostile terrorist actions and capabilities. The unlevel nature of the policy-alternative playing field is made worse when policy communities find chance-of-success judgments about the initial steps in unilateral coercive action programs inherently clearer and more reliable than those for programs featuring multilateralism and less directly coercive emphases.

We also can make use of a substantial body of knowledge about the self-interest calculus of elected politicians and large bureaucracies. Those are of

---

[4] The excessive extrapolation from early steps marks administration conduct and interpretation of the far-from-over Afghan campaign.

course primarily the actors in the U.S. who generate, select, and implement terrorism-relevant courses of action. Studies in the rational-choice tradition on elected officials in democratic political systems emphasize their concern with reelection of themselves and colleagues in their faction and party. For incumbents, reelection-conducive strategies are those most promising in avoiding blame for what the electorate would view as policy failures, and in gaining credit for perceived policy successes. Relative gains in those respects matter as well—placing blame on competitors for office and denying them credit for any successes. The harvests of blame and credit are of course in large part a function of what is focused on by the electorate, and that too becomes a target of manipulation.

From such perspectives, 9/11 posed several challenges to the Bush II administration, as it would also have to a Gore administration. The first was to avoid blame for defective prevention, for precaution deficits. Among the general strategies for blame avoidance by a new set of incumbents, that of attributing losses to a previous presidency was much less than fully available, given the historical record (Bobrow 2002a). We would expect emphasis then to be on blame-avoidance strategies that were more available. One such strategy is to characterize the source of the bad events (the Al Qaeda network) as being of such great capability and commitment that it would have been unreasonable to expect prevention. That is often accompanied by characterizing the bad event as unprecedented and marking the advent of a new era, circumstances under which it was reasonable to have had a precaution deficit. Another is to portray precaution deficits as stemming from well-intentioned conformity to public preferences along the lines of "we were only doing what you wanted" by not interfering with customary civil functions (for example airport operations) and not relaxing constraints on internal-security services. Still another is to shift blame to third parties. Those can be lower-level, subordinate organizations, particularly ones already of low repute (such as the Immigration and Naturalization Service, or INS). All those "escape hatches" have been used by the current American administration.

It seems worth noting that these blame-avoiding strategies commend themselves in part because they play to an area of overlapping interests between a current administration and the political party opposing it, especially recent and current opposition officeholders. More specifically, prominent Democrats had something to gain by keeping attention away from what they had done by way of prevention while controlling the Executive and Congressional branches.[5] In effect, elected politicians of both parties had a "class interest" in avoiding blame for 9/11.

---

[5] As early as 1993, U.S. Government exercises reported widely to relevant executive-branch agencies showed awareness of the possible use of commercial airliners "as bombs to destroy major landmarks" (Abshire 2002, 21).

Yet perhaps the most effective blame-avoiding strategies are those that shift attention from the past to the present and future and to credit-gaining actions. It becomes easier to gain credit for nonrecurrence of bad events if their source is portrayed as truly thirsting to cause more harm and having the capacity to do so.[6] Actions to regain what has been lost and may be lost in the future can more readily provide credit if they are visible and dramatic (creating a Department of Homeland Security) and seem to be immediate successes (displacing the Taliban and invading and occupying Iraq rather then enduring protracted WMD inspections and containment). Of course such credit is fragile and subject to erosion. Retaining such additions to a political bank account can be aided by shifting the attention of the media, and thus voters, to other terrorist threats and counterterrorist opportunities (like the "Axis of Evil') before erosion or ennui develops (as with the accomplishments of the Afghan campaign).

The blame/credit game probably cannot be avoided; indeed, it is likely to be played vigorously in a world of rational-choice politics. That will happen even if politicians and the electorate accept the previously mentioned yardsticks of an appropriate response to terrorism received. In any event, terms in the ratio of terrorism inflicted to terrorism reduced become targets for manipulation, as does the boundary between terrorism and defense. Consider the efforts of the Bush II administration to proclaim Saddam Hussein's regime to have a major and almost certainly deliverable WMD capability, and sharing it with Al Qaeda. Consider efforts to show determined attention to reduce the suffering of foreign civilians from American counterterrorist military actions in Afghanistan and Iraq, and to portray uncooperative members of the United Nations Security Council as being to blame for the lack of a multilateral imprimatur and sufficiently vigorous inspections of Iraq to avoid invasion and occupation.

Rational-choice perspectives also speak to the tendencies of large bureaucracies to relate to a policy problem. Some of those tendencies relate to avoiding blame for a policy failure, and to earning credit for policy achievements. Surely publicly announced FBI and CIA actions since 9/11 fit with these tendencies, as does resistance to Congressional investigation. There also are tendencies for bureaucracies to capitalize on opportunities provided to secure larger budgets, and to make themselves central to an issue area of great interest to a president and Congress. Bureaus do so largely by bringing out of their files pieces of their repertoire and items on their "wish lists" from the past, which had been shelved under political and societal pressure.

Events like 9/11 may be genuinely repugnant to individual members of a rational-choice bureaucracy, but they also are opportunities. Prevention

---

[6] Such a maneuver can also lessen the degree of blame for any recurrence.

failures can be used to justify agency claims on additional resources for redoubled efforts.[7] Once given, such increases will tend to be allocated in ways that enlist interest groups viewed as helpful for future budget cycles. Budgets have of course increased substantially for the new and old agencies most associated with the administration's response to terrorism, and indeed some Democratic politicians compete with the administration for the status of biggest-increase advocate. The bulk of those increases go to uses favoring the stakeholders seen as likely to be especially useful in an agency's pursuit of resources, even when those are not the uses of maximum immediate relevance to reducing anti-American terrorism at home or abroad or the damage incidents can cause (for a review of the 2003 Bush budget proposals and some alternatives see O'Hanlon 2002a, 2002b).

From an agency perspective, playing a central role in a matter of the highest presidential priority holds clear attractions for potential direct and indirect benefits. None will want to be left out of or seem inattentive or irrelevant to the war on terrorism but will instead strive to get a good seat on the bandwagon.[8] No agency will want to be displaced by rival agencies, but it can be motivated by that threat to be more "helpful" (a probable CIA reaction to Secretary of Defense Rumsfeld's intelligence-analysis shop). Here too there will be a sense of opportunity, a choice to resurrect courses of action that were previously envisioned and desired but were blocked. For example, at the FBI and perhaps some American foreign-intelligence agencies one would expect a revival (and indeed extension) of programs for monitoring an expanded list of persons of interest, disrupting groups that are not reliably supportive of the war on terrorism, and overstepping innocent-until-proven-guilty limits on deten-tion. All of those have historical precedent for the Bureau (and indeed for presidents). Profiling by demographic-group similarity to known terror-ists (in this case Moslems and persons of Middle Eastern appearance) can be expected to seem efficient, and even to be encouraged at the field level by Washington-set performance measures by a blame-avoiding FBI. More broadly, there will be moves to portray already desired programs as having a major, terrorism-relevant dual-use element (for example, by the Centers for Disease Control). All of these responses have been visible since 9/11.

Of course, neither politicians, bureaucrats, nor members of the electorate come to counterterrorism choices with a blank slate. Beliefs already held matter as they enter into the tendencies discussed earlier. The

---

[7] The subtext for such maneuvers is to persuade appropriators that providing budget increases will avoid leaks placing blame on them for the previous inadequacy of resources.

[8] For agencies with a longer view and aware of the changes in White House agendas over time, there will simultaneously be efforts (perhaps through leaks) to maintain professional credibility in ways for which cabinet members can deny responsibility.

import of these beliefs depends on their content for Americans.[9] Four sets of already held beliefs are especially relevant to our theme: (1) the available and appropriate American world role and its associated rights and obligations; (2) positive and negative images of foreigners; (3) major external threats to America; and (4) the proper role of government in domestic matters. Politicians of all stripes prefer to place their policies in the zone of permission provided by public opinion. When their preferences are for policies outside that zone, they endeavor to portray them in ways that move their policies into it. In sum, politicians tend both to cater to and to manipulate public opinion. Also, they may themselves hold beliefs similar to those held by many of their constituents. The combination of genuinely held beliefs and successful manipulation (marketing) can then deter high officials from public-policy reversals. They, and perhaps their country, become entrapped by their previous proclamations.

For persistent majorities of Americans, the U.S. has been seen as the most important country in the world, notable for its generosity and benign intentions for the rest of the world. What is good for America is predominantly good for the world, since Americans are the champions of progress, and our activism is indispensable for achieving it. One would then expect politicians to play with considerable success after 9/11 to a sense of national innocence and to a right and obligation to strike back at those who would terrorize us or even fail to support any counterterrorist response Washington might choose to adopt. Because we are good and benign, our having the capacity and the will to crush those who now or in the future may threaten us is not merely acceptable; it is a cardinal presidential responsibility. Because we are good and benign, those who actively seek to hurt us are inherently evil. Because we are good and benign, those who actively support or passively tolerate such activists are at best misinformed and at worst evil as well. Counterterrorist prescriptions that are focused on systemic causes rather than evil actors would be unlikely to resonate widely among the American public. The persuasiveness of systemic-cause explanations for dislike of the U.S. encountered another limitation in the prevailing belief that America was for the most part liked and respected abroad.

The public view of warranted American military intervention before 9/11 emphasized three conditions : (1) response to a direct attack on Americans at home or abroad; (2) response involving multilateral support and United Nations approval; and (3) response without more than a few U.S. military casualties. For elites, those conditions were less important as warrants for such steps. In the post 9/11 context, we would expect elites to turn to military interventions even in the absence of the first two

---

[9] Opinion-survey data for the period before 9/11 can be found in Bobrow and Boyer forthcoming.

conditions, while making substantial efforts to comply with the third. At the same time, they would prefer that the public believe that the first condition was being honored by fostering the view that targets of interventions were directly linked to recent or looming attacks on Americans. They would also have incentives to show that a good-faith effort had been made to seek multilateral support and even a U.N. mandate. Given their preferences for intervention and the enhanced credibility 9/11 provided for assertions of a direct-attack threat, they would be inclined to proceed anyway. Of course, the special receptivity to power confirming anticipated reactions would favor overestimates of the likelihood of multilateral support, (for example, by Turkey) and a U.N. mandate. That tendency would be reinforced for the continuing prosecution of the war on terrorism as the earlier steps, such as the Afghan campaign, confirmed those anticipations.

With regard to images of others, public opinion in general located them on a dimension of relations with the U.S.—friendly to hostile, allies to enemies. Those images do not include much about others' domestic political context or pressing foreign-policy issues in the regions in which they were located. As for particular foreign nations, those especially well-regarded members of a "with America" club were the major members of the Organization for Economic Cooperation and Development—that is, the rich industrialized democracies of the global North. None of those nations has a predominantly Moslem population or is located in the Middle East. Those regarded especially negatively were Iraq, Iran, North Korea, and Cuba. We would expect terror-inflicting responses to 9/11 to emphasize the negatively viewed nations as targets. When there had been little in the way of specific opinion about particular terrorist networks or states hosting them, we would expect responses to 9/11 to emphasize the cultural distance between them and ourselves. A U.S. administration would view support from club members as especially confirming of chosen policy, and would face a special burden of justification without it.[10]

Before 9/11, public perceptions of external threats to America featured international terrorism and proliferation of weapons of mass destruction. Accordingly, after 9/11, the Bush II administration would be expected to try to fuse the two threats, thus magnifying the importance of each. Opponents would have the burden of distinguishing between the two threats and discrediting U.S. policy on both counts. The administration could make doing so especially difficult by characterizing the sources of each threat as clearly outside a pro-American club and cultural community.

---

[10] Given their presumed closeness to the U.S., a reaction of shock and being betrayed might also be expected.

Finally, prior beliefs about the role of the American government in domestic matters clearly imposed a set of constraints on central government domestic powers and "interference from Washington". That is, the mandate for national defense was much less hedged than that for domestic matters. Further, public opinion had tended to give national politicians credit for domestic policy ventures even if their implementation in large measure involved unfunded mandates placed on subnational levels of government.

For responses to 9/11, these patterns suggest administration efforts to make domestic measures part of national defense falling under its mandate. Expanded central-government authority curtailing civil-liberty norms would be portrayed as directed against foreign enemies actual or potential residing in the U.S. with ties to international terrorism and even WMD proliferation. That could be made easier if the targeted populations were to fit with those nations and cultures already viewed negatively. Tolerance for domestic security measures could be sought by portraying them as preserving rather than infringing on the rights of "real Americans". Finally, there would be a temptation to practice policies that amount to unfunded mandates, and to pursue political credit without providing the resources to the state and local organs of government on the front lines of enhanced domestic safety.[11]

International-Relations Criteria and Policy Evaluation

The previous section presented likely policy tendencies and provided some illustrations of post-9/11 policies in line with them. That discussion does not in itself provide a basis for concluding that their aggregate consequences amount to the U.S. losing to terrorism. It does suggest that the policies chosen are neither surprising nor easily discarded. Reasoning from the past to the present is of course easier than reasoning from the present to the future. Yet we have available to us some criteria for policy effectiveness that are well-established in international-relations analysis based on substantial historical experience. Foresight about the war on terrorism can at least start by examining how well the policies chosen fit with those criteria.

There are several major schools in international-relations analysis (each with its own sub-sects).[12] Realists emphasize relative and absolute gains in power to advance vital national interests. For them, the U.S.

---

[11] Damage limiting domestic safety consequences would be particularly small as the delegated increase in responsibilities coincided with a period of acute financial stress at the state and local levels or pertinent private-sector firms, such as airlines. There is of course both irony and risk in an administration emphasizing terrorist homeland threats acting in this fashion.

[12] Such scholastic sectarianism should not be allowed to obscure the actuality that all three perspectives are grasping part of the international-relations elephant (Bobrow 1996).

losing to terrorism would amount to acting in ways that work to generate relative and absolute losses. Neoliberal institutionalists emphasize the construction of institutionalized security communities that adhere to common standards, treat cooperation with others in the community as a central policy, and engage in collective action against outsiders who violate community standards. Here the U.S. losing to terrorism would amount to fracturing of existing historically valued security communities and their institutions, marginalizing cooperation, and turning to unilateral rather than collective action. Constructivists emphasize ensembles of ideas that are normative and pragmatic about the national self and others, about ends, and about means for their pursuit. For them, the U.S. losing to terrorism would amount to adopting ends and means that clash with valued elements of our national self-conception, involve unwarranted characterizations of others, or are mutually incompatible–and fostering among non-Americans constructions of the U.S. as arrogant, hostile, dangerous, or even evil.

Realist Criteria

For realists, the pursuit and application of power are always matters of strategic interaction; that is, policies should take into account their effect on future power ratios over a series of moves and countermoves. They assume others will do so as well, in a game without end. The best-practice rules suggested by that perspective include the following:

First, avoid actions that increase the chances of others coming together to check your power, or accelerating acquisition of power resources, lest you try to overwhelm them in the future (Wolfers 1962; Aron 1966). As 9/11 recedes into the past, a number of current and emerging major powers have found additional reason to explore joint action to pose a balance to the U.S. Some others, most obviously North Korea and Iran, have chosen to accelerate their WMD programs. The display of overwhelming military power does not necessarily produce more than temporary compliance with the U.S., but it can instead impel efforts to emulate it or find new "asymmetric" counters to it (e.g., Nair 1991).

Second, avoid actions that even if at first highly damaging to your enemies are likely to fuel a future flow of resources to them. The actuality of American invasion, occupation, and planned rule of Iraq has substantial chances of generating new cadres for anti-American terrorist networks. Indeed, the focus on bin Laden and Al Qaeda has already elevated their standing as champions of opposition to the U.S., and terrorism as a means of challenging American might.

Third, recognize that associates in ad hoc coalitions with you are doing so to advance their own interests, and do not assume that these are always similar to yours.[13] That applies even more to allies rented for the occasion through economic incentives. Failure to do so may lead to inattention to your in effect being used. Some of the "partners" in the war on terrorism raise such possibilities, for example, Pakistan, China, and Russia. The general point suggests skepticism about the merits of cultivating new partners (especially ones who contribute little additional power) if it means alienating previous ones who have more to contribute.

Fourth, respect two Clausewitzian principles—that war is a continuation of politics in order to achieve political ends, and the "fog of war". If the political end is a stable and pro-American Islamic world, specific measures should be conducive to that end. Many measures now seem not to do that, including those asserted to lead to a wave of democratization. There is ample evidence of the instability associated with transitions to democracies for polities lacking substantial domestic roots and located in undemocratic neighborhoods (Mansfield and Snyder 1995). In any event, democracies often are more responsive to domestic opinion than autocracies are, and there is little reason to think that Middle Eastern publics are less "anti-American" than many currently ruling nondemocratic elites in that region. The fog of war applies not just to the conduct of a U.S. military campaign but also to uncertainties and surprises about third-party behavior and the adaptive gambits of targets of the war on terrorism. Claims to "know" that opponents will crumble and that a military campaign will conform to scenarios preferred by the U.S. scant the fog of war factor.

Fifth, avoid military actions against your enemy that if they fail to eliminate the enemy will disperse it without disabling it, and thus make it harder to find and target, monitor and contain. The Afghan campaign failed to eliminate either bin Laden or Al Qaeda, and it had those other consequences.

Sixth, recognize that power is not just material capability but its credibility as well. Since the U.S. began the war on terrorism when it was widely thought to be the world's greatest power, credibility arguably called for effective and successful countermeasures to the perpetrators of 9/11. The flip side of that coin is that it makes power credibility very vulnerable. Claimed and perceived superiority lessens what an opponent needs to impose on the U.S. by way of costs and to demonstrate in terms of survival than the opponent would if perceived American power were less. The requirements of a "victory" that would bolster American credibility become more demanding the more an administration uses its power assets to achieve it. It is not enough to militarily defeat an

---

[13] That would include recognizing that the support of some European states for the American war on Iraq may have less to do with their view of the merits of that action and more to do with a desired redistribution of power in the newly enlarged Europe away from France and Germany.

enemy—that result was already taken for granted. Maintaining credibility requires the clear achievement of the objectives of a declared U.S. war on terrorism, not just winning battles and campaigns. Erosion of credibility requires only that the opponent demonstrate some degree of survival, or perhaps only "bloodying" America and Americans. Success in those endeavors is especially persuasive when it is certified by the actions of American authorities—for example, proclaiming a continuing imminent threat to homeland security and acknowledging WMD proliferation by an axis of evil state like North Korea.

Seventh, assume that opponents are closely monitoring your domestic systems for strains that would create pressure to back off from your chosen power-exercising policies. With regard to the watch kept on the U.S., relevant signs of strain include weak economic performance and domestic dissent as they present political incentives to abandon policies in use. Perceived strains encourage opponents. The limp performance of the American economy since 9/11 does that. So too does a pattern of protest. U.S. administration policies that mobilize dissent at home are inadvisable. Further, resort to controversial measures to suppress or cow domestic dissent is welcomed by opponents and creates an administration "off-message" with respect to the declared focus and concentration of resources on current and future terrorists.

Neoliberal Institutionalist Criteria

For neoliberal institutionalists, the pursuit of security focuses on the broadening and deepening of security communities. Doing so will increase a community's propensity and capacity for collective action against violations of its common norms, and will affirm that they are based on shared, mutual interests and international futures that advance them. Collective-action institutions are viewed as security assets, assets that represent substantial investments in the past warranting protection from erosion by friction and antagonism among members about any single issue or case. The best-practice rules suggested by that perspective include the following:

First, treat disagreements among members about specific matters as reasoned disagreements among peers rather than as arbitrary and illegitimate nay-saying. Important elements of the Bush II administration have instead attacked the motives and character of other member governments of NATO and the U.N.

Second, refrain from unilateral actions except in the face of irreversible and highly dangerous imminent threats. Absent overwhelming evidence of such threats and the inadequacy of communitywide-agreed measures to temper them, show restraint. That rule has been at the heart of the debate about WMD inspections in Iraq versus the U.S. decision to abort reliance on inspections and associated measures in place since the Gulf War.

Third, avoid creating a record that suggests a lack of commitment to the community's norms and to deepening and broadening them. The Bush II administration has instead created just such a record with regard, for example, to the Kyoto environmental agreement, the International Criminal Court, the reproductive rights of women, and of course the invasion of Iraq and announced plans for post-invasion governance of it. With specific respect to 9/11, the administration responded to the unprecedented European commitments immediately following it, which invoked NATO Article 5 to come to the defense of the U.S., with what amounted to contempt ("Breaking Up . . ." 2003).

Fourth, preserve rather than discard international institutions that on balance have a historical record of usefulness and are likely to be turned to for assistance in the future. The U.N. and NATO have those characteristics, including—for major ongoing aspects of the war on terrorism—pacification and reconstruction of what have been state sanctuaries for terrorists, interfering with terrorist finances, and intelligence sharing. Yet important players in the Bush II administration and their domestic supporters have suggested that they have failed a litmus test of worth, and are instead making themselves "irrelevant."

Fifth, make clear that any unilateral departure from respect for a security community's norms and laboriously established processes is a regrettably necessary, temporary exception rather than an overdue precedent. A variety of doctrinal statements and public declarations by prominent members of the administration, including President Bush, Vice-President Cheney, and Secretary of Defense Rumsfeld have emphasized setting precedents for future unilateral military actions.

Constructivist Criteria

For constructivists, nations, populations, and their governments exist in believed worlds, worlds in which they have particular rights and obligations and warranted expectations. The rights and obligations follow from values prominent in self-conceptions of self—what one's polity has properly championed, currently represents, and should embody in the future. Those favor apparently compatible courses of instrumental action, and they pose troubling tensions with others. The former are more likely to secure widespread domestic support and seem righteous. The latter are more likely to encounter domestic dissent and condemnation, at least to the point of self-doubt and perhaps to the point of guilt. How particular courses of action get coded is largely a function of widely and deeply held historical memories and the images they evoke of oneself and salient

others. Those memories and images in turn suggest warranted expectations about the consequences and likely retrospective evaluations of
particular courses of action. We have a stake in seeming to conform to
our beliefs about ourselves in the world, and we have a stake in others
holding a compatible view of our role in the world. Acting accordingly, or
at least being seen to act accordingly, has substantial attractions for
politicians as strategic actors, and perhaps even in terms of their own self-
evaluation. Miscalculations and nasty surprises are especially likely when
the very policies American leaders and publics view as conforming instead
fuel incompatible constructions of the U.S. by others.[14] The best-practice
rules suggested by a constructivist perspective include the following:

First, invoke widely believed rights as the motivation for action, but
not to the extent of making the invocation seem insincere or readily
discredited on evidentially plausible grounds. The war on terrorism has
certainly been rich with invocations of such widely believed American
rights as safety and self-defense. Yet actions consonant with those
justifications have not been consistently taken—for example, the passive
response to the North Korean nuclear program. The plausibility of such
justifications for the invasion and occupation of Iraq hinges on the
discovery of a substantial and imminent WMD threat to the U.S.

Second, invoke widely believed obligations as the rationale for action,
but with the same limiting conditions as the citing of rights. Here too the
invocations have been ample—for example, to implement U.N. resolutions, to lead the international community, to champion freedom, to
punish and end gross violations of human rights in ways that override
state sovereignty. The genuineness of commitments to such duties in
pursuit of the war on terrorism continues to be called into question by
selective rejection of international leadership on related issues, and the
embrace prior to and during the war on terrorism of regimes that
themselves engage in gross violations of human rights.

Third, avoid diluting the appeal of widely accepted rights and obligations by actions counter to others of substantial standing—or at least
appear regretful about doing so. Domestically, that rule seems to be
under eager violation in at least two major ways. One is of course cutting
back civil liberties and due process—reducing being free in the hope of
being safe as the American Civil Liberties Union would put it. A second,
is the claim to a divine mandate rather than a civil one for major parts of
the war on terrorism, especially in the face of counter judgments by major
religious figures. A third violation is less willful than an unavoidable
consequences of the means chosen—inflicting pain and suffering on
noncombatants in foreign theaters of war.

---

[14] For evidence on what prevailing American constructions have been see Bobrow and
Boyer forthcoming.

Fourth, respect the recognitions after similar violations in the past that their costs exceeded their benefits in terms of damage to declared American values, domestic divisiveness, and even some shame. With respect to civil rights, there was the Palmer response to some thirty-three domestic bombings around the end of World War I, the dispossession and detention of Japanese Americans during World War II, the blacklists of the McCarthy period, and the domestic spying of the Vietnam War era. As for "collateral damage", there was the discord and attenuation of popular support following widespread media coverage of some of the terror inflicted by massive bombing and free-fire zones in Vietnam and by misdirected weapons in the more recent attacks on Serbia. Disrespect for the post-hoc evaluation of those precedents casts doubt on claims that new violations will be minimal (for example, the Total Information Awareness program), especially when their administrative agents have violation records.

Fifth, exercise due diligence to avoid acting in ways that lead to foreign constructions which contradict your self-concept or place that concept in a zero-sum relationship with what foreigners hold to be their rights and obligations. For international affairs, abiding by these rules has two general implications. One involves bolstering rather than weakening those abroad who share our widely held domestic view of the proper and actual American world role. Instead, aspects of the war on terrorism undermine foreigners who have contended that the U.S. is committed to even-handed tolerance of religious and ethnic diversity, loath to invade foreign nations, respectful of international institutions and agreements, considerate of the needs of friendly governments to accommodate to popular opinion, and self-restrained and proportional rather than panicked and obsessive in its use of national power. The other general implication involves eschewing actions that salient foreign historical memories will tend to interpret as indicative of a zero-sum American stance. In the context of the war on terrorism, a number of administration behaviors instead have directly called up such memories of being conquered and subordinated, memories widely available for recall in the Middle East, Asia, and Latin America. Whatever the care shown in some administration actions, negative cues have been provided by mentions of the crusades, ultimatums to be either "with us or against us", plans for occupation governments, and coalitions with former, sometimes brutal imperial powers.[15] Sending such signals undercuts the legitimacy within their own countries and groups of those indigenous personalities and organizations receiving support from Washington.

---

[15] An obvious example of the last is the role assigned to Britain, the direct and indirect ruler of the newly created Iraqi state after World War I, in the general invasion campaign and in Basra in particular.

Sixth, take into account the prevailing constructions held by your primary opponent no matter how unwarranted or appalling one may find them, and credit your opponents, with manifest skill, commitment, and adaptiveness in acting in their terms. For the U.S. in the war on terrorism, that would include several understandings about enemies. From its enemies' perspective, the U.S. was at war with them long before 9/11 and will continue to be. Co-existence is not an option the U.S. will make available to them. From their perspective, it is legitimate and indeed responsible to conduct unconventional warfare contrary to what we claim to be established international rules of conduct, since to do otherwise amounts to accepting a path of elimination and ignores our violations of those rules. From their perspective, priority should go to efforts to understand how the U.S. will prefer to act against them and American cost sensitivities.

Conclusions Reached and Conclusions Avoided

This essay has argued that the U.S. is losing to terrorism. That is, the current administration has adopted policies unlikely to meet the test of successful security policy put forward a half-century ago on the eve of World War II—fostering a context in which Americans can live with substantial freedom from fear (Earle 1941). In large measure, that is because of incentives and dynamics built into our policy processes and deeply rooted popular beliefs. Whether for those or other reasons, the consequence has been to wage the war on terrorism in ways counter to established criteria for successful great-power statecraft. We are on a dangerous path for reasons far more troubling than those emphasized in critical allegations about the psychological dynamics of the current President Bush or the sincerity or moral character of his administration.

References

Abshire, David.. 2002. *Lessons for the 21st Century: Vulnerability and Surprise*. Washington, D.C.: Center for the Study of the Presidency.
Aron, Raymond.. 1966. *Peace and War*. New York: Doubleday.
Bobrow, Davis B. 1996. "Complex Insecurity: Implications of a Disease Metaphor." *International Studies Quarterly* 40, no. 4 (December): 435–50.
———. 2001. "Visions of (In)Security and American Strategic Style." *International Studies Perspectives* 2 no. 1 (February): 1–12.
———. 2002a. "America and Terrorism: Interpretation and Response." In *Im Schatten des Terrorismus* edited by Patra Bendel and Mathias Hildebrandt, 185–96. Wiesbaden: Westdeutscher Verlag.
———. 2002b. "A Changing American World Role?" *Zeitschrift fur Politikwissenschaft* 12, no. 1/02: 83–96.

———. and Mark A. Boyer. Forthcoming. *Defensive Internationalism: Providing Global Public Goods in an Uncertain World*. Ann Arbor, Mich: University of Michigan Press.

Earle, Edward Mead. 1941. "American Security—Its Changing Conditions." *Annals of the American Academy of Political and Social Science* 218 (November): 186–93.

"Breaking Up—How Iraq Divided a Durable Alliance and Isolated U.S." 2003. *Wall Street Journal* (March 27): 1ff.

Knorr, Klaus, and Patrick Morgan, eds. 1983. *Strategic Military Surprise*. New York: Transaction Books.

Levy, Jack S. 1996. "Loss Aversion, Framing, and Bargaining: The Implications of Prospect Theory." *International Political Science Review* 17, no. 2 (April): 179–95.

Mansfield, Edward D., and Jack Snyder 1995. "Democratization and the Danger of War." *International Security* 20, no. 1 (): 5–38.

Nair, V.K.. 1991. *War in the Gulf: Lessons for the Third World*. New Delhi: Lancer International.

O'Hanlon, Michael. 2002. *Defense Policy Choices for the Bush Administration*. 2nd edition. Washington, D.C.: Brookings Institution Press.

———. et al. 2002. *Protecting the American Homeland*. Washington, D.C.: Brookings Institution Press.

President of the United States. 1998. "A National Security Strategy for a New Century." In *America's Strategic Choices* edited by Michael E. Brown et al. revised edition 351–411. Cambridge, Mass.: MIT Press, 2000.

———. 2002. *The National Security Strategy of the United States of America*. www.comw.org/qdr.

Wolfers, Arnold. 1952. "National Security as an Ambiguous Symbol." *Political Science Quarterly* 67, no. 4 (December): 481–502.

———. 1962. *Discord and Collaboration*. Baltimore, Md.: Johns Hopkins University Press.

11

PREEMPTIVE WAR, AMERICANISM, AND ANTI-AMERICANISM

DOMENICO LOSURDO

The Myth and Reality of Leftist Anti-Americanism

The March 2003 invasion of Iraq was accompanied by a curious ideological phenomenon: the attempt to silence the large and unprecedented protest movement by accusing it of anti-Americanism. With still new wars on the horizon, this supposed anti-Americanism was and continues to be depicted as something more than just a flawed political position; it is considered a disease, a symptom of maladjustment to modernity and a deafness to the rationales of democracy. This disease—it is claimed—subsumes anti-Americans from the right and from the left, and marks the worst pages of European history. Thus—the conclusion is drawn—to criticize Washington and preemptive war represents an actual menace. It would be easy to respond to this by calling attention to the anti-Europeanism mounting on the other side of the Atlantic, one with a long tradition behind it. It is quite significant that, in this political and ideological climate, no one remembers the terror perpetrated by the Ku Klux Klan in the name of "pure Americanism," or the "one hundred percent Americanism" opposed to blacks and whites guilty of challenging white supremacy (in MacLean 1994, 4–5, 14). In a similar manner, no one seems to remember the McCarthy witch hunt for those nurturing un-American ideas or sentiments.

Let us consider the main question here. Is there any historical foundation to the anti-democratic equating of left-wing and right-wing anti-Americanism? Indeed, the young Marx declares the United States to be the "country of complete political emancipation" and "the most perfect example of the modern state," one that ensures the dominion of the bourgeoisie without excluding a priori any social class from the benefits of political rights (see Losurdo 1993, 21–22). Already here one can notice a certain indulgence: hardly absent, in the United States class discrimination takes on a "racial" shape.

Engels's position is even more drastically pro-American. After distinguishing between the "abolition of the state" in the Communist sense, in the feudal sense, and in the bourgeois sense, he adds: "In bourgeois countries the abolition of the state means a reduction in state power to the

Translated, from the Italian, by Jon and Marella Morris

level of that in North America. There, class conflicts develop only
incompletely; the collisions between classes are constantly camouflaged
by the emigration to the West of the proletarian overpopulation. The
intervention of the state power, reduced to a minimum in the East, does
not exist at all in the West" (Marx and Engels 1955, 7: 288). More than
just an example of the abolition of the state (even though in the bourgeois
sense), the West seems to be synonymous with an increase in the sphere of
freedom: there is no mention of the plight of the American Indians, just as
there is silence regarding the slavery of blacks. The position is similar in
Origins of the Family, Private Property, and the State: the United States is
referred to as the country where, at least during certain periods of its
history and in certain geographical areas, the political and military
apparatus removed from society tends to disappear (Marx and Engels
1955, 21: 166). The year is 1884: at this time blacks are not only deprived
of the political rights they had acquired immediately after the Civil War
but are also bound to a system of apartheid and subjected to a violence
that even includes the cruelest forms of lynching. In the American south
the state was perhaps weak; much stronger was the Ku Klux Klan, an
expression of a civil society, yet a civil society which can itself be the locus
of applied power, and brutal power at that. Just one year prior to the
publication of Engels's book, the United States Supreme Court declared
unconstitutional a federal law that would have prohibited the segregation
of blacks in the workplace or in services (like railways) managed by
private companies, on the grounds that, by definition, such companies
were removed from any and all government interference.

Above all it is important to observe that, at the level of international
politics, Engels seems to echo the ideology of manifest destiny as it
emerges in his celebration of the war against Mexico: thanks also to the
"courage of American volunteers," "beautiful California was wrenched
from the indolent Mexicans who knew not what to do with it." By taking
advantage of the new, enormous conquests, "the dynamic Yankees" have
brought new life to the production and circulation of wealth, to "world
trade," and to the diffusion of "civilization" (*Zivilisation*) (Marx and
Engels 1955, 6: 273–75). Engels overlooks a fact decried in the same time
period by American abolitionists: the expansion of the United States
meant the expansion of the institution of slavery.

As for the history of the Communist movement as such, the influence
of Taylorism and Fordism upon Lenin and Gramsci is well known. In
1923, Nikolai Bukharin goes even further: "We need Marxism plus
Americanism" (in Figes 2003, 24). A year later, Stalin seems to regard
the very same country that participated in the intervention against Soviet
Russia with so much admiration that he tells the Bolshevik cadres if they
really aspire to the heights of the "principles of Leninism," they will have
to learn to assimilate "the pragmatic American spirit." Here, "Americanism" and the "pragmatic American spirit" signify not only concreteness

but also the intolerance of prejudices, and they ultimately call to mind democracy. As Stalin explains in 1932, the United States is certainly a capitalistic country; however, "the traditions of industry and the practice of production have something of democracy about them, which cannot be said of the old capitalist countries in Europe, where the genteel spirit of feudal aristocracy lives on" (see Losurdo 1997, 81–86).

Somehow, Heidegger is right to criticize the United States and the Soviet Union for representing, from a philosophical viewpoint, the same thing: "the unleashing of technique" and "the transformation of man into mass" (see Losurdo 2001, 105). There is no doubt that the Bolsheviks find the American notions of melting pot and self-made man highly appealing. On the other hand, they find other aspects of Americans to be thoroughly repugnant. In 1924, *Correspondance Internationale* (the French version of the Communist International organ) published an article written by a young Indochinese immigrant to the United States: while he has great admiration for the American Revolution, he is horrified by the practice of lynching blacks in the South. One of these mass spectacles is brutally described: "The Black is cooked, browned, burned. But he deserves to die twice instead of once. He is therefore hanged, or more exactly, what is left of his corpse is hanged. . . . When everybody has had enough, the corpse is brought down. The rope is cut into small pieces which will be sold for three or five dollars each." Yet the loathing of the system of white supremacy does not result in a general condemnation of the United States: yes, the Ku Klux Klan possesses all "the brutality of fascism," but it will eventually be defeated, not just by blacks, Jews, and Catholics (all victims at various levels) but by "all decent Americans" (in Wade 1997, 203–4). This is hardly indiscriminate anti-Americanism.

A "Wonderful Country of the Future"

It is an Indochinese man who compares the Ku Klux Klan to fascism, but the similarities between the two movements are evident to American writers of the time as well. More than just occasionally, and both positively and negatively, the white-robed men in the American South are compared to the Italian "black shirts" and the German "brown shirts." After pointing out the similarities between the Ku Klux Klan and Nazi movements, a present-day American scholar comes to the following conclusion: "Had the Depression not hit Germany as hard as it subsequently did, National Socialism might today be dismissed as the Klan sometimes is: a historical curiosity whose doom was foreordained" (MacLean 1994, 184). In other words, more so than a different political and ideological history, what explains the failure of the Invisible Empire in the United States and the coming of the Third Reich in Germany is the different economic contexts. This claim might be a bit excessive. And yet when the essential contributions by the United States and other countries (first of all the Soviet Union) in the struggle against Hitler's Germany and the Axis powers is brought up in order to silence criticism against Washington's current policies, only part of the truth is spoken. The other part of the story consists in the important role that reactionary movements and American racists played by inspiring agitation in Germany that would eventually lead to the rise of Hitler.

Already in the 1920s relationships, exchanges, and collaborations promoting antiblack and anti-Jewish racism were forming between the Ku Klux Klan and right-wing German extremists. Even in 1937 the Nazi ideologist Alfred Rosenberg hails the United States as a "wonderful country of the future," one that has the merit of formulating the brilliant "new idea of a racial state," an idea that will now need to be put into practice, "with young might" and through the expulsion and deportation of "blacks and yellows" (Rosenberg 1937, 673). One need only consider the laws passed immediately after the Third Reich's rise to power to realize how similar the situation is to that in the American South. Obviously, in Germany the position of Germans of Jewish origin corresponds to the position of African-Americans in the American South. Hitler clearly distinguishes, even on a juridical level, the position of Aryans with respect to that of Jews and the few mulattos living in Germany (at the end of World War I troops of color belonging to the French Army had participated in the occupation of the country). "The black question," writes Rosenberg, "is the most urgent of all the decisive issues in the United States"; and once the absurd notion of equality is eliminated with regard to the blacks, there is no reason why "the necessary consequences" should not be drawn "for yellows and Jews" as well (Rosenberg 1937, 668–69).

None of this should come as a surprise. Since the foundation of the Nazi plan was the construction of a racial state, what other possible models existed at the time? Rosenberg does mention South Africa, which must remain firmly held in white and "Nordic hands" (thanks to appropriate "laws" against the "Indians" as well as "blacks, mulattos, and Jews"), and serves as a "solid bulwark" to fend off the threat represented by the "black awakening" (Rosenberg 1937, 666). Yet, to some extent Rosenberg knows that the segregationist policy in South Africa was largely inspired by the system of white supremacy born in the United States after Reconstruction (Noer 1978, 106–7, 115, 125). Therefore, he focuses primarily upon the latter.

There exists yet another reason why the American republic represents an inspiration for the Third Reich. Hitler's goal is not a generic colonial expansionism but rather a continental empire to be created by the annexation and Germanization of the contiguous eastern territories. Germany is called upon to expand into eastern Europe as if it were the Wild West, and to treat the "natives" in the same way the American Indians were treated (see Losurdo 1996, 212–16), without ever losing sight of the American model, which the Führer hails for its "unprecedented inner force" (Hitler 1939, 153–54). Immediately after the invasion, Hitler proceeds to dismember Poland: one part is directly incorporated into the Great Reich (and from it the Poles are expelled); the rest becomes a "General Government" within which, declares Governor General Hans Frank, the Poles live as in "a sort of reservation": they are "under German jurisdiction," though they are not "German citizens" (in Ruge and Schumann 1977, 36). Here, the American model is followed almost literally: we cannot fail to notice a strong resemblance to the condition of the American Indians.

The Racial State in Germany and the United States

The American model leaves a deep mark even at the categorical and linguistic levels. The term *Untermensch*, which plays such a central and ruinous role in the theory and practice of the Third Reich, is nothing more than a translation of *Under Man*. The Nazi Rosenberg is well aware of this, and he expresses his admiration for the American author Lothrop Stoddard, who first coined the term, which appears as the subtitle (*The Menace of the Under Man*) of a book first published in New York in 1922 and then in German translation (*Die Drohung des Untermenschen*) three years later. As for its meaning, Stoddard states that it serves to indicate the mass of "savages and barbarians," "essentially uncivilizable and incorrigibly hostile to civilization," who must be dealt with in a radical manner in order to avoid the collapse of civilization. Even before being praised by Rosenberg, Stoddard had been commended by two American presidents (Harding and Hoover). He was later welcomed and honored in Berlin, where he met not only the most renowned representatives of Nazi eugenics but also the highest officials of the regime, including Hitler, who had already begun his campaign for the decimation and subjugation of the *Untermenschen*, the "natives" of eastern Europe.[1]

In the United States of white supremacy, as in the Germany gripped by the increasingly more powerful Nazi movement, the program to reestablish racial hierarchy is firmly linked to the project of eugenics. First of all, the best must be encouraged to procreate, so as to avoid the risk of "racial suicide" (*Rasseselbstmord*) that looms over whites. Sounding the alarm in 1918 is Oswald Spengler, who cites Theodore Roosevelt (Spengler 1980, 683). Indeed, Roosevelt's warning against the specter of "race suicide" or "race humiliation" goes hand in hand with his denunciation of the "diminution of the birth rate among the highest races," that is, "among the old native American stock." Obviously, the reference here is not to

---

[1] On the eugenics between the United States and Germany, see Kühl 1994, 61; the flattering judgment of President Harding is found at the beginning of the 1925 French version of Stoddard's book (*Le flot montant des peuples de couleur contre la suprématie mondiale des blancs*, translated by Abel Doysié. Paris: Payot, 1925).

Native American "savages" but to WASPs (see Roosevelt 1951, 1: 487, note 4, 647, 1113; 2: 1053).

Second, an unbridgeable gap must be created between servant races and master races, cleansing the latter of any waste and preparing them to face and break the revolt of the servant races, which, following the Bolshevik lead, have begun to spread around the world. Here, too, the findings of unbiased historical research are surprising. *Erbgesundheitslehre*, or *Rassenhygiene*, another keyword of Nazi ideology, is nothing more than a translation into German of *eugenics*, the new science invented in England during the second half of the nineteenth century by Francis Galton. Not by chance is this new science received most favorably in the United States, where the relationship between the "three races" and "natives," on the one hand, and the increasing mass of poor immigrants, on the other, is particularly problematic. Well before Hitler's rise to power, on the eve of World War I, a book is published in Munich entitled *Die Rassenhygiene in den Vereinigten Staaten von Nordamerika* (Racial hygiene in the United States of North America), which already in its title points to the United States as a model for "racial hygiene." The author, Géza von Hoffmann, vice-consul of the Austro-Hungarian Empire in Chicago, extols the United States for the "lucidity" and "pure practical reason" it has demonstrated in confronting, with the necessary energy, a very important problem that is instead so often ignored: for in the United States, to violate the laws that forbid sexual intercourse and interracial marriages can be punished with up to ten years in prison. And not only the people responsible for the act are liable to prosecution; so are their accomplices (Hoffmann 1913, 9: 67–68). Ten years later, in 1923, a German doctor, Fritz Lenz, complains that so far as "racial hygiene" is concerned, Germany is well behind the United States (Lifton 1986, 23). Even after the Nazis take power, the ideologues and "scientists" of race continue to hammer away: "Germany too has much to learn from the measures taken by the North Americans: they know their business" (Günther 1934, 465).

The eugenic measures passed immediately after the Nazi *Machtergreifung* aim to prevent the risk of "Volkstod" (Lifton 1986, 25), the "death of the people" or of the race. Once again the theme is that of race suicide. To prevent the suicide of the white race, which would mean the end of civilization, one must not hesitate to implement the most rigorous of measures, the most drastic of solutions, with regard to the "inferior races": if one of them—Theodore Roosevelt proclaims—should assault the "superior" race, the latter would respond with "a war of extermination," called upon "to put to death man, woman and child, exactly as if they were crusaders" (Roosevelt 1951, 2: 377). It is worth pointing out that a vague notion of "ultimate solution" regarding the black question had already appeared in a book published in Boston in 1913 (Fredrickson 1987, 258 note). Later, of course, the Nazis theorized and attempted to put into practice the "final solution" (*Endlösung*) to the "Jewish question."

Nazism as a Project of "White Supremacy" on a Worldwide Level

In the course of its history, the United States has directly had to face the problems resulting from the contact between different "races" and the influx of numerous immigrants from every part of the world. On the other hand, the angry racist movement that emerges at the end of the nineteenth century is a response to the Civil War and its radical Reconstruction period. Whereas the former property and slave owners suddenly find themselves, as rebels, without political rights, blacks go from being slaves to being full citizens with political rights. They often become part of the representative bodies, where, as legislators or managers, they somehow gain power over their former owners.

Let us now consider the experiences and emotions behind the unrest that leads to Nazism. During the nineteenth and twentieth centuries, the Ku Klux Klan and the theorists of "white supremacy" label the post-slavery United States, with its onslaught of immigrants coming from Europe's marginal countries and even from the Orient, a "mongrel civilization" (MacLean 1994, 133) or a "cloaca gentium" (Grant 1917, 81). Analogously, in *Mein Kampf* Hitler describes his native Austria as a chaotic "conglomeration of peoples," a "Babylon of people," a "Babylonian kingdom" torn by "racial conflict" (Hitler 1939, 74, 79, 39, 80). In Austria, catastrophe seems imminent: the "Slavization" and "erasure of the German element" (*Entdeutschung*) is progressing, and thus the twilight of the superior race that had colonized and civilized the Orient is at hand (Hitler 1939, 82). The Germany where Hitler comes to live has witnessed unprecedented upheaval since the end of World War I, an upheaval somehow comparable to that visited upon the American South after the Civil War. Worse even than the loss of colonies, Germany is forced to endure a military occupation by the multiracial troops of the victors and seems to have been transformed into a "racial hodgepodge" (Hitler 1939, 439). Inflaming this fear that the end of civilization is at hand is the October Revolution, which calls for the rebellion of colonized people and seems to confirm ideologically the "horror" of a black military occupation. The October Revolution breaks out and takes hold of an area populated by people traditionally considered at the margin of civilization. Just as in the American South abolitionists are branded "Negro lovers" and traitors to their own race, social democrats and especially Communists are considered by Hitler to be traitors to the German and the Western race. In the final analysis, the Third Reich appears to be an attempt, under the conditions of total war and international civil war, to prevent the end of civilization and the suicide of the West and of the superior race by creating a regime of white supremacy on a worldwide scale, and under German hegemony.

Anti-Semitism and Anti-Americanism? Spengler and Ford

The campaign against those who dare to criticize Washington's policy of preemptive war typically links anti-Americanism to anti-Semitism. Here again, one cannot help but be amazed at the lack of historical memory. Does anyone recall the Ku Klux Klan's praise for "the genuine Americanism of Henry Ford?" (MacLean 1994, 90). Widely admired, the automobile magnate condemns the Bolshevik Revolution as being first and foremost the product of conspiring Jews, and he even founds a magazine, the *Dearborn Independent*, that publishes articles collected in 1920 into a single volume entitled *The International Jew*. The volume immediately becomes a seminal reference book of international anti-Semitism, to the extent that, more than any other, it is credited with contributing to the success of the notorious *Protocols of the Learned Elders of Zion*. It is true that Ford will eventually be forced to renounce his campaign, but by then his book will already have been translated into German and will have become quite popular. Well-known Nazi figures like von Schirach and even Himmler will later claim to have been inspired or motivated by Ford. Himmler in particular claims to have comprehended the "the danger of Judaism" only after reading Ford's book: "For National Socialists, it was a revelation," as was the reading of the *Protocols of the Elders of Zion*. "These two books showed us the way to free a humanity plagued by the greatest enemy of all time, the international Jew." Himmler follows a formula that echoes the title of Ford's book. These testimonials might be self-serving in part, but one thing is for sure: in Hitler's interviews with Dietrich Eckart, the anti-Semitic Henry Ford is among those most often cited as having had the greatest influence on him. And, according to Himmler, Ford's book, along with the *Protocols*, played a "decisive" (*ausschlaggebend*) role not only in his own personal development but in the Führer's as well.[2]

Here, too, the banality of a schematic contrast between Europe and the United States is revealed, as if the plague of anti-Semitism did not directly involve both Europe and the United States. In 1933 Spengler feels the need to clarify this point: the Judeophobia to which he openly confesses should not be confused with the "materialistic" racism typical of "anti-Semites in Europe and America" (Spengler 1933, 157). The biological anti-Semitism that rages impetuously on the other side of the Atlantic is considered excessive even by an author like Spengler, who speaks out

---

[2] See the account by Felix Kersten, Himmler's Finnish masseur, in the Paris Centre de documentation Juive et contemporaine (*Das Buch von Henry Ford*, 22 December 1940, no. CCX-31); see also Poliakov 1977, 278, and Losurdo 1991, 83–85.

against Jewish culture and history throughout his works. For this reason, among others, Spengler is considered timid and inconsequential to the Nazis. Their enthusiasm lies elsewhere: *The International Jew* continues to be published with honor in the Third Reich, and with prefaces that emphasize the distinct historical merit of its author (for having brought to light the "Jewish question"), as well as what is perceived to be a direct line of continuity leading from Henry Ford to Adolf Hitler! (See Losurdo 1991, 84–85.)

The current polemic concerning anti-Americanism and anti-Europeanism is naïve: it seems to ignore the cultural exchanges and reciprocal influences America and Europe have had on one another. In the immediate aftermath of World War I, Croce has no problem pointing out the influence that Theodore Roosevelt had on Enrico Corradini, the nationalist leader who joined the fascist party (Croce 1967, 251). In the early twentieth century, the American statesman had made a triumphant trip to Europe, during the course of which he was awarded an *honoris causa* degree in Berlin and acquired—according to Pareto—numerous "flatterers" (Pareto 1988, 1241–42, §1436). The representation of the United States as a sort of sacred space, immune to the plagues and horrors of Europe, is above all a product of the cold war. One must never overlook the exchange of ideas flowing between the two continents: the American Stoddard coined a keyword of Nazi ideological discourse (*Untermensch*), but Stoddard in turn had studied in Germany and read the theories so dear to Nietzsche regarding the superman (*Uebermensch*) (Losurdo 2002, 886–87). Moreover, while Germany gazes with admiration upon the land of white supremacy, it reacts with repugnance to the notion of the melting pot. Rosenberg recounts with disgust that in Chicago there is a "big [Catholic] cathedral" that "belongs to the niggers." There is even a "Negro bishop" who celebrates Mass: it marks the "breeding" of "bastard phenomena" (Rosenberg 1937, 471). In turn, Hitler denounces the "Jewish blood" that flows in the veins of Franklin Delano Roosevelt, whose wife is said to have a "negroid look" about her (Hitler 1952–54, 2: 182, conversations dated July 1, 1942).

The United States, the West, and "*Herrenvolk* Democracy"

At this point it becomes clear that the theory according to which rightwing anti-Americanism and left-wing anti-Americanism coincide is based upon ideology and myth. In fact, the very same elements criticized by the leftist tradition that begins with abolitionism and carries on to the Communist movement are instead viewed positively and even enthusiastically by the right. What is cherished by one side is despised by the other, and vice versa. Yet both sides find themselves facing the paradox that has characterized the United States from its very foundation, a paradox that was articulated in the eighteenth century by the British writer Samuel

Johnson: "How is it that we hear the loudest yelps for liberty from the drivers of the negroes?" (in Foner 1998, 32).

It is a fact: democracy developed within the white community concomitantly with the enslavement of blacks and the deportation of American Indians. For thirty-two of America's first thirty-six years as an independent country, the presidency was in the hands of slave owners. And it was also slave owners who drafted the Declaration of Independence and the Constitution. Without slavery (and the subsequent racial segregation) one can understand nothing about "American freedom": the two go hand in hand, the one supporting the other (Morgan 1975). While this "peculiar institution" ensures firm control over the "dangerous" classes at places of production, expansion westward serves to defuse social conflict by transforming a potential proletariat into a class of landowners, though at the expense of peoples who must be removed or crushed.

After the War of Independence, American democracy comes to experience a further development with Jackson's presidency in the 1830s: the expansion of suffrage and the elimination, in large part, of property restrictions within the white community are concomitant with the rigorous deportation of American Indians and with increasing resentment and violence directed against blacks. The same might be said for the period dating from the end of the nineteenth century to the end of the first fifteen years of the twentieth century. This so-called Progressive Era is undeniably characterized by numerous democratic reforms (which ensure the direct election of the Senate, the secret ballot, the introduction of primary elections and the institution of the referendum, and so on); yet it is an especially tragic period for blacks (the targets of Ku Klux Klan terror squads) and American Indians (stripped of their remaining homeland and subjected to a ruthless leveling intended to deprive them even of their cultural identity).

Concerning this paradox of their history, numerous American intellectuals have spoken of "*Herrenvolk* democracy," that is, democracy only for the "genteel population" (to use an expression of the sort Hitler was fond of) (Berghe 1967; Fredrickson 1987). A clear line of demarcation between whites, on the one side, and blacks and redskins, on the other, fosters the development of relations based on equality within the white community. Members of an aristocracy of class or color tend to consider themselves "equal"; the inequality imposed upon the excluded is the flipside of this relation based on equality among those who wield the power to exclude "inferiors."

Must we then juxtapose Europe to the United States in a positive-negative contrast? This would be a grave mistake. In fact, the category of *Herrenvolk* democracy can be of assistance in explaining the history of the West as a whole. From the end of the nineteenth century and into the beginning of the twentieth, the extension of suffrage in Europe goes hand in hand with colonization and the imposition of servile and semiservile work relations upon subjugated peoples. Government by law in Europe is tightly interwoven with bureaucratic will and police violence, and with a state of siege in the colonies. In the final analysis, it is the same phenomenon that occurs in the United States, except that in Europe it is less evident becasue the colonized people live across the ocean.

Imperial Mission and Christian Fundamentalism in American History

It is on a different level that we grasp the real differences in the political and ideological development between Europe and the United States. Profoundly marked by the Enlightenment, Europe at the end of the nineteenth century experiences an even more radical secularization: the disciples of both Marx and Nietzsche are convinced that "God is dead." In the United States the situation is very different. This is how in 1899 *Christian Oracle* magazine explains its decision to change its name to *Christian Century*: "We believe that the coming century is to witness greater triumphs in Christianity than any previous century has ever witnessed, and that it is to be more truly Christian than any of its predecessors" (in Olasky 1992, 135).

At this time, war is being waged against Spain, which is accused by American leaders of having unjustly denied Cuba its right to liberty and independence, and moreover to have resorted, against an island "so near our own borders," to such measures as disgust the "moral sense of the people of the United States" and represent a "disgrace to Christian civilization" (in Commager 1963, 2: 5). Here, the indirect gesture to the Monroe Doctrine and the call for a crusade in the name of democracy, morality, and religion are woven tightly together to excommunicate, so to speak, a Catholic country and to bestow a saintly character upon a war that was to confirm the powerful role of imperial America. Later, president McKinley will explain the decision to annex the Philippines by way of an illumination from "Almighty God," who, after hearing the kneeling president's ceaseless prayers, at last, on a particularly restless night, frees him of every doubt and indecision. It would not be right to leave the colony in the hands of Spain or to surrender it "to France or Germany, our commercial rivals in the Orient." Nor, for that matter, would it be right to leave the Philippines to the Filipinos themselves, who are "unfit for self-government" and would let their country slide into a state of "anarchy and misrule" even worse than the result of Spanish dominion:

> There was nothing left for us to do but to take them all, and to educate the Filipinos, and uplift and civilize and Christianize them, and by God's grace do the very best we could by them, as our fellow men for whom Christ also died. And then I went to bed and went to sleep and slept soundly. (In Millis 1989, 384)

Today we know of the horrors perpetrated during the suppression of the independence movement in the Philippines: the guerrilla war carried out by the Filipinos was met with the systematic destruction of fields and livestock, the massive confinement of the population in concentration camps where they fell victim to starvation and disease, and in certain cases even the murder of all males over the age of ten years (McAllister Linn 1989, 27, 23).

And yet, despite the extent of "collateral damage," the march of imperial-religious war ideology triumphantly resumes during World War I. Immediately after U.S. intervention, in a letter to Colonel House, Wilson says of his "allies": "When the war is over we can force them to our way of thinking, because by that time they will, among other things, be financially in our hands" (in Kissinger 1994, 224). At any rate, there is no doubt about the fact that "a strong element of *realpolitik* was at work" (Heckscher 1991, 298) in Wilson's position concerning Latin America and the rest of the world. This, however, does not stop Wilson from carrying out the war as if it were an actual crusade even in the literal sense of the term: the American soldiers are "crusaders," the agents of a "transcendent achievement" (Wilson 1927, 2: 45, 414), of a "holy war, the holiest in all history" (in Rochester 1977, 58), a war destined to champion peace, democracy, and Christian values throughout the world. Once again, material and geopolitical interests and imperial ambitions are inextricably linked to a missionary and democratic conscience.

The same ideological platform is applied to other American conflicts in the twentieth century, the cold war being particularly noteworthy in this regard. One of its protagonists, John Foster Dulles, is said by Churchill to be "a dour Puritan." Dulles is proud of the fact that "nobody in the Department of State knows as much about the Bible as I do." His religious fervor is by no means a private affair: "I am convinced that we here need to make our political thoughts and practices reflect more faithfully a religious faith that man has his origin and destiny in God" (in Kissinger 1994, 534–35). Along with faith, other fundamental theological categories seep into the political struggle at an international level: the neutral countries that refuse to take part in the crusade against the Soviet Union are conspiring in "sin," while the United States, at the head of the crusade itself, represents the "moral people" by definition (in Freiberger 1992, 42–43). The leader of these people who are so distinguished by their morality and nearness to God is, in 1983, Ronald Reagan. He will spark the climax of the cold war, a climax destined to mark the defeat of the atheist enemy, with words resounding with theology: "There is sin and evil in the world, and we are enjoined by Scripture and the Lord Jesus to oppose it with all our might" (in Draper 1994, 33).

Moving on to more recent times, in his first inaugural address, Clinton is no less religiously inspired than were his predecessors or his successor:

"Today we celebrate the mystery of American renewal." After recalling the pact between "our founders" and "the Almighty," Clinton emphasizes: "Our mission is timeless" (Lott 1994, 366). Realigning himself with this tradition, and further radicalizing it, George W. Bush conducts his electoral campaign with a truly authentic dogma: "Our nation is chosen by God and commissioned by history to be a model to the world of justice" (Cohen 2000).

In the history of the United States it is clear that religion is called upon to play a fundamental political role at an international level. We witness an American political tradition that expresses itself in overtly theological terms. More so than the declarations issued by European leaders, the "doctrines" pronounced by American presidents time and time again call to mind the encyclicals and dogmas proclaimed by the leaders of the Catholic church. American inaugural addresses are really and truly sacred ceremonies. I shall limit myself to two examples. In 1953, after inviting his listeners to bow their heads before "Almighty God," Eisenhower addresses Him directly: "All may work for the good of our beloved country and Thy glory. Amen" (Lott 1994, 302). Here, the identification that exists between God and America is particularly striking. Half a century later, not much has changed. We have seen how Clinton's inaugural address begins, but it is worth looking also at how it ends. After citing "Scripture," the new president finishes by saying: "From this mountaintop of celebration we hear a call to service in the valley. We have heard the trumpets, we have changed the guard. And now each in our own way, and with God's help, we must answer the call. Thank you, and God bless you all" (Lott 1994, 369). Again, the United States is hailed as the city upon the mountain, the blessed city of God. In his address immediately following his reelection, Clinton feels the need to thank God for having made him be born an American.

This ideology, or this missionary theology, has always made Europe uncomfortable. Clemenceau's irony concerning Wilson's fourteen points is well known: God Himself was content with only ten commandments! In 1919, in a private letter, John Maynard Keynes calls Wilson "the biggest imposter on Earth" (in Skidelsky 1989, 444).

Freud is even more explicit with regard to Wilson's tendency to view himself as being invested with a divine mission: this is "unmistakable insincerity, ambiguity, and an inclination to deny the truth." Kaiser Wilhelm II had already claimed to be "a man favored by Divine Providence" (Freud 1995, 35–36). But here Freud errs, and risks confusing two very distinct ideological traditions. True, the German emperor is also prone to attributing religious motives to his expansionist ambitions: before the troops departing for China, he invokes the "blessing of God" for what will be a ruthless undertaking to crush the rebellion of the Boxers and defend "Christianity" (Röhl 2001, 1157). It is also true that the emperor considers the Germans to be "the people chosen by God" (Röhl

1993, 412). Hitler, too, claims to have felt himself called upon to carry out "the work of the Lord," and he states his desire to obey the will of the "Omnipotent" (Hitler 1939, 70, 439), all the more so since the Germans are "the people of God" (in Rauschning 1940, 227). The slogan *Gott mit uns* (God with us) is well known.

Yet, one should not overemphasize the importance of these declarations and ideological motivations. In Germany (the home of Marx and Nietzsche) the secularization process is well under way. Wilhelm II's invocation of the "blessing of God" is not taken seriously even by extreme nationalists. According to one of the cleverest among them (Maximilian Harden), the return of the "days of the Crusades" is ridiculous, as is the grandiose attempt to "win the world over to the Gospel"; "thus visionaries and crafty speculators stroll around God" (in Röhl 2001, 1157). True, even before ascending the throne, the future emperor hails the Germans as "the people chosen by God"; but one of the first to mock him is his own mother, the daughter of Queen Victoria, who if anything would like to lay claim to the preeminence of England (Röhl 1993, 412).

This last point is worth reflecting upon further. In Europe, imperial genealogical myths neutralized one another to some extent; the royal families were all related to one another, and therefore each of them faced missionary ideals and imperial genealogical myths that were both diverse and contradictory. Such ideals and genealogies were further discredited by the catastrophic experience of two world wars. And, despite its defeat, the ten-year struggle by communist agitators, fighting against imperialism and in the name of the equality of nations, has left a mark on the European conscience. The result is evident: in Europe, any imperial mission or direct election by God of one nation or another is unbelievable. There is no place left for this imperial-religious ideology, which instead plays such a central role in the United States.

With regard to Germany, the historical transition from the Second Reich to the Third Reich is characterized by an oscillation between nostalgia for a warlike paganism, centered around the cult of Wotan, and the aspiration to make Christianity a national religion called upon to legitimize the imperial mission of the German people. The latter ambition was most thoroughly developed by the *Deutsche Christen*, or "German Christians." It was not a very realistic aim, given that secularization had made its way not only throughout German society but also throughout Protestant theology itself (Karl Barth and Dietrich Bonhoeffer come to mind). In addition, since the leaders of the Third Reich tended to support paganism, the Christian aim could hardly be expected to command a great following. The history of the United States, on the other hand, is marked by the tendency to transform the Judeo-Christian tradition into a sort of national religion that consecrates the *exceptionalism* of the American people and the sacred mission with which they are entrusted. Is this interweaving of religion and politics not synonymous with fundamentalism? It is not by chance that the term *fundamentalism* is first used in American and Protestant spheres as a proud and positive self-characterization.

The shortcomings of Freud's and Keynes's position can now be better understood: of course any American administration will have its hypocrites, its schemers, and its cynics; but this is no reason to doubt the sincerity of Wilson or, today, of Bush Jr. One must not lose sight of the fact that the United States is not a very secular society: 70 percent of Americans believe in the devil, and more than a third of adults claim that God speaks to them directly (Gray 1998, 126; Schlesinger Jr. 1997). Still, this is an element of strength, not one of weakness. The placid conviction that one represents a sacred and divine cause facilitates not only the formation of a united front during times of crisis but also the repression or trivialization of the darkest pages of American history. Undeniably, during the cold war Washington sponsored bloody coups in Latin America and put ruthless military dictators in power; in Indonesia, in 1965, it promoted the massacre of hundreds of thousands of Communists or Communist sympathizers. Yet, as unpleasant as they might be, such details do not mar the sanctity of the cause embodied by the "Empire of the Good."

Weber is closer to the truth when during World War I he decries American "cant" (Weber 1971, 144). "Cant" is not a lie, nor is it conscious hypocrisy: it is the hypocrisy of those who are able to lie even to themselves. It is similar to the false conscience of which Engels speaks. In Keynes and Freud we see both the strength and the weakness of the Enlightenment. While largely immune to the imperial-religious ideology raving on the other side of the Atlantic, Europe is nevertheless unable to comprehend thoroughly this mixture of religious and moral fervor, on the one hand, and of lucid and overt pursuit of political, economic, and military world domination, on the other. Yet it is this mixture, or rather this explosive combination, this peculiar fundamentalism, that constitutes the greatest threat to world peace today. Rather than to a specific nation, Islamic fundamentalism refers to a community of people who, not without reason, claim to be the targets of a policy of aggression and of military occupation. American fundamentalism, instead, transfigures and intoxicates a well-defined country that, appointed and empowered by God, regards the current international order and purely humane law to be irrelevant. It is within this framework that the delegitimization of the United Nations, the disregard for the Geneva Convention, and the threats made not only against enemies but even against Nato "allies" must be situated.

The Campaigns against "Drapetomania" and against Anti-Americanism

In addition to fighting "evil" and defending Christian and American values, the war against Iraq (not to mention wars on the horizon) aims also to expand democracy around the world. To what extent is this latter claim believable? Let us return for a moment to the young Indochinese man who in 1924 denounced the lynching of blacks. He later returned to his homeland, and there he took on a name that would come to be known throughout the world: Ho Chi Minh. During the relentless American bombings, did the Vietnamese leader perhaps remember the horrors perpetrated against blacks by the champions of white supremacy? In other words, did the emancipation of African Americans, and their acquisition of civil and political rights, truly mark a change, or is the United States still a *Herrenvolk* democracy, with the exception that now the excluded are no longer to be found within, but outside, the mother country, as had been the case with European "democracy"?

We might examine the question from a different perspective, by considering a reflection made by Kant: "What is an *absolute* monarch? It is he who, when he commands that war must be, war follows." Kant is targeting not the states of the ancien régime but rather England, with its century of liberal development behind it (Kant 1900, 90 note). According to Kant's position, the current president of the United States should be considered a despot on two counts. First, because of the emergence in the past ten years of an "imperial presidency" that, when embarking upon military actions, often presents Congress with a fait accompli. We are more concerned here with the second aspect: it is the White House that sovereignly determines when U.N. resolutions are binding or not; it is the White House that sovereignly determines which countries constitute "rogue" states and whether it is lawful to subject them to embargoes that will cause the suffering of an entire population, or to the hellfire of depleted uranium and cluster bombs, the effects of which will inflict damage and suffering for years after the conflict has ended. Sovereignly, the White House decides upon the military occupation of these countries for as long as it deems necessary, sentencing the countries' leaders and their "accomplices" to lifelong prison sentences. Against them, and against "terrorists," even "targeted killing" is legitimate, or rather, killing that is anything but targeted, such as the bombing of an ordinary restaurant where it was believed that Saddam Hussein might have been found. Clearly, legal rights do not apply to "barbarians." In fact, a closer look at, for example, the Patriot Act, reveals that the rule of law does not apply even to those who, while not "barbarians" in the strict sense of the word, are suspected of participating in their game.

The origin of the expression *rogue states* is interesting. In Virginia between the seventeenth and eighteenth centuries, when semi-slaves, that is, temporary, white-skinned slaves, tried to flee and were caught, they were branded with the letter *R* (for Rogue): immediately recognizable, they no longer had any chance to escape. Later, the problem of identification was finally solved by substituting white semi-slaves with black slaves: skin color made branding unnecessary; to be black was itself synonymous with being a rogue. Now, entire States are branded rogue. *Herrenvolk* democracy is slow to die.

This is an old story. What is new is the growing intolerance that Washington has for its "allies." They too are called upon to kowtow to—without beating about the bush—the will of God's chosen nation. The perplexity and negative reaction provoked by the American president's unrestrained behavior as the world's sovereign, unchecked by any international body, is now clearly understandable. This is the scandalous disease that the ideologues of war condemn as anti-Americanism. While unique, the reaction is not without similar historical precedents. In the middle of the nineteenth century the system of slavery was alive and vital in the American South. Yet doubts did begin to emerge: the number of fugitive slaves was increasing. Not only did this alarm the white-supremacist ideologues of slavery; it confounded them. Why would a "normal" person flee from a society so well ordered and in tune with the hierarchy of nature? It must be some sort of plague, a psychological disturbance. But what? In 1851 Samuel Cartwright, a surgeon and psychologist from Louisiana, claimed he finally had an explanation, which he shared with the readers of an important scientific journal, the *New Orleans Medical and Surgical Journal*. Taking his cue from the ancient Greek word δραπετησ (*drapetes*), meaning runaway slave, Cartwright triumphantly concluded that the psychological disturbance, the disease that caused black slaves to run away, was "drapetomania" (in Eakin 2000). The current campaign being waged against anti-Americanism has much in common with the one carried out against drapetomania more than a century and a half ago.

References

Berghe, Pierre L. van den. 1967. *Race and Racism: A Comparative Perspective*. New York, London, Sydney: Wiley.

Cohen, Richard. 2000. "No, Mr. Lieberman, America Isn't Really God's Country." *International Herald Tribune* (8 September): 7. (The article incorrectly speaks of Lieberman, but this is corrected the next day, on p. 6.)

Commager, Henry S. (ed.). 1963. *Documents of American History*. Seventh edition. New York: Appleton-Century-Crofts.

Croce, Benedetto. 1967. *Storia d'Italia dal 1871 al 1915*. Originally published in 1927. Bari: Laterza.

Draper, Theodore. 1994. "Mission Impossible." *New York Review of Books* (6 October).

Eakin, Emily. 2000. "Is Racism Abnormal? A Psychiatrist Sees It as a Mental Disorder." *International Herald Tribune* (17 January): 3.

Figes, Orlando. 2003. "The Greatest Relief Mission of All." *New York Review of Books* (13 March): 22–24.

Foner, Erich. 1998. *The History of American Freedom*. London: Picador.

Fredrickson, George M. 1987. *The Black Image in the White Mind: The Debate on Afro-American Character and Destiny, 1817–1914*. Hanover, N.H.: Wesleyan University Press. Originally published in 1971.

Freiberger, Steven Z. 1992. *Dawn over Suez: The Rise of American Power in the Middle East, 1953–1957*. Chicago: Ivan R. Dee.

Freud, Sigmund. 1995. "Einleitung zu 'Thomas Woodrow Wilson': Eine psychologische Studie." Translated into Italian by Renata Colorni as *Introduzione allo studio psicologico su Thomas Woodrow Wilson*, in *Opere*, edited by Cesare Luigi Musatti, vol. 11. Turin: Bollati Boringhieri. Written in 1930, originally published in 1971.

Grant, Madison. 1917. *The Passing of the Great Race or the Racial Basis of European History*. London: Bell.

Gray, John. 1998. *False Dawn: The Delusion of Global Capitalism*. London: Granta Books.

Günther, Hans S. R. 1934. *Rassenkunde des deutschen Volkes*. Munich: Lehmanns. Originally published in 1922.

Heckscher, August. 1991. *Woodrow Wilson: A Biography*. New York and Toronto: Scribner's.

Hitler, Adolf. 1939. *Mein Kampf*. Munich: Zentralverlag der NSDAP. Originally published in 1925.

———. 1952–54. *Livres propos sur la guerre et la paix*, edited by François Genoud. Paris: Flammarion. (These are Hitler's table talks collected by Martin Bormann.)

Hoffmann, Géza von. 1913. *Die Rassenhygiene in den Vereinigten Staaten von Nordamerika*. Munich: Lehmanns.

Kant, Immanuel. 1900. *Der Streit der Fakultäten*. In *Gesammelte Schriften*, vol. 7. Berlin and Leipzig: Akademie-Ausgabe. Original 1798.

Kissinger, Henry. 1994. *Diplomacy*. New York: Simon and Schuster.

Kühl, Stefan. 1994. *The Nazi Connection: Eugenics, American Racism, and German National Socialism*. New York and Oxford: Oxford University Press.

Lifton, Robert Jay. 1986. *The Nazi Doctors: Medical Killing and the Psychology of Genocide*. New York: Basic Books.

Lott, Davis Newton (ed.). 1994. *The Presidents Speak: The Inaugural Addresses of the American Presidents, from Washington to Clinton*. New York: Henry Holt.

Losurdo, Domenico. 1991. "Marx et l'histoire du totalitarisme." In *Fin du communisme? Actualité du Marxisme?* edited by Jacques Bidet and Jacques Texier. Paris: PUF.

———. 1993. *Democrazia o bonapartismo: Trionfo e decadenza del suffragio universale*. Turin: Bollati Boringhieri.

———. 1996. *Il revisionismo storico: Problemi e miti*. Rome and Bari: Laterza.

———. 1997. *Antonio Gramsci dal liberalismo al "comunismo critico."* Rome: Gamberetti.

———. 2001. *Heidegger and the Ideology of War: Community, Death, and the West.* Translated by Marella and Jon Morris. Amherst: Humanity Books.

———. 2002. *Nietzsche, il ribelle aristocratico: Biografia intellettuale e bilancio critico.* Turin: Bollati Boringhieri.

MacLean, Nancy. 1994. *Behind the Mask of Chivalry: The Making of the Second Ku Klux Klan.* New York and Oxford: Oxford University Press.

McAllister Linn, Brian. 1989. *The U. S. Army and Counterinsurgency in the Philippine War, 1899–1902.* Chapel Hill and London: University of North Carolina Press.

Marx, Karl, and Friedrich Engels. 1955. *Werke.* Berlin: Dietz.

Millis, Walter. 1989. *The Martial Spirit.* Chicago: Elephant Paperbacks. Originally published in 1931.

Morgan, Edmund S. 1975. *American Slavery, American Freedom: The Ordeal of Colonial Virginia.* New York and London: Norton.

Olasky, Marvin. 1992. *The Tragedy of American Compassion.* Washington: Regnery Gateway.

Noer, Thomas J. 1978. *Briton, Boer, and Yankee: The United States and South Africa, 1870–1914.* Kent, Ohio: Kent State University Press.

Pareto, Vilfredo. 1988. *Trattato di sociologia generale*, critical edition. Edited by Giovanni Busino. Turin: UTET. Original 1916.

Poliakov, Léon. 1977. *L'histoire de l'antisémitisme*, volume 4, *L'Europe suicidaire.* Paris: Calman-Levy.

Röhl, John C. G. 1993. *Wilhelm II: Die Jugend des Kaisers, 1859–1888.* Munich: Beck.

———. 2001. *Wilhelm II: Der Aufbau der persönlichen Monarchie, 1888–1900.* Munich: Beck.

Rauschning, Hermann. 1940. *Gespräche mit Hitler.* Second edition. New York: Europa Verlag. Originally published in 1939.

Rochester, Stuart I. 1977. *American Liberal Disillusionment in the Wake of World War I.* University Park and London: Pennsylvania State University Press.

Roosevelt, Theodore. 1951. *The Letters.* Edited by Elting E. Morison, John M. Blum, and John J. Buckley. Cambridge, Mass.: Harvard University Press.

Rosenberg, Alfred. 1937. *Der Mythus des 20. Jahrhunderts.* Munich: Hoheneichen. Originally published in 1930.

Ruge, Wolfgang, and Wolfgang Schumann (eds.). 1977. *Dokumente zur deutschen Geschichte, 1939–1942.* Frankfurt a. M.: Rödelberg.

Schlesinger, Arthur Jr. 1997. "Has Democracy a future?" *Foreign Affairs* (September–October): 2–12.

Skidelsky, Robert. 1989. *John Maynard Keynes: Hopes Betrayed, 1881–1920*. Vol. 1. London: Macmillan. Originally published in 1981.

Spengler, Oswald. 1933. *Jahre der Entscheidung*. Munich: Beck.

———. 1980. *Der Untergang des Abendlandes*. Munich: Beck. Originally published 1918–23.

Stoddard, Lothrop. 1925. *The Revolt against Civilization: The Menace of the Under Man*. German translation by Wilhelm Heise, *Der Kulturumsturz: Die Drohung des Untermenschen*. Munich: Lehmanns. Originally published in 1922.

———. 1984. *The Revolt against Civilization: The Menace of the Under Man*. New York: Scribner's. Originally published in 1922.

Wade, Wyn Craig. 1997. *The Fiery Cross: The Ku Klux Klan in America*. New York and Oxford: Oxford University Press.

Weber, Max. 1971. "Zwischen zwei Gesetzen." In *Gesammelte politische Schriften*, edited by J. Winckelmann. Third edition. Tübingen: Mohr (Siebeck).

Wilson, Woodrow. 1927. *War and Peace: Presidential Messages, Addresses, and Public Papers (1917–1924)*. Edited by R. S. Baker and W. E. Dood. New York and London: Harper.

12

ON THE SO-CALLED WAR ON TERRORISM

TOM ROCKMORE

Although a war on terrorism in response to the massive terrorist attacks in the United States on September 11, 2001, could be justified, the war currently under way is unjustified, ineffective, and not obviously a war on terrorism at all. The current war, as well as what is known of what is being contemplated, looks likely to remain simply ineffective, as there is no evidence, none whatever, that the U.S. and its allies are closer than before to eradicating or even to diminishing terrorism. And there is reason to think that what is being called a war on terrorism, but which increasingly serves other interests, is itself a major source of further terrorism, a help not a hindrance to the creation and spread of terror around the world.

There is no problem about justifying a war on terrorism. But there is also no prospect of adequately justifying the present so-called war on terrorism other than through some form of the ancient, but spurious, idea that might makes right. After its initial phase, which was directed mainly against arbitrary targets, what is called the war on terrorism appears not, or mainly not, to be directed against terrorists. Since the outbreak of the war in Afghanistan, everything has been happening as if the so-called war on terrorism has less and less to do with terrorism and serves increasingly as a convenient pretext for American imperialist ambitions. The standard to justify a war on terrorism, to which I shall return in a moment, is not particularly high. But it is too high to be met in the current war. Unless one is a pacifist, which is not the line I shall be taking here, a war on terrorism could be justified for the simple reason that a person, a group, or a country has a right, when and if it is attacked, to defend itself. The right of self-defense is one of the most elementary human rights. Yet only some among the many possible wars on terrorism are justified, and hence just. Some minimal conditions that must be met for a just war on terrorism are that the war be wholly or at least primarily directed against terrorism and not undertaken for other ends, that it be waged in defense against the attackers, not against others, that the war take place on grounds which can be rationally justified, and that terrorism be correctly identified.

What is routinely called the war on terrorism has so far been a manifest failure. First, it has been mainly directed against those who did not attack the U.S. Second, it has increasingly not been directed against terrorists at all, unless anyone the U.S. government does not like can fairly be called a terrorist. Third, it has so far failed to find an adequate justification, a reason or set of reasons that could justify the type of war that is being waged. Fourth, it has conflated the response to terrorism with a pre-emptive strike on Iraq. And, fifth, it has failed to provide a plausible account of the sources of, or even correctly to identify, terrorism.

A War against the Terrorists?

In claiming that it only makes sense to wage a war on terrorism against those who in fact attacked the U.S., I am hardly breaking new ground. Yet it is important to point out the obvious, since so far many innocent people—many more than were killed in the U.S. during the terrorist attacks on September 11, 2001—have been struck down by the U.S. and its allies in the course of the so-called war on terrorism.

The ongoing war in Afghanistan was and is unjust because it simply lumps together those who may have attacked the U.S. with those who clearly did not do so and hence should not have been attacked in return. There is no reason to think that the U.S. was attacked by Afghanistan. The U.S. attacked Afghanistan in response to an attack attributed to a terrorist group called Al Qaeda led by Osama bin Laden in a war that is still continuing. Everything about this attack is doubtful. It has still not been shown that a mad Saudi was able from a cave in Afghanistan to coordinate a large-scale attack on the U.S. on September 11, 2001. If we assume for the purposes of argument that he did, then we have to ask if the attack on Afghanistan in general is justified. I believe it is not, since we cannot equate Afghanistan as a whole with whatever Al Qaeda is supposedly responsible for. There is no right to harm, much less to destroy, anyone other than those who attacked the U.S., including through what is euphemistically called collateral damage. Is the life of an Afghan worth less than that of an American? And if, for purposes of argument, we look away from collateral damage and simply abstract from what is right, is the war useful? The answer must be no. For there is simply no reason to think that this war has reduced terrorism in the world, and hence achieved its stated goal.

The first phase of the war in Afghanistan coincides with an initial, very rapid military response. Here the U.S., perhaps to avoid the impression of being a helpless giant, a mere paper tiger, struck out very nearly blindly with the help of a hastily arranged coalition of friendly nations. The expected result, quickly achieved, was largely to destroy the economic infrastructure —hence the little indigenous economy this very poor country possessed—mainly through a massive aerial bombardment and follow-up ground engagements. The further unexpected result was that, despite determined efforts, it proved impossible to find, to kill, to bring to justice (however defined), or to "neutralize" those the U.S. had in its sights. These include

Osama bin Laden, whom the U.S. considers to be the main perpetrator, the world's official enemy number one; and Mullah Omar, whose crime seems to be that he is a high official of a form of Islam popular in the region but unpopular among current U.S. government officials.

The planning in the first phase of the war was hasty, and the attention devoted to identifying the enemy was even hastier. The U.S. quickly identified as its enemy Osama bin Laden and a terrorist organization, Al Qaeda, that he may or may not have headed and still possibly heads. Here the details are somewhat vague. Although capital punishment is involved, since the U.S. was (and still is) assassinating its foes and imprisoning its enemies without anything resembling due process, there does not seem to be any proof, nor has any been presented, that could stand up in a court of law.

The U.S. also assimilated among its enemies for the purposes of its war on terrorism in its Afghan phase the Taliban, who had formed a religious organization that was engaged in enforcing a particularly repressive form of Islam on the Afghan population. In time of war, when one is in need of enemies, people to blame, foes to assault, it matters little whether those picked out actually have any relation to the causes of the conflict. Three things are important in this respect. First, since no one alleges that the Taliban regime attacked the U.S., it was unfairly singled out as the enemy for a war on terrorism. Second, like Osama bin Laden, a former CIA operative, the Taliban government was once a friend of the U.S. It was largely set up and financed by the the U.S. through the CIA at the time it was engaged in countering the Russian expeditionary war in Afghanistan. When the U.S. was friendly with the Taliban, what now seem like violations of human rights in Afghanistan were no more important to the U.S. than Russia's crushing of Chechnya or Turkey's oppression of the Kurds. But times have changed, and the U.S. has become friendly with the Russians and remained friendly with the Turks but has become unfriendly to the Taliban. It is a little like saying that once the U.S. no longer likes its former allies, they can be assimilated to terrorists. Third, although the U.S. with the help of its allies succeeded in crushing Al Qaeda and the Taliban, as well as installing its chosen representative Hamid Karzai as president, it did not win the war in Afghanistan, despite the overwhelming display of military might. Karzai can hardly go out of his own home without his contingent of American soldiers. The war has not come to an end but is still constantly simmering. And there is no reliable reason to believe that terrorism in the region has decreased.

How can one justify an attack, not on terrorists who attacked the U.S. but on an entire country like Afghanistan? The most candid thing one can say, which falls short of a rational justification for killing innocent people, is that there was great psychological and political pressure on the U.S. government to do something dramatic. Psychological catharsis was needed, and inaction could easily have been politically dangerous for the party in power. It is astonishing, since the pressure to act quickly no longer exists, that the second phase of the so-called war on terrorism seems not to be better planned, and certainly not better justified, than the first phase. It still is not clear who the enemy is. The list seems to change frequently—every month, sometimes even daily. Possible enemies, countries on the American hit parade (or is it the hit list!), so far include Iraq, Iran, and North Korea, the trinity composing the "axis of evil," and also, according to Secretary of Defense Donald Rumsfeld, as many as forty or fifty other countries. In fact, little effort seems to be expended on responding to that crucial question of who or what the target is, which seems to be anyone, any group, or any country anywhere in the world the current government thinks is inimical to American interests. Interestingly, terrorism—however understood—seems to be increasingly less relevant to that designation.

Like the first phase of the so-called war on terrorism, the second phase, in which the war is to be expanded into other countries, is still under way. There is no way of telling how long the second phase will last. There is also no way of predicting when the third phase, in which the war finally comes to an end, will begin. It is difficult to tell when that might occur, since in order to bring the war to an end one must know what that end would mean. What would it mean to win the war on terrorism? Must one defeat the terrorists, that is, those who actually attacked the U.S.? Must one defeat terrorism around the world? Must one defeat those who might later turn to terrorism? Which kind of terrorism? Must one defeat all those the U.S. does not like or considers opposed to its present or future interests? Unless and until the answers to these questions can be formulated, the war on terror seems likely to continue with no end in sight, until the American public puts a stop to it, or at least until the 2004 elections.

Justifying a War on Terrrorism and Morality

It is one thing to go to war against terrorism, or at least to make a rhetorial claim to do so, and something else to justify that war, to provide reasoned arguments that an impartial observer might find convincing to legitimate the proposed form of action. Like all significant courses of action, war, any war, requires a justification. War is too important to be waged unless reasons can be given that justify it as the proper course of action. "Justification" can be understood in a wide variety of ways—among them, as the whim of the supreme leader, the felt need to make good on an affront to the elder president Bush, what the party in power is able to do when bolstered by high standings in public-opinion polls, the ability to force a course of action through the legislative branch of government in which one possesses a majority, or a series of reasons of whatever kind. Reasons that have been or could be offered might be moral, prudential, utilitarian, and so on.

To justify a military response, three tests must be met. First, as I have already stated, the war must be waged against the aggressors, in this case against those who have attacked the U.S. and its allies. Since in the present case this test has only partly been met, this particular war is not justified. Second, the justification provided must be linked to the particular situation. In saying this I mean to eliminate ultimately general attempts at justification that apply to all situations in all times and places, and hence apply to none of them in particular. Third, in assessing the correct way to respond to terror, one must keep in mind the adamantine link between politics and ethics. In virtue of its ethical component, military action must respect ethical norms at the risk of itself becoming akin to, even indistinguishable from, the terrorism to which it seeks to respond. While it is always just to respond to terrorist acts, only some responses are just. A just response through military action must meet identifiable ethical standards; and a response through military action that fails to meet identifiable ethical standards cannot be just.

The third point, the idea that there is an unbreakable link between military action (or waging war) and ethics, is controversial. Unlike Kant, who regards ethics as an autonomous domain, Aristotle thinks that ethics is intrinsically political, because it always occurs in a political space. But politics cannot dispense with ethics. The rationale for war can never only be that it is possible but must only be that it is justifiable, hence right. To put the same point in other words, the justification of war of any kind, which can never rely on whim or caprice, can only take place on moral grounds.

There is an obvious relation of legality to morality. The legal framework governing relations among individuals and ultimately among countries codifies considered views of institutionalized morality. The situation for an individual, a group, and a country is in this respect similar. Just as an individual requires a justification for acting in one way rather than another, so do groups and nation-states. A company like IBM, which decides on a course of action for commercial advantage, needs to respect the laws of a given country, hence ultimately views of what is right or wrong. It would be a mistake to think that when a nation invokes national interest, or *raison d'état*, it somehow escapes from either the legal framework binding on all nations in the contemporary world or the ordinary demands of morality. A course of action, which may or may not be legal or illegal, is not morally just because it is decided on in the name of one or another country but is just if and only if it is morally justified for an agent to act in such and such a way. It might well be in the interest of the U.S. partly or wholly to redraw the map of the Middle East in arrogating to itself Iraqi oil reserves and Iranian gas reserves, but merely because it might be able to bring this off would not mean it is morally justified in doing so.

A very short list of proposed justifications for war might include the view of war as an instrument of national policy on the theory that might makes right, a theory as old as Plato's *Republic*; the defense, legitimate or otherwise, of what is loosely known as national interest; the stance that war is morally justified in certain circumstances; and so on. One of the most widely known moral justifications, the so-called just-war theory, has roots in both Christian and Muslim thinking. For Augustine, a war is just when it is undertaken for the common good by a nation-state that represents God in establishing order and justice on Earth. Just-war theory is currently understood as offering a series of principles aimed toward providing a plausible moral framework for armed conflict in which the rules governing the justification, or legitimation, of war can plausibly be distinguished for fair conduct in war. A moral framework —such as that which seems to be at work in the thinking of Muslim extremists, American governmental officials, and the American public—is not necessarily related to, say, justifying war through claims of national interest. Such a justification might claim that, whatever the morality involved, it behooves the U.S. to act in certain ways. A moral justification, to the contrary—such as an appeal to any conception of just war—eschews efforts at justification through national interest in favor of justification through what is morally correct. From a moral point of view, what is identified as national interest never trumps what is right.

A moral justification is narrower than, and substantially different from, a justification on grounds of national interest. The latter merely needs to show that what is occurring or proposed agrees with, say, a normal way of construing the national interest. There can be disagreement about where the national interest lies. But once that is determined through agreement among the responsible parties or in some other way, it need not further be shown that the proposed course of action is consistent with any particular moral code. A moral justification, to the contrary, has the double burden of showing that the proposed course of action is not only consistent with national interest, since otherwise there would be no reason to embark on it, but also further justifed by its perceived agreement with some conception of morality. Views of morality differ widely, but a moral justification, hence a war that claims moral justification, must agree with at least one such moral code.

Just-war theories, which have always been rooted in theology, are often problematic. Since they have a theological component, they uniformly invoke the support of sacred texts in different religious traditions. War is justified from the perspective of just-war theorists because the particular war, or war directed toward a particular goal, is sanctioned by divine authority. In primitive, intuitive form, the concept of just war is present in the thinking of the Bush administration, in the thinking of the American public that so far supports the Bush administration in its so-called war on terror, including both the war in Afghanistan and the war in Iraq, and in the thinking of Osama bin Laden and other Muslim extremists who call for a *jihad* against the U.S.

Yet the appeal to just war is problematic in practice. There is, for instance, no clear way to distinguish between Bush's and bin Laden's views of which war is just, perhaps no way at all to determine among Christian, Muslim, and other theological affirmations that one or another side represents God's view of the matter. It needs to be explained why we should believe anyone who claims to know what God thinks about a particular situation. It needs to be shown how we can reasonably distinguish among competing accounts of God's view of the war on terror.

A theological justification of war is obviously convincing only to someone who buys into the theological framework on which it rests. Someone who doubts asserted claims to know God's opinion and desires will not be convinced by references to sacred texts. In the absence of a theological justification of war, military action can nonetheless be justi-fied on secular grounds.

A secular criterion which is often advanced, and which I mentioned above, is self-defense. The United Nations Charter and decisions by the World Court in the Hague "prohibit international force that is not under-taken in self-defense after the occurrence of an armed attack against a national boundary or pursuant to a decision by the U.N. Security Council."[1] In plain language, while not ruling out the use of force by one sovereign country against another, the U.N. Charter and the World Court allow it in only two specific instances: it must either be authorized by the U.N. Security Council or be in response to a direct attack. Any action that fails to meet one of these two tests is considered to be illegal.

Like the U.N. Charter and the World Court, Christian theories of just war reject any claim for war as even possibly just if it is not waged in self-defense. The idea of self-defense, hence of just war, entails a reaction to an attack, as opposed, say, to a pre-emptive strike. A more nuanced view of self-defense, hence of just war, might include a reaction to an imminent attack. This amended view of just war is often used to justify the Israeli attack on Arab soldiers massed on its borders in 1967. Such a view leaves open the difficult question of how to determine that an attack is imminent and thus allows for a pre-emptive strike, which also falls under the heading of self-defense and justifies such an action as belonging to a just war. Although it is sometimes possible to justify a first strike on grounds of imminent attack, no form of just-war theory—or indeed any other effort to justify war on moral grounds—can legitimately be invoked to justify a war merely because a given country might some day pose a threat.

---

[1] Richard Falk, "The New Bush Doctrine," in *Nation*, July 15, 2002.

Conflating Terrorism and a First Strike on Iraq

The Iraqi connection to terrorism, cited as justification for a first strike on Iraq, is difficult to perceive, visible perhaps only to the anointed, or those happy few who, like President Bush, Vice President Dick Cheney, and National Security Adviser Condeleezza Rice, have close ties to the U.S. oil industry. A good indication that what is euphemistically called the war on terrorism is increasingly being used to serve other ends is the way it has been enlisted to support the idea (and the reality) of a pre-emptive war on Iraq. As concerns the war on Iraq, everything happened as if the long build-up from September 11, 2001, to the outbreak of hostilities, including the complicated and finally unsuccessful diplomatic ballet, was designed to prepare American public opinion for something that had already been decided in advance. If this is the case, then the various efforts to win support in the Security Council were never regarded as decisive but rather as an occasion to garner support for what the U.S. intended to do anyway.

A first strike in Iraq was proposed for a number of reasons, none of which justifies a first strike. These reasons include claims that Iraq had (or soon would have, or someday would have) weapons of mass destruction; that it was in league with Al Qaeda; that Saddam Hussein is evil, very evil, and was dreadful to his citizens; that he had been a troublemaker in the region; that the U.S. needs a more reliable and cheaper source of oil; that what is euphemistically called regime change in Iraq is part of the Republican party platform; that the current president's father erred in failing to take out Saddam Hussein during the Gulf War in 1991; and that this first strike was a possible first step (presumably to be followed rapidly by others if the war is deemed a success) toward what is euphemistically called redesigning the map of the Middle East in ways favorable to the U.S.

No credible proof has ever been presented for the claim that at the time the U.S. was planning to go to war against Iraq, Iraq in fact possessed so-called weapons of mass destruction. The suggestion that there is in fact credible proof but that it cannot be presented publicly is itself not credible. Tony Blair, who has acted as the U.S. front man in making the case—according to the French, Blair functions as Bush's poodle, or *caniche*—has not been persuasive enough to convince more than a small fraction of the British public, strongly opposed to going to war without the approval of the U.N. Security Council. It should not be overlooked that while Blair has been faithful to Bush, there have been massive defections in the Labour Party in Britain and widespread public opposition to the war, including among academics who regard it as illegal.

There was no way to verify the claim of Iraq possessing weapons of mass destruction short of finding something in the 2001–2002 round of

U.N. inspections. Yet there is no reason to believe that the U.S. was ever prepared to rely on inspections and follow through on resolution 1441 of the Security Council, which mandated them. One of the difficulties in the present situation is that the failure to find something was never taken as a reason to put off hostilities but rather as a reason to commence hostilities. That means (and in fact meant) that if the inspections succeeded—if, after very thorough scrutiny, nothing, or nothing substantial, was uncovered or discovered—they simply failed. This explains the striking U.S. indifference about the results of the U.N. inspections, as if finding or not finding something was never the principal objective, as if, despite proclamations to the contrary, disarming Saddam Hussein were not in fact the aim in view. Further, if mere possession of such weapons were the problem, perhaps the U.S. should bomb not only Baghdad but London and Paris as well. It should certainly also attack North Korea, where there seems not to be any doubt about whether there are weapons of mass destruction.

It seems true that Hussein is evil by any reasonable standard and acted in dreadful ways with respect to his citizens. But that does not give the Americans any right to attack him. It is also inconsistent with the U.S. policy of supporting dictators around the globe with no concern for what happens to people under their control. There is absolutely no evidence that the U.S. was ever concerned about the welfare of Iraqis until it became convenient to express such an interest. There is also no legal reason to believe that, now that the U.S. has begun to manifest such interest, it has any right to interfere by itself—that is, apart from a mandate voted by the U.N.—in the affairs of a sovereign nation.

It is true that Iraq has been a troublemaker in the region. But when that troublemaking suited the U.S., it supported Saddam Hussein. Now that this no longer suits the U.S., it no longer supports him. But where is it written that the U.S. has the right to invade Iraq merely to correct its own prior mistakes? There is certainly no reason to think that, when the U.S. invaded, Iraq was or recently had been involved in aggression against its neighbors, which might justify intervention, say, on the side of Kuwait. And there is utterly no way to justify a first strike, since there is no reason to think that Iraq either had attacked or was about to attack the U.S.

If a first strike cannot be justified through linking Iraq to terrorism, perhaps it can be justified in some other way, say, through a claim of national self-interest, such as gaining access to enormous proven oil reserves, or through the idea of bolstering a lagging U.S. economy, or in order to stabilize a chronically unstable region, or to help the party in power turn attention away from various problems at home.

None of these suggestion can be justified morally, but political leaders are not often deterred by such nuances. If one were cynical enough to think it didn't matter how resources were acquired, it might indeed be interesting to gain access to enormous oil reserves, especially if that could be done at little cost to oneself. This essentially economic reason is obviously linked to how a pre-emptive strike on Iraq would factor into the U.S. economy, which was in very bad shape at the time the U.S. attacked Iraq. As the pre-emptive war in Iraq was beginning, the number of variables in play, including the economic consequences, was so great that literally no one could believably claim to understand them. No one had any idea of what was likely to occur.

If the U.S. aim in starting the war were economic, then it would be important to point out there is no reason to think such a war would help the economy. The length of the proposed war is an important factor. If it were to take longer than the Gulf War, which was very short, in large part because the Iraqis made their stand in the desert, a first strike in Iraq might not solve but rather create new economic problems. If the Iraqis were to decide to make a stand in the cities, the length of time, hence the overall cost, and the difficulty in actually winning the war and appropriating Iraqi oil might prove prohibitively expensive.[2] We also do not know if stability in the region will increase, remain approximately the same, or even decrease, perhaps sharply, because Jordan, Saudi Arabia, and perhaps other countries may be destabilized as a result of military action. And while it may indeed be in the interests of the party in power to turn attention away from mounting problems at home, it simply beggars the imagination to think this could be reason enough to plunge Iraq, the Middle East, and perhaps other regions as well into war.

What Is Terrorism?

These remarks on the so-called war on terrorism, like the war itself, presuppose an understanding of "terrorism." The current rush to counter terrorism of whatever kind and wherever it appears is shaped by three hypotheses: we know what terrorism is; it is justified to meet it by counterterrorism, in effect to terrorize the terrorists; and we know who the terrorists are. So far everything has been happening as if all it takes to come to grips with terrorism is to collect resources and friendly nations, in short to exercise the military option. But what if we do not know what terrorism is?

What one means by "terrorism" is a variable that obviously depends on the observer and the perspective adopted. If a Chechen objecting to the Russian occupation of Chechnya uses force, that might be labeled terrorism. But as Michael Stohl points out, the threat or use of force by a great power is held to belong to diplomacy, evading the charge of terrorism.[3] This questionable view justifies Russia crushing Chechnya,

---

[2] See William D. Nordhaus, "Iraq: The Economic Consequences of War," *New York Review of Books* 49, no. 19 (December 5, 2002): 9–12.

[3] Noam Chomsky, *9-11* (N.p.: Seven Stories Press, 2001), 16–17.

the U.S. carpet bombing Cambodia (as well as Henry Kissinger being awarded a Nobel Peace Prize), and the U.S. bombing an aspirin factory in the Sudan. And it is also a view presupposed in the possibility of a first strike on Iraq.

Different definitions of terrorism are routinely adopted. "Terrorism" is defined according to the *U.S. Code* (1984) as follows: "[An] act of terrorism means any activity that [A] involves a violent act or an act dangerous to human life that is a violation of the criminal laws of the United States or any State, or that would be a criminal violation if committed within the jurisdiction of the United States or any State, and [B] appears to be intended (i) to intimidate or coerce a civilian population; (ii) to influence the policy of a government by intimidation or coercion; or (iii) to affect the conduct of a government by assassination or kidnapping."[4]

The definition of terrorism in the *U.S. Code* is neither the most inclusive nor the most carefully formulated. Definitions which are not tied to American laws are for that reason broader in scope. The problem of terrorism is not, and should not be regarded as, a specifically American problem. Though the U.S. is obviously involved, since it was attacked, the problem is clearly a general one that concerns all people in all countries that have been or in the future might be exposed to terrorism in all its many different forms. In practice, definitions of terrorism are often linked to treaties established by international bodies, especially the General Assembly of the U.N., in the form of international conventions, binding on all countries throughout the world. Such treaties define types of terrorism, or terrorism within a specific framework, such as against a specific type of individual (for example, diplomats), or with specific means (for example, bombs and nuclear weapons or biological and chemical weapons).

The treaty collection of the U.N. to date includes conventions on the prevention and punishment of crimes against internationally protected persons (including diplomatic agents), the financing of terrorism, and so on. These are treaties that in the main the U.S. has so far tended to support. Yet there are other U.N. treaties on terrorism that the U.S. has signed and ratified but later taken steps to impede or prevent from taking effect. The interest in looking at treaties on terrorism ratified by the General Assembly is that they present definitions of terrorism that may broadly respond to, but are independent of, specific U.S. concerns. Such definitions, which are negotiated among all the members of the U.N. at the time of their adoption, are intended to apply to all countries, not only the U.S. If we assume that all human beings are equally important, that

---

[4] *United States Code Congressional and Administrative News*, 98th Congress, Second Session, 1984, Oct. 19, vol. 2, par. 3077, 98 STAT. 2707 (St. Paul, Minn.: West Publishing Co., 1984).

none is more important than any other, then, if there is a choice, obviously a more inclusive view of terrorism, a view that can be applied more or less across the board to everyone, not only to some people, is better than a less inclusive view.

It seems clear that U.S. support for the treaties on terrorism adopted by the General Assembly, like the U.S. support for the U.N. and international law in general, has so far been very limited. The U.S. either recognizes conditionally, or no longer clearly recognizes, or even clearly no longer recognizes views of terrorism embodied in treaties that it has helped to negotiate and it has signed and ratified. Even the treaties on terrorism it does recognize it recognizes only conditionally since, when they contradict U.S. law, they are superseded by the *U.S. Code*, which conflicts on important points with other views of terrorism.

Three points seem important as concerns the current U.S. practices and stated views on terrorism. First, the U.S., whose founding documents embody a series of universal claims (for example, "all men are created equal"), fails to observe its stated concern with universality in its dealings with other countries. The interest in human rights so prominent in American politics, at least since Jimmy Carter's presidency and until very recently, seems suddenly to have been forgotten, to have vanished from American rhetoric. It is as if, to use Orwellian language, some were more equal than others. This is the obvious idea behind the reprehensible practice of treating the bombing of innocent civilians as so much collateral damage. It is ironic that many of the same people who insist on opposing abortion for whatever reason on the grounds of the supposed sanctity of human life seem less interested in protecting human life in other contexts.

A second series of problems follows from the definition in the *U.S. Code* of terrorism as a function of U.S. criminal law. Although criminal law might be a factor, the problem of terrorism is misidentified as a problem of obeying or disobeying U.S. criminal law. This approach is doubly incorrect. On the one hand, it misidentifies criminality with terrorism by linking terrorism to U.S. criminal law. On the other hand, it restricts "terrorism" to any type of violent act that fits the U.S. and the U.S. alone.

Third, the suggested link between terrorism and violence is problematic. The relation between terrorism and violence is neither a simple equivalence nor symetric, but rather asymetric. Not all violence is terrorist, but all terrorism is violent, more specifically violence exerted with respect to individuals or groups. The *U.S. Code* offers a trio of tests for identifying terrorism: it is violent; it is intended either to intimidate or to coerce individuals or governments; and it is intended to influence government policy through assassination or kidnapping. This ad hoc combination seems unsatisfying as even an informal description of terrorism, much less as a legal description that serves as the basis of criminal prosecutions. There is no obvious relation, none whatsoever, between terrorism exerted against individuals or groups and efforts to influence government policy. The people who disappeared during the Argentine dictatorship, *los desaparecidos*, did not disappear in an effort to influence government policy but rather in the course of its being carried out. There is no difficulty in admitting that terrorism is intended to coerce or intimidate. Yet there is a deep problem in regarding criminal violence as an identifying characteristic, or even as the hallmark, of terrorism. On the contrary, terrorism is merely another form of violence.

Since the U.S. is one of the most violent societies that has ever existed, it is not surprising that violence of various kinds is a common occurrence in daily life. In the U.S., where some twelve thousand people are shot to death every year, the right to bear arms means that in certain circumstances just about everyone, on occasion even young children, might be armed.

One must be careful in analyzing the link among violence, criminal violence, and terrorism. The *U.S. Code* is concerned with physical violence, whose link to criminality and terrorism is far from obvious. Not all violence is physical, and not all terrorism necessarily employs physical violence. No one thinks American football, a very violent game, is criminal.

Violence is not necessarily physical at all. The list of forms of violence, which is very long, includes mental violence, which is alleged in petitions for divorce based on mental cruelty; violence in textual interpretation; violent forms of speech, like the proverbial example of crying "Fire!" in a crowded theater; violent emotions, of the kind likely to be depicted by good actors playing characters in a tragedy; the violence of nature, such as a violent storm, desecration, or profanation, dear to romanticism; economic violence; and so on.

Terrorism, which is always violent, it is often neither physical nor violent, as "violence" is normally defined in criminal statutes. Some types of economic violence are permitted, even encouraged, by—and hence are an integral part of—the same system of laws designed to suppress criminal violence. Economic violence might be one of the factors operating in the present case, where, when the competition basic to free-enterprise capitalism no longer seems attractive, the U.S. seems inclined simply to confiscate Iraqi oil reserves for itself. Economic violence, or violence in the name of profit, comes in many forms, none of which apparently falls under the U.S. definition of terrorism, but all of which constitute terrorism of a basic kind.

Economic violence is central to capitalism, which depends on the accumulation of capital for the owners of the means of production. The drive for profit leads automatically, even inexorably, to the continued search for new markets, raw materials, and cheap labor. One form of this search is colonialism, in which a country exploits foreign colonies for the purpose of economic gain, often after the colonized country has become independent. One example among many is the French zone of influence in French West Africa, where all the countries in the region continue to depend on France, as witness the recent French "intervention" in the Ivory Coast. Another form is the imperialistic desire for what already legally belongs to others; the U.S., which is dependent on foreign oil supplies, apparently now covets the huge proven reserves of fossil fuel in the Middle East. Still another form of violence is the creation of farm price supports for agricultural products in first-world countries which, since they maintain prices at an artificially high level (much higher than the level of the so-called free market), quite literally condemn farmers in the third and fourth worlds, and those who depend on them, to death by starvation.[5]

Condemning the inhabitants of sub-Saharan Africa to death by starvation because of the political desirability of domestic price supports is more violent than the infinitely more "newsworthy" attack on the World Trade Center. The dreadful attack on the World Trade Center was a single occurrence, which will perhaps never recur. But the starvation of Africans as a direct, foreseeable result of price supports, which hampers the free market that the U.S. officially desires but unofficially thwarts through various forms of economic protectionism, is an ongoing but terrible by-product of free-enterprise capitalism in which profits are made at the expense of the quality of life (and even life itself) of the poor of this world.

All terrorism is violent, but not all its types are physical, or even criminal, at least according to the laws currently in force. Hence, terrorism in general cannot merely be assimilated to violation of the *U.S. Code*, or even to criminal violence. If the desire to combat terror were not limited to checking passengers boarding airplanes or invading foreign countries, then it would be useful to combat forms of violence which are not sanctioned, say, by the *U.S. Code* but which, deeply rooted in the modern world, adversely affect the daily lives of literally billions of people around the world.

Terrorism is only one form of the violence endemic in the modern world. There are different ways to explain the terrible wave of violence washing over the world at the beginning of the new millennium. A religious believer might look to a punishment sent by God, in the way some Christians consider AIDS to be rooted in divine displeasure. And a Heideggerian might point to the supposed turn away from being. Yet it would be more plausible to relate the current spread of religiously inspired and other forms of terror to recent history. We recall that much

---

[5] For illuminating comments on issues concerning the attitude of first-world countries toward third- and fourth-world countries, including the effect of price supports for agricultural products in first-world countries on other parts of the world, see Joseph E. Stiglitz, *Globalization and Its Discontents* (New York: Norton, 2002).

of the last century was taken up by a confrontation between two very different politico-economic systems: capitalism in all its many forms and "official" Marxism. The disappearance of official Marxism leaves largely unresolved the persistence of poverty after (and in virtue of) the Industrial Revolution, the very problems for which Marx formulated his theories in the middle of the nineteenth century. It further leaves the only remaining superpower increasingly unrestrained by other nations, increasingly free to do what it chooses, increasingly likely to work its will in myriad ways, if not by persuasion then by resorting to force against other nations. The short answer, although I cannot argue the point here, is that a number of the problems we are witnessing are due less to the disparity between one or another form of religion and the modern world than to the failure of capitalism, the central economic motor of modernity, to benefit more than a selected few. This form of violence is not contingent, a historical accident, but rooted in capitalism itself.

Some Concluding Remarks

I have argued four related points: the war in Afghanistan cannot be understood merely as a war on terrorism; in a pre-emptive war in Iraq, terrorism appears increasingly as a mere pretext; a war against terrorism that is not defensive cannot be morally justified; and the problem of terrorism can probably not be overcome through military action alone, of whatever kind, since it is rooted in the nature of modern life. To anyone who discounts government rhetoric and examines the issues, it is abundantly clear that the so-called war on terrorism has increasingly little to do with terrorism and increasingly more to do with securing and increasing the preeminence of the U.S. in the current and future international situation.

I would like to conclude with a comment about a pressing international problem. It needs to be explained how the U.S., which depicts itself as a peace-loving, democratic nation, has suddenly been transformed into a country with increasingly little regard for international treaties, the rights of sovereign nations, the World Court, the U.N., and the international legal framework established with great difficulty as one of the chief achievements of modern times.

A partial response can be found in the way in which the current president came to power through means "outside" the normal democratic process. The very fact that the president was not elected but appointed creates a situation in which whoever occupies that office is not constrained by the normal process of checks and balances. Democracy depends on regular changes from one party to another freely decided by the people. Since George W. Bush was appointed, everything has been happening as if one of the main goals of the present administration were precisely to perpetuate that exceptional situation in changing the political process to its advantage in a way that will impede and perhaps even prevent the normal alternation in political office.

Terrorism is a real, not apparent, problem, which is not being met by the inability of the U.S. and its allies to devise either a morally justifiable, or even a useful, reaction to a real current problem, hence to undertake more than an apparent war on terrorism. Rather than a moral justification for incessant and ceaseless military actions, one encounters religious, or quasi-religious, claims that are invoked for situations that often have less to do with terrorism than with the expansionist desires of the U.S. and its friends. But religion, which is presented as moral, is not necessarily moral. And an appeal to religion where a moral justification cannot be devised merely shows the helplessness of the world's only remaining superpower in responding to a crisis rooted not in the appeal to an outmoded form of religion but in the nature of the modern world.

What we are witnessing is not the death throes of capitalism, nor the end of a way of life as we know it. It is rather a case of the most powerful nation the world has ever known striking out against real and/or imagined foes while pursuing its own perceived self-interest, if necessary at the considerable expense of seriously weakening the international legal framework in a so-called war on terror that is highly likely not to decrease but rather to increase terrorism around the world. This unjustified war, which simply cannot be won as it is currently conceived, finally only demonstrates the weakness of the U.S. and its allies in their inability to resolve the very problems that give rise to terrorism.

13

TERRORISM AND THE NEW FORMS OF WAR

JOSEPH MARGOLIS

I

From the first moment of the original event, 9/11 has conveyed a dawning sense of its transformative power. It was quickly labeled (from the American side) an act of terrorism, and almost as quickly an act of war. It was a substantial and deliberate strike—hardly the first—of an invisible, even symbolic, war pressed against the United States, at the very least, directed against its heartland, pursued by material means, and yet impossible to classify in any conventionally recognized way that would otherwise have involved hostilities between well-defined states. It instantly signified to all a "war" very definitely begun and definitely continued, though by uncertain and unpredictable means. The matter is still vague in essentials, although its potential threat is hardly uncertain. Indeed, the threat is thought by many to be altogether genuine and pointed.

Nevertheless, *as* a war, its "nature" is hardly clear. It lacks a determinate perpetrator of the right kind; it makes no explicit claims or demands; it advances no official rationale or grievance; it has no geographical home or source; it implicates no state's initiative; and it gives no hint of any possible final or rational resolution. It has, however, been taken, with rather little quarrel, to justify almost at once a retaliatory invasion by the United States, acting against the Taliban, of a sovereign state (Afghanistan) and a forced change in its regime, all in the name of a new kind of war, a "war against terrorism" not yet defined or internationally sanctioned. It has also been made to yield a justification for further possible strikes against—by penetrating at will the territory of—sovereign states that, in the light of the admitted facts, were not implicated in any specific terrorist acts that issued from their space (Yemen, for instance, in an incident involving a direct attack on an American warship in port).

Indeed, read in terms of the problematic new category (or category-to-be), 9/11 was being pressed in an even more adventurous way to yield a justification for a preemptive strike (by the United States) against another state (Iraq) that had not been convincingly shown to constitute an imminent or direct threat of war of any kind specifically directed against it, or to have conspired with any terrorist group to commit the acts involved in 9/11 or any related acts. Somehow, the justificatory argument has managed to conflate the notably vague, almost indefinable—even arbitrary—sense in which a political entity that is *not* a state (Al Qaeda or Hezbollah or some such entity) arguably constitutes a terrorist threat against a particular state (the United States, say) and the usually crisp sense in which one state is said to threaten, or to have actually committed an aggression against, another state (Iraq, for instance, against Kuwait, before the 1991 Gulf War, and, arguably, Saudi Arabia).

The world sees in these events the inescapable need to reexamine the concept of war and the right of states to defend themselves against "terroristic wars" and the threat of such wars. The world finds itself confronted by an entirely new run of technologies involving instant global communication and the ready manufacture and marketing of "weapons of mass destruction" made accessible to states and nonstate bodies that would ordinarily never have been able to pose such a threat of war before. Nonstates (certainly Al Qaeda) are now, and will increasingly be, in a position to carry out military strikes, even sustained campaigns, as effectively as conventional states; in fact, the miniaturization and "democratization" of nuclear, chemical, and biological weaponry in the hands of skilled, perhaps even suicidal, "terrorists" threaten to offset in the profoundest way the military capacity of any state, even the most powerful, to mount a conventional war or a conventional defense against attack.

We are moving into a world in which ordinarily disadvantaged, otherwise weak, poor, impoverished, helpless populations may have found a way to transform themselves into a force that might conceivably topple or severely wound even a superpower—though by normally outlawed means. So the need to define a "war on terrorism"—and, correspondingly, certain new forms of "state terrorism"—cannot be postponed. (These innovations clearly go together, and are, indeed, subject to the same sort of vagueness and metaphoric application.) The "just-war" concept was already severely challenged during the time of the French Revolution and was at least in need of the most radical reinterpretation by the time of the Second World War.[1] "Just war" is now effectively moribund (though many deny it), which is not to say (or deny) that bodies like the United Nations, NATO, and individual states rightly claim to rely on one or another notion of justice in war (perhaps too facilely converted into a version of just war) according to which they anticipate international support and confirmation of their way of conducting hostilities. The trouble is that, in speaking of a war against terrorism, it no longer makes sense to say that a modern state can actually conduct a war along just-war lines.

[1] See Walzer 1977.

The realities of modern warfare have decisively defeated two essential doctrines of the just-war concept: that of a clear demarcation between combatant and noncombatant populations and that of the feasibility of confining the effects of admissible military strikes (hostilities) to any reasonably demarcated combatant population or installation. Neither of these conditions can be satisfied in our present world, however we fiddle with what to put in their place. Now, with the advent of 9/11—in fact, well before it—we have been forced to acknowledge, in a sense that is hardly speculative, that political bodies that are not states are quite capable of waging a serious war, are plainly willing to do so, and, as a result, have begun to alter in the most radical way imaginable the parity and effectiveness of different forms of "military" power. But they have come to that pass—it may be that it could not have been avoided—by refusing to draw *any* defensible distinction between combatant and "innocent" populations or installations and by rejecting *any* normative restriction on what to count as "legitimate" instruments of war (*jus in bello*).

The logic of the situation invites just those dubbed "terrorists" *by* the very states they have attacked (Al Qaeda, say, as the presumed perpetrator of the attack on the Pentagon and the World Trade Center towers) to refuse to be governed by their enemy's conceptions of just-war or related constraints. These nonstate bodies view themselves not as terrorists but rather as "freedom fighters," counterterrorists, guerrillas, champions of one or another sort of victim population, acting against the "state terrorism" of the other.

They *cannot* rule out, a priori, the use of anthrax, smallpox, plague, sarin, VX, nuclear weapons, poisoning of the water supply, random murder, or suicide bombings: they cannot, because they could not otherwise *be a plausible match* for the powers they mean to oppose or defeat. Accordingly, they must invent (and believe in) an ideology capable of justifying such extreme measures. The likeliest doctrines of course would make every pertinent encounter an apocalyptic confrontation between irredeemable evil and whatever was qualifiedly good in the human way; and that, of course, would be a policy made to order for a religious war of the kind that, however erroneously, is now regularly named *jihad* (to counter versions of the West's *crusade*).[2] The fact is that the growing disparities of wealth and power among states, which bear directly on the technology of modern warfare, create a setting in which disadvantaged states and nonstate bodies are driven to invent a would-be legitimation for forms of warfare that have been or would assuredly be canonically disallowed.

You may quarrel with all this; but one thing is absolutely certain: present circumstances signify the inevitable radicalization of the kind of

[2] See Huntington 1996.

war we must now acknowledge, a war in which we shall be unable to control the spread of the use of weapons of mass destruction and even seemingly senseless murder, and shall be unable to anticipate the terrorist populations from which an effective strike will come. If you grant the point, you must surely realize that the present American policy toward Iraq and the Muslim world is being brilliantly staged in such a way as to be utterly counterproductive. America is fulfilling Al Qaeda's wildest dreams faster than Al Qaeda could ever have done on its own.

II

The American strike against Iraq launched in March 2003 is well on its way to destabilizing a large part of the world. It challenged the United Nations in a way the U.N. could not possibly meet, since the U.N. proved powerless to restrain the United States from carrying out its intended attack, which, arguably, it had effectively authorized (though not explicitly) as a preemptive strike that, at the end, it was unwilling to endorse again, and which the United States may never validate in a convincing way. America's maneuver has also exposed the near-irrelevance of NATO and may have decisively split the unity of Western Europe as it has functioned until now; it is well on its way to producing a profound division between the "old" and the "new" Europe (as Donald Rumsfeld has put the matter). The strike against Iraq threatens to destabilize the Muslim world by reawakening Kurdish fears and aspirations, ethnic and religious divisions within Iraq itself, and the struggle between secular and fundamentalist currents bearing on republican and monarchical regimes throughout the Middle East. It has done all this all the while exacerbating the terrible conflict between the Israelis and the Palestinians, which had an absolutely central role in the move toward "regime change" in Iraq. It has provoked North Korea to play a nervy version of nuclear chicken, under cover of America's preoccupation with Iraq and its presumed inability to attack without Chinese complicity; and it has, of course, quickened the radicalization of the Muslim world itself and a potentially brisk commerce in weapons of mass destruction (initiated, in part, by North Korea). It has already set a dangerously low barrier against the use of the preemptive strike as a rationale for conventional aggressions on the part of strong states—potentially, then, on the part of a state like China, acting against Taiwan or the Philippines. It risks destabilizing the world's economy in a period of notable weakness, and it could well lead the American economy into a prolonged depression.

Instabilities of all these sorts are likely to multiply and deepen, regardless of the outcome of the strike against Iraq. To be sure, no one can say with assurance how all these worries will turn out. But the risks are as real and as deep as any the world has had to face since the Second

World War. The dangers are profoundly global, but the fuse will have been lit by a single pair of hands, witnessed by a small number of compliant governments and an unpersuaded chorus of the peoples of the world.

The forces that will have been loosed by America's strike against Iraq are incalculable and impossible to identify completely. But what remains troublingly unexplored is the significance of the grave fact that we have been confronted, suddenly, unexpectedly, in the most extreme way, and (to all intents and purposes) unilaterally, by a novel legal and moral crisis affecting the very conception of global war and peace. Every consideration pertinent to the continued role of the U.N., for instance, has been knocked into a cocked hat. The possibility of such a crisis was, indeed, bruited in World War II and the Cold War—frozen, until now, in all our conjectures, by the need to come to terms with the dawning threat of nuclear annihilation.

The developing technologies of war are evidently more humane: they now promise calibrations of destruction in keeping with the scale of the imagined advantages of actually going to war and the rational necessity of actually surviving. They also oblige us to concentrate on the logic of admitting that even a middle-sized war in our time may be more about the anticipated crippling damage of a first strike (well beyond the Iraqi episode, which may not have been foreseen at all) than about the imperatives of responding to actual hostilities within any war's span.

The American argument exposes the irrelevance of the just-war model and pointedly confirms the likelihood that the most powerful states of the world will, as a matter of course, be unwilling to tolerate uncertainty regarding the intentions and weapons of seemingly hostile states and their nonstate allies (like North Korea at the moment) capable of acquiring and using weapons of mass destruction for an initial or preemptive strike of their own.

In this sense, Iraq signifies the international community's inability to stalemate future aggressions prepared to obscure the difference between state terrorism and any legitimate preemptive strike *in extremis*. It's obvious that the argument of self-defense will have to yield in this direction; but any such concession is bound to increase the likelihood of initiatives like Al Qaeda's, miniaturized as far as possible, opposed to drawing a line between admissible and inadmissible weapons of war, and made increasingly difficult to monitor in advance of any actual strike. Under these circumstances, the strongest states will be inclined (the United States, for instance, already in the matter of linking Iraq and terrorism) to impose domestic restrictions on personal rights and liberties affecting citizens and alien residents alike, in an effort to minimize terrorist dangers at home. There's an inevitable spiral of lost liberties there. (Internal doubts and questions begin to prove unpatriotic or disloyal.)

Even a legitimate war on terrorism tends, like state terrorism, to produce a siege mentality in which the manufacture of weapons of mass destruction will require their increased proliferation as well as the increased threat of their being used. The reality of terrorism feeds on the fear of terrorism; and since it is an idea that cannot be regularized in accord with canonical notions of war, there is no obvious way in which the intended use of a preemptive strike against alleged threats of this new sort can be made adequately responsible to the community of nations- —especially when such a strike is not sustained by the greatest powers. In this sense, peace in our time requires commitments that, in the past, were never deemed essential to resolving a war—as they now must be. For one thing, the erosion of democratic liberties at home is likely to encourage a strong state (the United States once again) to favor its own unilateral decision to use the preemptive strike (according to its own conscience) even when opposed by a significant number of the members of the world community; and, for a second, the very legitimacy of construing a war against terrorism as a reasonable extension of the concept of canonical war cannot but oblige the world community to act together to reduce the cause of terrorism itself.

In a word, the reduction of extreme disparities in goods and rights affecting survival, quality of life, and perceived injustice is no longer a matter of extraneous benevolence but rather one of war and peace and survival itself. *We can no longer live in peace if most of the world does not live nearly as well as its most privileged part.* The metaphors of war are becoming literal forms of war in order to collect the underlying motives for terrorism—at the price of becoming impossible to control by any collection of states. Normal prudence dictates the acknowledgment of these new forms of war by terroristic means—and, as a result, dictates the need for adequate countermeasures, which are not yet under discussion.

The United States has confronted the entire world with a conceptual option that can no longer be ignored. It was already before us in the Israeli strike against Iraq's original nuclear factory and, in a way, in the Cuban missile crisis. But the latter event was read by all as a fortunately brief episode internal to the Cold War, which the rest of the world saw itself as powerless to control; and the former was read by nearly all as a problematic (also fortunately short and successful) skirmish, local to an inactive but threatened war between two relatively minor states. The American challenge is completely different, a breakthrough of the profoundest conceptual and practical kind, promulgated by a state capable of acting unilaterally on its own conviction, in circumstances that link imminent threat to potentialities not yet actual, defended in terms of technological realities.

The problematic category—war against terrorism—applied to states and nonstate entities alike, is so broadly construed that it could easily be interpreted to justify a preemptive strike by Iraq against the United States. Or, conceivably, by North Korea against the United States, a possibility Korea has already aired—at least rhetorically. But the joke is a good one, if that is what it is. Read more soberly, the American threat (and acts of war) provide an obvious cover (if one were needed) for similarly legitimated strikes—for example, in the running feud between India and Pakistan or, conceivably, in the uncertain relations between the United States and Iran or Syria. The American war against terrorism could easily change into a new form of imperial terrorism of its own. The United States may deny any such intention, but much of the world doubts the disclaimer.

The lengthening short history of the American war on terrorism will, for the reasons given, surely weaken both domestically and internationally our most assured moral-political convictions: it will mark them with a troubling sense of their own contingency, questionable validity, bias, potential irrelevance, characteristic opportunism and inconsistency, and, most important, probable intransigence against admitting the supposed grievances (in moral-political terms) of any states or peoples that, contrary to the American charge against the terrorists, view themselves as the actual victims of a kind of state terrorism now being attributed to the United States (and other states similarly committed to Western forms of hegemony and exploitation). The profound inconclusiveness of the American charge is plausibly matched by a countercharge that similarly belongs to a potentially new idiom: not to suggest that either claim would be idle, only that notions like "terrorism" and "state terrorism" (or "counterterrorism") cannot be easily regularized in any nontendentious way. Anyone, it seems, can play the game; and no one can win by the rules. We are spinning out of control.

III

What seems to be happening is this. The new technologies of war oblige us to admit the crippling, even mortal, dangers of a first strike involving weapons of mass destruction; hence, the legitimacy of a preemptive strike under conditions notably laxer than those of an imminent threat very strictly construed. Add to this what we know about the proliferation of such weapons; the ease of production, acquisition, transfer, use; difficulties of detection; growth of a viable market in such weapons; existence of rogue states and nonstate bodies that aspire to a kind of weapons parity, are willing to use such weapons, and are prepared to justify their use; and the reluctance of states committed to world peace to act together in a preemptive strike, even if strongly (however problematically) urged by one of their number in the name of self-defense: you cannot fail to see how the uncertainties of a correct response are bound to mount with the perceived difficulties of defusing the precipitating dangers by other means.

The point is that we are being drawn inexorably in the direction of the "logic" of the American argument, even if not in the direction of that particular argument itself. The resources of international law are being stretched to the breaking point; and war itself is being transformed into an instrument of moral or political conscience that may be invoked unilaterally by states of sufficient power. The problematic category—war against terrorism—risks leading the entire international community to the brink of political chaos. There are no adequate safeguards to fall back to, and it is not clear that there could be any, at least in terms of the various sorts of threats that go by the names of "terrorism" and "state terrorism."

What all this suggests is: first, that the question of the validity of war is, *now*, in principle inseparable from questions regarding the accessibility and right distribution of the goods and resources of the world among all affected peoples; second, that the new technologies of global communication and the production and acquisition of weapons of mass destruction have made it impossible any longer to segregate perceived distributional injustices, widening material disparities beyond all reasonable tolerance, ad hoc and unconvincing rationales in favor of the global economic status quo, and similar complaints from the idea of the infectious themes of a defensive "war" against the new forms of political and economic penetration that are congealing, particularly in the Middle East, into the syndrome of what we may call Western "state terrorism"; third, that complaints of what are called "terrorism" and "state terrorism" are now so standard and widespread that defensive "wars against terrorism"—against states and nonstate entities alike—now occupy the full attention of the world and cannot be expected to recede without moving to correct (in a public and international way) what are perceived to be unacceptable disparities in wealth, power, and access to the world's resources and goods that have provoked both conventional wars and the new wars that confront us now; and, fourth, that we cannot hope to ensure peace in this desperate world we share without attempting to narrow as much as possible the extremes of poverty, drought, starvation, peonage, political autonomy, disease, pollution, capital development, access to resources and markets, helplessness, incapacitation, and the like—consistent with an acceptable quality of life for all peoples.

In short, the transformation of the very concept of war by the technologies of terrorism obscure the deeper fact that the new forms of defensive war against what is increasingly perceived as state terrorism are morally and politically inspired—well beyond the range of canonical aggression associated with the just-war concept—in terms of growing disparities in freedom and self-determination and quality of life and ethnic respect linked to the new possibilities of terrorism.

In different ways, the members of the disadvantaged world are rising up against the hegemonies of the West (largely) in the only way they can: namely, by radicalizing the legitimacy of every conceivable means of resistance, even where it effectively enlists hitherto morally unacceptable means. The rationale (as I have already noted) must take the form of an argument *in extremis* or in the shape of an apocalyptic resistance against unpardonable evil. You cannot fail to see, therefore, that the conditions of debate are being transformed before our eyes in a way that can no longer fall back to entrenched forms of justice and morality.

It is not altogether wrong, therefore, to claim that many in the United States who uphold the war against Iraq fear that the Muslim world, increasingly radicalized by Al Qaeda and other terrorist groups, may be prepared to risk tearing the entire fabric of the world to pieces in order to bring down the hegemonic powers of the West. But, then, it is difficult to deny that something of the opposite sort has also motivated the current American administration, which believes the United States to be the target of Muslim terrorism—and couches (unconvincingly) its attack on Iraq in terms of correcting Saddam Hussein's tyrannical treatment of his own people.

The touchstone of this entire convergence is surely the interminable conflict between the Palestinians and the Israelis. For it is there, rather than in the political rhetoric of applying the logic of the war against terrorism (the would-be response to 9/11) to the war against Iraq, that one finds the natural confluence between the counterterrorism of the Muslim terrorists and the mounting resistance, worldwide, to the geopolitical penetration of the Middle East. Seen in these terms, Israel appears as an outpost of a would-be American empire. You have only to think of the extraordinary fact that the United States (together with its principal ally, Great Britain) is prepared to change the political structure of Iraq unilaterally, if necessary, and outside the framework of the United Nations; whereas it adamantly opposes doing the same against North Korea. The irony is perfectly clear: the Koreans are bent on selling nuclear weaponry to any state or nonstate body that can afford to buy; and the Iraqis no longer have a nuclear arsenal of their own. This begins to explain the curious attempt on the part of the Bush administration to demonstrate, against all reason, that Iraq is the terrorist ally of Al Qaeda: hence, it explains why the aggression against Iraq was initially presented as a defensive "war against aggression." Perceived through Muslim eyes, the new state terrorism of the Americans is masquerading as a preemptive strike against the threat of Iraq's weapons of mass destruction! All perfectly valid, except for the fact that Iraq had the barest remnants of its former weaponry.

IV

We seem to be at the beginning of an evolving phase of the globalization of war and peace, a phase in which hostilities between conventional states are conflated with the complication of "terrorism" construed both as a metaphoric extension and/or transformation of conventional hostilities between states ("state terrorism") and as a defense, *in extremis*, conducted primarily by nonstate bodies against what they perceive to be the evolving forms of state terrorism. In these terms, terrorism is (i) an aggression, or the perceived threat of an aggression, employing weapons of mass destruction, potential even if not actual or imminent, involving conventional states, now advanced as grounds for a preemptive strike under cover of self-defense; (ii) an aggression, or perceived threat of aggression, employing unusual or heterodox means of war that override or repudiate all conventional distinctions between combatants and noncombatants, admissible and inadmissible forms of warfare (including but not restricted to weapons of mass destruction), pursued independently by nonstate bodies or in collusion with states that favor terrorism themselves; (iii) a figurative transformation, constituting a new form of war, of all forms of political and economic penetration and control exercised by states, blocs of states, or populations however distributed worldwide, whose activities are perceived to be causally responsible for intolerable disparities, inequities of power, cultural indignities and affronts, and injustices regarding the freedom, political self-determination, and quality of life of the peoples of the world; and (iv) the figurative transformation of all measures designed to combat manifestations of (i), (ii), or (iii) in any form or combination.

The American strike against Iraq, premised on Iraq's instantiating (i), illustrates a version of (iv), viewed through American eyes, and a version of (iii), viewed through Muslim eyes; the American perception of 9/11, usually read as effectively linked to Iraq's illustrating (i), best illustrates (ii), which, seen through Muslim eyes, is a form of (iv); and the Muslim perception of Palestinian suicide attacks against Israel, or Al Qaeda's attacks on the United States (allowing the charge) involving 9/11, the American warship in Yemen, and the embassy in Kenya; and the American strike against Iraq, read in terms of (i) and (ii), best illustrate (iv).

These innovations are of a mixed sort, essentially because wherever terrorism is construed as itself a form of war, it constitutes a figurative charge intended to transform and extend the canonical accounts of war (*jus ad bellum, jus in bello*) in terms of the moral-political concerns of distributive justice applied holistically to personal freedom, political self-determination, access to resources and goods, conditions of survival, and quality of life. Extreme disparities here, perceived as due to the hostile activities of strong states that would normally *not* constitute war in any canonical sense, are now being metaphorically transformed into a new form of war. Here, terrorism and counterterrorism are deemed wars, even if the precipitating "hostilities" are relatively invisible, not deliberately intended, not canonically admissible, cast entirely or primarily in terms of moral and political injustice of an extreme and intolerable kind. They are judged to be inherently evil, to entail responsibility equivalent to committing an aggression, and to invoke the reasonable conjecture that "canonical" wars themselves implicate a conceptual link to questions of distributive justice and allied values applied to the conditions of life. The very idea of globalization leads to the not unreasonable postulate that the whole of humanity must take care of its own. The fact is that all the peoples of the earth profess to be committed to some version of that doctrine.

There remain two further complications. For one, there is no known account of morality in which objective obligations requiring a "defensive war" against terrorism worldwide—answering to item (iii) of the tally given just above—*can* be convincingly imposed on the world community itself.[3] For another, the norms of collective justice and injustice are remarkably diverse, criterially interpreted, irreconcilable by any straight-forward means, subject not merely to the conflicting interests of estab-lished states but also to the more intractable diversity of the histories of the peoples involved. This begins to fix the sense in which terrorism, along the lines of item (iv) of the tally given, itself reflects the sense of outrage of the disadvantaged and exploited peoples of the world—in an age of global hegemony, of extraordinary disparities approaching conditions *in extremis* and confirming diverse convictions about radical evil, of the ready accessibility of weapons of mass destruction, *and* of the clear evidence of the unnecessary disparities and waste made possible by modern productive technologies.

Terrorism (iv) is likely to be a more or less permanent feature of the political landscape from here on out—and will doubtless become riskier and riskier, until (and unless) the world relents (if it ever will). But it signifies, conceptually, that the age of *applying* the would-be canonical principles of justice and morality to the conditions of war in our time (possibly in any time in which hegemony cannot be counted on to behave humanely) is all but over. Terrorism is, then, an interim condition in a process of fundamental change in political paradigms that is now being tested. The reasonable sign of a successful transformation of the sort required will be gauged by the degree to which terrorism itself subsides. Here, the political strategies are largely pragmatic: What, relative to the history of past wars and their resolution, *and* relative to the new forms of war that terrorism begets, will be permitted to form a new international order prepared, within reasonable limits, to enforce the redress of pertinent grievances? That is what the United Nations, divided in conventional ways within itself, has not yet addressed. And that, I venture to say, *is* what Muslim "terrorism" ultimately signifies. You

---

[3] One of the latest efforts at a moral universalism (drawn from Aristotle) has been tendered in Nussbaum 1996 as well as in a number of Nussbaum's recent books. I must be candid: apart from its obviously humane intention, Nussbaum's brief merely confirms the inconsequentiality of any such attempt in a world at war with itself. One despairs in reading such accounts, which merely expose the pretensions of familiar models of moral and political life (developed in the West) intended to legislate for the whole of the world. That's simply no longer acceptable, unless Western hegemony can remain assured.

must bear in mind that Al Qaeda, Hezbollah, Hamas, and similar groups have merely been experimenting with the first possibilities of a defensive war by terroristic means. Consider that the desperately disadvantaged peoples of the rest of the world may have other inventions to offer by which to concentrate the mind.

References

Huntington, Samuel P. 1996. *The Clash of Civilizations and the Remaking of World Order*. New York: Simon and Schuster.

Nussbaum, Martha C. 1996. *For Love of Country?* Edited by Joshua Cohen. Boston: Beacon Press.

Walzer, Michael 1977. *Just and Unjust Wars: A Moral Argument with Historical Illustrations*. New York: Basic Books.

14

AFTERWORD:
THE ROAD FROM SEPTEMBER 11 TO ABU GHRAIB

ARMEN T. MARSOOBIAN

The essays contained in this volume were written during the two-year period following the attacks of September 11, 2001. In one way or another, they primarily focus upon the American response to those attacks—a response that has come to be known as the war on terrorism. The authors have grappled with the thorny issues that arise from the choice of the term *war* to characterize this response. Just as important, they also have tried to make sense of the object of this war, that notoriously hard to define word *terrorism*. The manner in which this war has been conducted by the Bush administration has been especially troubling. Whether it is the more or less "successful" intervention in Afghanistan or the much more problematic undertaking in Iraq, the nature of the American response raises fundamental political, moral, and legal questions. Though many of the preceding essays were written either during the build-up to the March 2003 invasion of Iraq or during its immediate aftermath, that is, during the so-called "mission-accomplished" period, they foretell much of what has gone wrong in this war. What is more important, they identify many of the causes of this failure. My remarks here are not intended to rehearse the many telling insights of these essays. I will use some incidents that have occurred subsequent to the completion of the essays as a springboard for reflection upon the insights contained in this volume. I will begin with the scandal of American abuse of detainees in Baghdad's Abu Ghraib prison, which is still unfolding as I write these words.

As Joseph Margolis has pointed out in his article, "Terrorism and the New Forms of War," we have journeyed down a very dangerous path as a result of George W. Bush's declared "war against terrorism." Margolis holds that this problematic new category of war has no clearly defined rules of conduct, no "adequate safeguards to fall back to." This has been borne out by our treatment of prisoners in Abu Ghraib, Guantánamo Bay, and other, often undisclosed, locations around the world. With one stroke of the pen, President Bush on November 13, 2001, through an executive order, exempted all detainees of this so-called war on terrorism from the protections acknowledged under the Geneva Conventions regarding the treatment of prisoners of war (Bush 2001). As a clarification of that executive order, the White House press secretary released a policy statement regarding the "status of detainees at Guantanamo" on February 7, 2002, in which Bush specifically claimed that the Third Geneva Convention of 1949 regarding the treatment of prisoners of war (POWs) does not apply to Al Qaeda detainees but does apply to Taliban detainees (Office of the Press Secretary 2002). By a rather bizarre piece of logic, Bush claimed that although the convention does indeed apply to the Taliban, the Taliban detainees are not entitled to POW status because of their "failure to wear uniforms" and to "conduct their operations in accordance with the laws and customs of war." Yet according to those same criteria, many of America's own special-operations forces also would not be entitled to POW status. As Ronald Dworkin has pointed out in his article, such an interpretation of the Geneva Conventions is contrary to "the spirit of the principles behind those rules," albeit rules that were written with more conventional wars in mind. The Geneva Conventions clearly state that if there is any doubt as to the status of prisoners, they should be treated as POWs until the issue is resolved by a "competent tribunal," not by fiat of a secretary of defense, as is the case at Guantánamo.

Some two years later the flawed reasoning behind the president's orders has now become clear. In a series of memorandums that have only recently been made public, the legal arguments behind the president's words have been revealed (Yoo and Delahunty 2002 and Gonzales 2002). These arguments highlight a rejection of the fundamental principle of law and, in a deeply troubling way, strike at the heart of the moral basis of a law-abiding society. I will label these arguments the "pick-and-choose" approach to international law and the "double-standard" approach to international law. In the pick-and-choose approach, a party to an agreement or contract, after the fact, decides what parts of the agreement he or she will live up to and what parts he or she will ignore. In the double-standard approach, the contracting party exempts himself or herself from adhering to the terms of the agreement but insists that the other contracting party be prosecuted for failing to adhere to those same terms. Both of these approaches are evident in memos crafted by the Office of Legal Counsel of the U.S. Department of Justice and later affirmed in a memo to the president by the White House counsel, Alberto R. Gonzales. They serve as the basis for our treatment of the detainees of the war on terrorism. This is not the place, nor do I have the legal competence, to rebut in a detailed fashion the legal arguments made in these memos, but I will highlight aspects of these arguments that fall under the dubious approaches mentioned above.

In the memo prepared by John Yoo and Robert J. Delahunty of the Office of Legal Counsel, they argue that Geneva Conventions III (the Convention Relative to the Treatment of Prisoners of War) and IV (the Convention Relative to the Protection of Civilian Persons in Time of War) as well as the U.S. War Crimes Act, 18 U.S.C. § 2441 (Supp. III

1997) (the federal law enshrining many of the Geneva safeguards), do not apply to the war in Afghanistan. Yoo and Delahunty further argue that customary international law, which served as the basis of the Geneva Conventions, does not bind the president or restrict the actions of the U.S. military in this war. Among the arguments given to reach these conclusions is the argument to the effect that the president can choose temporarily to suspend the Geneva Conventions for the war in Afghanistan and by extension other fronts in the war on terrorism. The reasoning behind this claim goes as follows: "There is no textual provision in the Geneva Conventions that clearly prohibits temporary suspension. The drafters included a provision that appears to preclude State parties from agreeing to absolve each other of violations. They also included careful procedures for the termination of the agreements by individual State parties, including a provision that requires delay of a termination of a treaty, if that termination were to occur during a conflict, until the end of the conflict. Yet, at the same time, the drafters of the Conventions did not address suspension at all" (Yoo and Delahunty 2002, 32). Because there is no explicit provision forbidding suspension, it is argued that suspension is permissible. The elementary logical fallacy here is an *argumentum ad ignoratiam* (an appeal to ignorance). What is the meaning of being a signatory to a treaty if one can pick and choose when it is in effect and when it is not, when certain provisions should apply and when they should not? Common Article I of the Geneva Conventions states that the signatory parties pledge "to respect and to ensure respect for the present Convention in all circumstances." As Plato's Socrates eloquently argued in the *Crito*, a change in circumstances does not warrant the breaking of an agreement that does not suit our present purposes, whether that agreement is explicit or implied.

In a concluding section of the same memo, after Yoo and Delahunty have established that customary international law also does not apply to our actions in Afghanistan, they address the question, Do the customary laws of war apply to Al Qaeda or the Taliban militia? They conclude: "Although customary international law does not bind the President, the President may still use his constitutional warmaking authority to subject members of al Qaeda or the Taliban militia to the laws of war. While this result may seem at first glance to be counter-intuitive, it is a product of the President's Commander in Chief and Chief Executive powers to prosecute the war effectively" (2002, 39). The enemy can be prosecuted in military tribunals for breaches of the customary laws of war while at the same time the United States can exempt itself from those same laws. A clear double standard has been applied. Again, this strikes at the heart of the concept of law and the moral basis for our agreement to live as members of a nation governed by law. We cannot tell our enemies to abide by laws that we ourselves are unwilling to abide by. Let alone our enemies, what a dreadful message to send to our friends around the world!

In a memo to the president prepared by White House counsel Gonzales on January 25, 2002, arguments in summary form similar to those in the Yoo and Delahunty memo were made. Gonzales was attempting to address the concerns raised by Secretary of State Colin Powell about the proposed policy of exemptions from the Geneva Conventions. Gonzales concluded that Powell's arguments were unpersuasive and that the policy should not be reversed. There is one telling phrase in which Gonzales summarizes one of Powell's points: "A determination that GPW [Geneva Convention III] does not apply to al Qaeda and the Taliban could undermine U.S. military culture which emphasizes maintaining the highest standards of conduct in combat, and could introduce an element of uncertainty in the status of adversaries" (2002, 3). In response, Gonzales maintains that there will be no confusion as to the status of our adversaries, because the president has directed our armed forces to apply the principles of the Geneva Conventions, and they always do what they have been directed to do.

Although I will make no causal argument that leads from the loosening of the rules of war and the blurring of the status of the detainees to the American abuses in Abu Ghraib, there is ample evidence to suggest that this slippery slope may not be a fallacious fancy at all (Barry, Hirsh, and Isikoff 2004). The ambiguities that have been introduced by the new category of detainee, the so-called illegal combatant, may well have led to the poisoning of the "military culture" that Powell was so worried about. In spite of the administration's claim that the detainees, whether the POWs in Iraq or the illegal combatants in Guantánamo, would be treated humanely, this shift in status contributed to confusion on the ground and opened the door to abuse. As Gonzales himself maintained, "this new paradigm renders obsolete Geneva's strict limitations on questioning of enemy prisoners and renders quaint some of its provisions" (2002, 2). Once we imported the terms *terrorism* and *terrorist* into the rhetoric of the Iraqi war and occupation, we sowed the seeds of hatred that now mark both sides of this conflict.

The Bush administration's callous and manipulative treatment of legal obligations and agreements poses a significant threat to our American democracy. This threat poses as grave a challenge to our way of life as those acts of terrorism that shook our nation on September 11, 2001. I hope that we are up to such a challenge.

References

Barry, John, Michael Hirsh, and Michael Isikoff. 2004. "The Roots of Torture." *Newsweek* (May 24, 2004). Online at www.msnbc.msn.com/id/4989422/site/newsweek/ (accessed May 24, 2004).

Bush, George W. 2001. Executive Order 66 FR 57833, 2001 WL 1435652, "Detention, Treatment, and Trial of Certain Non-Citizens in the War

Against Terrorism." November 13, 2001. The White House, Washington, D. C. Online at www.law.uchicago.edu/tribunals/exec_order.html
(accessed May 24, 2004).

Gonzales, Alberto R. 2002. Memorandum for the President. January 25,
2002. Online at www.msnbc.msn.com/id/4989436/site/newsweek/ (accessed May 24, 2004).

Office of the Press Secretary. 2002. Fact Sheet "Status of Detainees at
Guantanamo." February 7, 2002. The White House, Washington,
D. C. Online at www.whitehouse.gov/news/releases/2002/02/print/
20020207-13.html (accessed May 24, 2004).

Yoo, John, and Robert J. Delahunty. 2002. Memorandum for William J.
Haynes II, General Counsel, Department of Defense. January 9, 2002.
Washington, D. C.: Office of Legal Counsel, U.S. Justice Department.
Online at www.msnbc.msn.com/id/5032094/site/newsweek/ (accessed
May 24, 2004).

INDEX

Note: Page numbers in **bold** refer to the whole text of the chapter.